Entering the Field

EXPLORATIONS IN ANTHROPOLOGY
A University College London Series

Series Editors: Barbara Bender, John Gledhill and Bruce Kapferer

Entering the Field

New Perspectives on World Football

**Edited by Gary Armstrong and
Richard Giulianotti**

BERG

Oxford • New York

First published in 1997 by
Berg
Editorial offices:
150 Cowley Road, Oxford, OX4 1JJ, UK
70 Washington Square South, New York, NY 10012, USA

Berg is an imprint of Oxford International Publishers Ltd.

Library of Congress Cataloging-in-Publication Data

A catalogue record for this book is available from the Library of
Congress.

British Library Cataloguing-in-Publication Data

A catalogue record for this book is available from the British
Library.

ISBN 1 85973 193 7 (Cloth)
      1 85973 198 8 (Paper)

Typeset by JS Typesetting, Wellingborough, Northants.
Printed in the United Kingdom by WBC Book Manufacturers,
Bridgend, Mid Glamorgan.

Contents

Acknowledgements

The editors have many players and teams to thank. Our greatest gratitude is to the chapter contributors, who have made this collection possible. We are also grateful to Bob and Linda Anderson, Frances Cresser, Kathryn Earle, Gerry Finn, Mike Gerrard, John Gledhill, Rosemary Harris, Karen Kinnaird, Clive Norris, the staff at *Football Archives* and *When Saturday Comes*, and our anonymous referee at Berg, for their generous assistance in helping us see this project through from beginning to end. Thanks are also due to fans from all over the world, who have given their time, thoughts, and experiences to the editors and contributors. Special thanks are extended to fans in the editors' home cities of Sheffield and Aberdeen, and to two valued team-mates (Hani Darlington and Donna McGilvray) who have, as we write, still to take advantage of the Bosman free transfer ruling.

Gary Armstrong
Richard Giulianotti

Chapter 1

Introduction: Reclaiming the Game – An Introduction to the Anthropology of Football

Richard Giulianotti and *Gary Armstrong*

> *People who don't follow football think of it as just a game, something that can be packed away when it is finished and forgotten about. But the game, played out by twenty-two men in an hour and a half, is only the Kernel of Something greater. The game is the core, you might say, of the Game.*

(Pearson 1994: 152)

Football and UK Anthropology: A Late Call from the Bench

Until recently, anthropology had failed to address adequately the game of football or 'soccer',[1] or consider its supporters and players. It is over thirty years since anthropologists and sociologists at Manchester University were implored by their Professor, Max Gluckman, to attend the sporting pageants provided locally by the famous 'tribe' of Manchester United Football Club. Since then, UK anthropology's major contribution to the study of the game and its social minutae has lagged significantly behind that by its overseas colleagues, being restricted to the pop-ethnology of Desmond Morris (1981), or the British village studies by Frankenberg (1957) and Strathern (1982). Since these exploratory studies, it has been an increasingly forlorn wait until the preliminary work of Armstrong and Harris (1991). Alternatively, in Europe and the Americas, anthropological study of football has acquired a longer and more concerted, though still relatively recent, pedigree. The pioneering ethnography of Janet Lever in Brazil (1969, 1983) was not fully followed up until over a decade later, through the work

1

particularly of Archetti (1985) in Argentina, Bromberger (1987a, b, 1988) in Southern Europe, and Da Matta (1982) and Leite Lopes and Maresca (1987) in Brazil. These latter studies have been inspired by tracing the cultural and historical formation of regional and national identities through public engagement in football. Indeed, it is in the area of social history, which according to Evans-Pritchard (1962) is essentially an identical form of enquiry, that we can construct a parallel UK historiography of football anthropology. To go alongside the pioneering work of Pierre Lanfranchi on South European football, there are the scholarly UK researches by Mason (1980), Holt (1986), Korr (1986)[2], Vamplew (1988). Fishwick (1989) and Mason's (1994) most recent work, on the social history of football in South America, renders the academic distinction of social history and anthropology exactly that: academic. Encouragingly in 1994, a prize-winning popular book detailing football rivalries around the world drew on anthropological knowledge and was written by the son of a British anthropology professor (Kuper 1994).

The delayed arrival of football anthropology in the UK was largely due to an overriding concern with controlling and criminalizing spectators. Research funding was given mainly to policy-orientated research on football hooliganism, to the extent that the 'sociology of football hooliganism' acquired a degree of academic orthodoxy, coloured by personal diatribe and vilification (see *Sociological Review* 1991; Finn 1994a: 121n). Psychologists have also contributed to government enquiries into fan disorder (Popplewell 1986) while continuing, as Malinowski (1922) would argue, to entertain this research field merely to give apt illustrations to benefit *a priori* theory (see Canter, Comber and Uzzell 1989; Kerr 1994). Whether the project entails enforcing such classifications as 'lower-working class' or 'rough working class', and 'paratelic negativism' or 'psychopathy', the criticism of the resultant theoretical determinism remains: 'arranging butterflies according to their types and sub-types is tautology. It merely reasserts something you know already in a slightly different form' (Leach 1961: 5). The major methodological oversight is, therefore, ethnographic detail, or a willingness to pay due attention to the voice of the participants, be they players or fans.

In the post-hooliganism research field, sociologists and social historians have sought to fill this lacuna by embracing the contemporary theme of globalization, and its consequent potential for actuating localist and regional cultural values and discourses through a common framework of rules and customs within the sport (see Giulianotti and Williams 1994; Wagg 1995b). Anthropologists have started to attempt a *rapprochement*, through the ethnographic investigation of sport's diverse social and cultural forms and meanings (Blanchard 1995; MacClancy 1996). This collection seeks to extend the new genre, through the fields of research and by being multi-faceted in its methodological approach.

Football and Anthropology: Twin Existences?

Inevitably, some will ask what it is anthropology and anthropologists have to offer which is distinctive by comparison with what has gone before.

The anthropologist tries to represent what is seen and heard, to reconstruct action and interpret events. There is no definitive way of representing 'reality' just as there is no such thing as a culture that is finite. The anthropologist aims to be what Atkinson (1990) calls a 'credible witness', working within the cognitive parameters set out for ethnography, recognizing that it always produces a matter of greater or lesser misrepresentation.

The fundamental aim of the discipline is to investigate classifications, of which there are no shortage around the game. Played to clichés, reported on in similar fashion, football's followers and critics have always attempted to compare, compartmentalize and classify. Anthropology has to try to decode presumptions and prejudices, and go amidst the 'natives'. Such research requires pursuit of the 'imponderabilities of everyday life', of which football contains a multiplicity. Such fieldwork is, as a consequence, usually an extremely personal and traumatic experience, but an essential one if anthropology is to be differentiated from other subjects. From this experience the anthropologist becomes a knowing presence capable of understanding on the basis of minimal cues and cognizant of William Foot-Whyte's (1984: 83) maxim, that 'a great deal of what is important to observe is unspoken'. The achievement lies in the ethnographic method and imagination of the discipline, as commended by Sir J.G. Frazer (1922: ix): 'in practise an act has no meaning for an observer unless he shows or infers the thoughts and emotions of the agent.' The resulting narrative on the unknown may begin to buttress Murdock's (1972) observation, that anthropology's principal contribution to knowledge is colossal ethnography. An irony and paradox of anthropology, however, as Barley (1986) notes, to be classified as an 'expert' on a culture one has first to be a total foreigner to it. Anthropological enquiry needs to show how the idealized communion of being a football player, spectator, or fan is attempted; and via this, to consider football identity amongst the various other notions of selfhood.

From its origins in the city of Sheffield in the mid-nineteenth century, what became known as Association football developed over the course of 150 years to become the 'global game'. According to its President João Havelange, football's governing body FIFA is one of the world's three largest power blocs alongside the USA and the International Olympic Committee (Mason 1995: 134). The development of anthropology has not had quite the same impact, but the game and the discipline do share parallels. Both originated from the sons of the middle class, and were concerned with discerning discipline and order among those assumed to be lower on the evolutionary scale at home or abroad. Both assumed the mantle of the 'white man's burden' in 'civilizing' those with skin darkened by pigmentation or the filth of industrial production. The mantra 'customs none, manners beastly' was, no doubt, played across football club committee meetings as well as the colonial verandas.

As the game's popularity spread before the First World War, regions and countries became synonymous with particular styles of play. Individual teams held periodic dominance; whatever tactics were employed, the ultimate vindication was victory on the field. While the sun never set on the British Empire, so British club sides were virtually unbeatable and periodically toured the colonies and other nations to tackle the local first eleven. Similar processes were evident in British anthropology. Universities became internationally renowned, leading figures were the academic versions of star players, as they and their team-mates disputed their rivals' tactics, produced polemics and argued over what selections inspired the best academic results (Kuper 1983). Imported ideas were few and far between; by the 1960s, proclamations over the supremacy of British football were as hollow as those attesting to the superiority of anthropology.

Today, the football we watch in the UK, and the anthropology produced by British practitioners, bears little resemblance to a century ago. The professional game has changed beyond recognition, with the local and parochial being increasingly supplanted by the global and cosmopolitan. This process is underwritten by transnational television satellite networks and the sudden proliferation of football magazines. As a consequence, the lifelong working-class fan faces a future of exclusion as multinational sponsorship combines with the discovery of a form of lifestyle authenticity for the new British middle class, to hike up match entrance prices. This is where, in a sense, football and anthropology diverge; as the game divests itself of localist trappings, British anthropology turns ever more to the study of the indigenous culture.

Spheres of Influence: the Game and its Public Appeal

Given its imperial genealogy, football has been interpreted as generating a form of false consciousness among its mass custodians. At first glance, the evidence supports this thesis. Throughout the world the game has been used by colonial authorities and the politically powerful, to inculcate desired 'civilized' (*sic*) standards or distract the mob from higher, political activities (Stedman Jones 1974; Jones 1988; Holt 1989: 142–4). Ian Taylor (1971: 127), like Vinnai (1971), argues from a Marxist perspective that football in Britain was a way of keeping down the 'dangerous class' under Industrial Capitalism and was pursued by middle-class teachers and clerics who promoted a game they had learned at public school. However, as MacClancy (1996: 11) suggests, this is a relatively simplistic argument.

In Britain, as the historian W.J. Baker (1988) argues, the football ground afforded the late nineteenth-century workers a relief from drudgery. Only a generation removed from their former village and farm labouring existence, the new proletariat were suffering alienation from the impersonality of urban existence (see Malcolmsen 1971 and Jones 1988). One hundred years later this theory is equally applicable to the new urban dwellers of the developing world. Yet, in both epochs, the game has coexisted with the growth of socialist and anti-colonial movements; it 'became an arena for political contest between the colonizers and the colonized' (MacClancy 1996: 12). Indeed, for the historian Fishwick (1989: 66), watching football was, in Britain, a 'thundering denunciation of work'; match-going allowed an engagement absent elsewhere in life. The ninety minutes provided excitement, debate, achieve-

ment and freedom to behave as one wanted which consequently
brought a 'new kind of solidarity and a new kind of sociability'.
The game's 'spiritual qualities' provided a temporary escape from
life's realities.

Throughout the world, football clubs have emerged as the
repositories of various identities, many political, but all intrin-
sically spatial. The significance of football in connection with
'place' for the historian Holt (1989: 167) was epitomized by the
role it played in creating a civic pride and a sense of membership
for the industrial working class, as well as providing a topic all
men could talk about. Intra-city football rivalry, in particular the
'Derby' match, proved 'who ruled the locality both in a sporting
and in a wider symbolic sense' (ibid.: 170). The football ground
and the team that trots out on to the pitch therein offers a study
of 'Topophilia' (Bale 1982: 25–30), i.e. a person's affective ties
with the environment, which couples sentiment with place (see
Bachelard 1969; Tuan 1977; Shields 1991: 29). To borrow from
Portelli (1993: 100), the ground gives shape to the image of unity,
and 'spectacularises' the social relations of a city (see Bromberger
1993a: 130–1). This space encapsulates (football) culture, which
as Shields (1991: 274) argues is nothing until it is 'spacialised' and
allowed its 'regimes of articulation'. But what is articulated and
why and what is censored by the powers that be are narratives
that anthropologists must present and analyse. The football match
provides an enchanting dramatic activity in which standards can
never be hidden nor the customer deceived. Seduced by an
unscripted drama every motion is open to question, to ridicule
and, to constant disappointment.

The fan may be an illusory participant, and the managers,
players and the chairmen may be the real holders of power. This
does not stop thousands from enjoying the feeling that they are
important and 'belong'.

Retaining Possession: Discourses of Masculine and Class Control

The popular English historian, Arthur Hopcraft (1968: 179), has
argued that the football crowd is 'always going to have more
vinegar than Chanel'; football grounds have always reverberated
to witty, ribald and abusive commentary on players, officials, rival

fans, and events on the pitch. In addition to the traditional association of the game with the working class, the other obvious factor here is that football has traditionally been synonymous with men. Throughout the world the game provides an access to male credibility. Part of the process of becoming a fan is learning to speak in 'football tongues'. The game enables various male metaphors and flippant remarks relating to sexuality and physicality. Not all men use these phrases but their availability means many choose a vocabulary which has football as an inspiration, and which does not need explanation in the local culture. Other verbal inspiration and the ability to talk *footballese* comes from a fan's daily consumption of the sports media. This, together with the experience of playing the game, produces what Archetti (1994a) terms a 'privileged male participation'.

The sporting body is a metaphor for male power, and a form of collateral which can be disciplined against opponents for the gaze of spectators, male and female. The acts of both playing football and spectating provide in many cultures the most important, collective source of male imagery and masculine ideals. As Lever (1983: 155) reminds us 'virtually all male socialisation, not just sport, teaches boys to be competitive', thus, participation in the game of football is rarely played in the Corinthian spirit. Furthermore, as Adorno (1967) argues, sport provokes a desire to 'do violence to others' and to likewise be attacked and suffer. Suffering is common in local amateur adult leagues which for a minority are an occasion to manifest a very high level of footballing ability, but for the majority are a weekly reminder that time waits for no man. At both junior and adult level, throughout the world, the game is played across a series of clichés redolent of masculine double-talk and metaphor, adopted by players to heighten or disguise their competitive endeavours.

Whilst it is typically believed that manifestations of swinging moods and irrationality are essentially a female trait (see Lutz 1988: 73–6), football playing and spectating allow men to act out the same diversity of emotions. Football permits antagonisms to manifest themselves through what Bromberger (1993a: 133) calls 'ritualised warfare', but one with boundaries which are never fixed and are thus open to controversies. Fans would probably agree as to what is relevant to encourage their representatives on the pitch, but disagree as to what is necessary or indeed honourable outside the requirements of 'normal' fandom, particularly in relation to the issue of the world-wide, but ill-defined phenomenon of 'Hooliganism' (Redhead 1991: 479). The various conflicts the game gives rise to have become a paramount concern for those involved in the administration and control of the game. Violence and death have occurred at and around games the world over and the State has used its own agents of violence to respond. For decades disorder on and off the pitch has been part of the occasion (see Hutchinson 1975; Mason 1980: 166; Fishwick 1989). Attempts by police to control this disorder in and around football are nothing new. Complaints about the game and its associated rowdiness go back over one hundred years (see Storch 1976; Vamplew 1984). What is new, however, is the way the young male football fan has been presented by some sources as being the devil incarnate, the 'Other' against whom right-thinking people can evaluate their personal propriety. The 'hooligan' *qua* symbol has become a routine target of global demonology. Yet, the public nature of the game has a wider consequence, in that it lends itself to periodic excess and the carnivalesque. Such conflicts between violence and exuberance have manifold causes: some crowds manifest in them wider political struggles for legitimacy be it via the club's nomenclature, kit colours, songs sung or actions and sympathies displayed by the players; the world over the football crowd has facilitated the opportunity of the repressed in their taunting of the powerful.

Spectating has always provided an arena in which to shout, dance, gesture and abuse others; rights that are denied for the most part elsewhere today (see Giddens 1991: 38; Bromberger 1994). 'Fandom' produces forms of consciousness which are neither rational nor impartial in their modes of thought. Partisans do not sit on the fence, fans do not seek the approval of other men. The match was and still is a liminal zone in which much male behaviour and opinion is enlivened by ridicule, rejoicing and indignation. The chance to suggest to very fit, muscular men, that their sexuality is questionable, or that they are a disgrace to their profession is easily expressed without the fear of the receiver reciprocating and demanding redress for the insult. Emotions can run riot, and sometimes so do the fans. Fan testimonies abound with the observation that the game induces a kind of all-consuming, irrational and totally childlike happiness in adult persons (see Pearson 1994: 48). Fans attend to experiences of desperation, envy, despair, misery, euphoria, all wrapped up in two hours of love and hate mixed with sincerity, passion and humanity. The nature of support permits the committed to 'go with the flow' (Finn 1994a: 109) in the liminal experience the game offers. After the match, football becomes a vehicle for existential reflection, in Archetti's (1992: 233) terms, the game assists a fan to 'reflect on the limits of "rationality", provoking the heart that aches and memories that linger'.

Football Affects: Teamwork and Playmaking

There are a plethora of participants, spectators and academics who have attempted to encapsulate discursively the symbolic totality of football. The American anthropologist Janet Lever (1983: 146) has lent weight to the Durkheimian and functionalist perspective, by arguing that football fosters deeper social integration, particularly through the ritualizing of conflict: 'By giving dramatic expression to the strains between groups and regions, soccer confrontations sustain traditional pluralism, countering cultural homogeneity while accentuating the wholeness of the social system.'

However, the very act of donning team colours means that some form of opposition and intolerance will ensue. World tournaments are celebrations of nationalism where the industrialized and industrializing worlds compete; where the developed play the developing, and democracies play 'emerging' nations. The latter must contend increasingly with the fragmenting reality of economic and cultural globalization, as their best players become economic migrants plying their skills on wealthier continents, re-enacting the wandering minstrel who is appreciated at the moment of performance, fêted in his absence and welcomed home to retell his tales from afar. This lucrative, young man's walkabout, this freedom, to realize, financially, a peculiar talent, needs not the proof of scalps or skin, but a few goals recorded on film to reassure those who remain and wait. Returning players become the wise elders, permitted to pontificate via the unofficial courts of the TV's panel of experts. From here they pass judgement on the performance of the young and general injustices within the game.

The historian Richard Holt (1989: 173) relates the game to Geertz's (1972) idea of 'Deep Play' (see Armstrong 1996), arguing that football is like a mirror for its spectators. It gives a: 'celebration of intensely male values . . . where skill and cunning were valued, but hardness, stamina, courage, and loyalty were even more important. Fairness and good manners were not held in high regard.' What can be said safely is that football provides a variety of identities sometimes, but not always, founded on accident of birth and not necessarily based in family ties. Such personal investment in football is not attributable merely to its practice or spectacle but in Bromberger's (1993a: 117) terms to its 'dramatic qualities', which he equates with the 'genres of theatrical production' to provide a unity of time, space and action, favouring the communion between players and spectators. The game's appeal is rooted in its social plasticity, which demands attention and creation. 'Football is neither a ritual of open rebellion nor the much-mentioned opium of the masses. It is a rich, complex, open scenario that has to be taken seriously' (Archetti 1992: 232). The true 'meaning' of football as Archetti (ibid.: 212) argues 'always remains hidden, can lose its value, but never dies'.

Like the ritualized procedures of a sacred ceremony, footballing events carry similar roles and structuration: a hierarchy of officials; regulating conventions and taboos; a closed space of worship and a pitch which acts as the equivalent of a high altar. An esoteric language is used in this temporal sequence, played to a liturgical calendar in which those seen as the socially powerful are publically present at important games. The players participate in a pre-match retreat from which the 'polluting' sexuality of women is excluded: a form of superstition that goes beyond modern medical supervision. Often, the players follow a fixed sequence of actions, culminating in the post-match examination of conscience. The outcome, Archetti argues, corresponds to the fundamental binary dichotomy of Good over Evil. Conceptions of the virtuous and pernicious become embodied, through the attribution of praise and blame, and validated through reward and glory or contrition and absolution.

A Secular Religion: Football as Cosmology

In continuing the ritualistic metaphor, we encroach upon the popular narratives, strangely underdeveloped by anthropologists, on football *qua* secular religion. There is a quasi-religious aspect to involvement in football (see Lever 1969; Coles 1975: 61–77;

Morris 1981). Football loyalties are deeply engrained, whether these are to the act of playing, the sociability of bonding with players, clubs and spectators, or to the moral codes presumed by the game. Thus, football centres upon an affirmation of faith, an element of identity, both personal and collective, that is never fully communicable in effectively rational terms. In common with religion, football involves a ritual around cultural artefacts, that generate symbolic communication with performative dimensions (see Archetti 1992). Christian Bromberger (1993b: 45), in analysing the parallels of religion and football, noted that the 'faithful' congregation of supporters and the anointed community of players, each manifest codified gestures and a special language, with some being more fervent than others. Notions of fate and fortune are central to the event; achievement, whether as player or spectator, is rarely seen to be the provenance of merit or grace alone. The game toys with a delicious uncertainty, between the binary opposition of science and serendipity, for while it is codified to reward skill and endurance, it is often associated with the divine intervention of serendipity and the malefactory. As in the outside world, decorous behaviour does not always receive its due return, and status is a precarious resource.

Why, we need ask, are people attracted to these rituals of football, where the uncertainty of the game's outcome are equalled only by the intensity of personal investments? Anthony Cohen (1974: 137) provides some insights into the essential appeal of such ceremonies; they help individuals: 'to derive comfort, perform a social obligation, achieve recreation, discover their identity, pass the time, be with others, and for an endless variety of other private personal purposes.'

These purposes are always suspended within relations of power between both individuals and groups. In contrast to what Cohen (1974: 55) calls the 'contractual role' of occupation where the self is least involved, there exist 'non-contractual, non-utilitarian roles and activities in symbolic action'. Drawing upon the work of Victor Turner, Cohen notes how some individuals take 'periodic leave' from work relationships or contractual activities to seek *Communitas* in recreational pursuits with people with whom they are not usually involved contractually. In this era, social relations, such as gatherings around football, need not be founded in any particularly local scenario but may be constructed across time and space. In this way the participants pursue what Lyotard (1988:

43) would term the 'promise of a community', an analogous updating of Anderson's (1983) 'imagined community'. Elsewhere, Maffesoli (1996: 119) refers to forms of football association involving the 'neo-tribe', which gives rise to solidarity 'through the accentuation of proxemics', the day-to-day alchemy of imperceptible situations, written as history by the subordinate masses.

For the majority of people in Western industrial cultures there is now no testing epic of poverty and war. Enslaved by ideas of rationality, technology and economic systems, humanity loses creativity and can experience disenchantment (see Weber 1930: 181, 1948: 139). Public forms of sociation and entertainment are removed when they may be edged into private and personal spaces. The private, secular and civilized natures of social life come to render urban living as publicly shallow and interactively subdued. Advanced stages of modernity precipitate this Durkheimian 'social anomie', giving rise to what Mary Douglas (1970) terms the contemporary 'ritual poverty' of the developed, and potentially the developing, worlds. Similarly, Klapp (1969) describes how this sense of futility leads to 'symbolic poverty', and argues that modern society lacks vital gossips, meaningful relationships, fulfilling rituals, and a sense of place (ibid.: 318). Football can provide for these emotional needs. In their free time some people seek out elements of community, endeavour, shared discovery and self-determination to fight against feelings of powerlessness and bewilderment. The problem becomes one of transcending monotony. As Klapp (1969: 319–20) contends, the absence of identifications and arenas for public forms of self-validation can lead some to seek an alternative or compensatory activity, which may see them define themselves through some 'action or ordeal'. One way is through the construction of these obdurate football 'communities', bound through opposition to those perceived as 'others'.

Anthropologies of Football: in the Field, on the Pitch

This anthology looks at these football communities and societies across the world. The papers draw upon fieldwork and analysis by social researchers working in five continents, employing methods and interpretive approaches found in the disciplines of anthropology, social and cultural history and sociology, in particular. The methodological emphasis throughout is on the contributors' collection and usage of primary data, whether through historical excavation or contemporary fieldwork. Consequently, there is a decisive endeavour here to avoid the criticism justifiably levelled at many UK sports sociologists, on the basis of their sedentary research techniques. As MacAloon (1992: 110)[3] writes, 'one wonders whether any other subject of social inquiry produces so much armchair analysis based so largely on newspaper stories, television broadcasts, a few statistics, some historical documents, and critical common sense.' This kind of research procedure does little to dispel public misgivings about the general value of academic studies of society, particularly as many non-academics will spend a lifetime debating and perfecting their understanding of football and other sports, with a passion that few share for their profession. We agree with Merton's (1967: 118–26) insight, that academic enquiries must seek to produce a deeper understanding of social life than may be formulated by those he calls archaically 'the non-theoretic men of affairs'. The most propitious procedure for achieving such an end is to undergo the cerebral *rites de passage* within our contemplative institutions, before embarking upon ethnographic explorations of any form of social life. The latter transition may be an unsettling or humbling experience, to those otherwise accredited with an elevated standing. The study of football cultures is certain to provoke routine but enriching challenges and contradictions of the researcher's personal and professional assumptions. Yet, the researcher is required to sustain his or her own methodological mantra, even as it is drowned by the vituperative chants of the research subjects. To paraphrase the inveterate ethnographer Paul Willis (1996), how can one claim to do any form of cultural study without actually meeting and engaging with its 'subjects' through ethnography? Carrying out a depth of day-to-day research is essential if the academic is to rebut the accusation of lazily resorting to professional status, to the false witness to one's attempt to speak more perceptively than most others on subjects that they know, cherish and practise (Descola 1996: 144–5). Football may be the universal theme of this collection, but fieldwork is perhaps of equal importance, in transferring engagement with the game from the research group on to the page.

This book is separated into three sections. The first section introduces the reader to South American and European football, where the game has mass public appeal and international success. Public enchantment with the game of football is synonymous with popular media images of South America and the *jouissance* of its successes: the ticker-tape welcome by home fans for their team inside stadia at Argentina '78; the 'beach football' samba carnival of dancing Brazilian fans at World Cup grounds every four years (see Humphreys 1994: 66). The social and moral chemistry which enlivens the game is more eloquently expressed in South American discourses on football. As a collection by Brazilian essayist Eduardo Coutinho (1980) reflects, football's social form is impressed by religious observance and political exploitation, corporeality and eroticization, and the autotelic play of the young versus the intrigue and instrumentality of the old. The typified stereotypes of football *qua* public obsession in South America misses out on these social and existential nuances, and tends to gloss over the dark history in which football grounds have been the literal venues of State repression, particularly in Argentina, Chile, Paraguay and Peru (Archetti and Romero 1994; Romero 1994).

Football in South America has distinctive British origins. Mason (1994: 1) observes, 'The first groups of young men to play something like the modern game of football in nineteenth-century Latin America were probably British sailors.' The names of older South American football clubs tend to reflect this archaic influence, notably in Argentina with River Plate, Racing Club and Boca Juniors, and, to a lesser extent, in Brazil with Corinthians. Yet, as the respective chapters by Eduardo Archetti and Jose Serge Leite Lopes demonstrate, football in Argentina and Brazil is the popular cultural terrain upon which particular national, ethnic and individual identities are explored and expressed, showing what it is to be Argentinian or Brazilian, and to be enveloped by such adhesive national football cultures. The two papers investigate these themes through contrasting scholarly perspectives.

According to Archetti, the social and moral dilemmas that confront Argentinians are given form and meaning through their continuing interpretations of Diego Maradona, Argentina's greatest football player. The individual deity that is Maradona is assiduously studied and evaluated by Argentinians, not only with regard to his mercurial playing performances, but more valuably to construct and reconstruct narratives on his capricious career and lifestyle. Drawing strongly upon interviews with a socially diverse group of fans, Archetti captures the symbolism of Maradona for Argentinians: a boyish genius among hardened adults, displaying a blend of fragility, fantasy, self-expression and frustration. Archetti's contribution must also be located within his impressive wider project, which elsewhere explains Argentinian football in relation to the formation of national identity, the construction of masculine identity, the violent history of fans and the State, the debate among Argentinians over opposing styles of play, the history and successes of the national football team, and the popular nexus of the game to the dance of tango (Archetti 1985, 1992, 1994a, 1994b, 1994c; Archetti and Romero 1994).

In contrast, the chapter by Leite Lopes explores the historical dimension of Brazilian football, and in particular the transformation of the game from a white, aristocratic pastime to a professional sport appropriated by the working classes, blacks and non-white groups. In this sense, Leite Lopes' study departs from the ground-breaking studies of Brazilian football by Janet Lever (1969, 1983), which have been interpreted as emphasizing the social cohesion and bonding afforded by collective engagement in the game (Jarvie and Maguire 1994: 10). Brazil's history of slavery and racial stratification has been the key component in the troubled and contested genesis of a distinctive Brazilian football style, deemed in turn to be artistic and romantic, or disorderly and uncivilized (Leite Lopes and Faguer 1994). Yet, without this aestheticization of football, carried out socially from below, and with an exuberant disregard for functionality and results, there is no 'Brazilian style' (see Banck 1994). As Leite Lopes notes, the game has served partially to emancipate individual Brazilian mestizos and mulattos from their structural impoverishment, although the peerless national sides of 1958 to 1970 have inspired a partial recolonization of football by the white, élite groups.

In Europe, this public essence of football has its sizeable equivalent in Italy. As the chapter by De Biasi and Lanfranchi explains, the ceremonies of the stands within Italian stadiums have their cultural and civic origins in the Renaissance form of football (*calcio*) played across town piazzas north of Rome (Baker 1988: 63–5). The fan rivalries, of course, may be said to have a deeper genealogy, which can be traced back to the riotous backing given to antiquity's charioteers by ordinary citizens (Cameron 1976; Guttman 1986: 19–34). As De Biasi and Lanfranchi argue, modern

Italy's football culture reflects the civic and regional chauvinisms and antagonisms (*campanilismo*) which underwrite the public culture of this 'nation of cities'. Hence, unlike those ethnologies of North European and South American cultures which tie football to the relatively dispossessed, the Italian game carries little in the way of a working-class heritage (Dal Lago 1990). Similarly, Italian football fans have evolved a distinctive *ultrà* sub-culture, which combines local civic identity, extraordinary fan choreographies and pyrotechnics in the stands, and the nomenclature of 1970s Italian paramilitaries and international youth cultures (Roversi 1994). Recently, the competitive domination of the Milan team, owned by the rightist media tycoon and former prime minister Silvio Berlusconi, has led to 'a double process of the politicization of football and the footballization of politics' (Dal Lago 1994: 142). According to Porro (1994: 1), Berlusconi's intervention with the football-branded political party entitled *Forza Italia!* represents a 'post-modern' turn in Italian society, as 'the search for political legitimacy is coupled to the winning image of high performance professional sport.'

The second section of this book deals with football in the developing world, in Asia, Africa and Antarctica. Football's effectiveness as a ritual forum, enabling the promotion of particular senses of national and ethnic identity to emerge, is given fuller examination in the chapter by Dag Tuastad on Palestinians. A concertedly political role is readily identifiable in the football culture of Palestinian refugees in Jordan. The *al-Wihdat* football club has become an outlet for stateless Palestinian nationalism which is otherwise suppressed in Jordan. In this way, the club's cultural and nationalistic politics come to resemble those attributed to the history of European sides such as Barcelona, Glasgow Celtic and Schalke 04, in providing respectively the indigenous Catalans, the immigrant Catholic Irish in Scotland, and Polish labourers on the Rhur with a popular cultural space in which to reproduce their threatened cultural identity, and to compete and conflict with more powerful majority groups on a more equal basis (see Colome 1992; Finn 1991, 1994b; Gehrmann 1994). Dag Tuastad hints that this ritual conflict on the football field may have distinctively functional dimensions for the Jordanian regime, in dissipating the Palestinians' more profound political antagonisms to the state through sport. Yet, the tension remains, such that the ritual may germinate uncontained hostility among Palestinians towards the symbols of their erstwhile masters. This is the Janus head of the football carnivalesque, inviting entry to a ritual that may confirm or consume the power of the proprietors.

The cultural politics of football reflect more fundamental social divisions in Africa, which are grounded in the contest between colonial and African, and traditional and modern cultural forces. South Africa, where the game historically has been at its strongest, provides the extreme illustration of football's politicization, in a society rooted in the racism of apartheid (Kuper 1965). Moreover, within the African areas of enforced separate development, South African football has made a contested transition from the tradition of local township rivalries to modern identifications with sides competing nationally (Jeffrey 1992). In this sense, football may be utilized to implant a particular sense of nationhood, thereby supplanting deep structural inequalities and cultural differences on the basis of ethnicity, class and language.

The most recently successful sub-Saharan football nation has been Cameroon. Its national team, the 'Indomitable Lions', reached the quarter-finals at the 1990 World Cup Finals (Tomlinson 1994: 27–8). The team's triumphs, however, are not achieved through purely scientific player selection from a nation of under 12 million people and over two-hundred tribes. 'Every player, Minister of Sport and assistant masseur tries to get players of his own tribe into the Lions, and a manager who plays their games will not be picking the team on merit' (Kuper 1995: 123). In their chapter on Cameroon football, Paul Nkwi and Bea Vidacs explore how tribal and presidential politics impact upon the game, particularly along the ethnic faultlines left by French and British 'colonialists'. Two decades earlier, Clignet and Stark (1974) noted how football was a cultural force promoting and evidencing early processes of social modernization. Cameroonians used their involvement in the game to symbolize their valuation of other aspects of their modern lifeworld. Players will be given nicknames which reference metonymically their educational status or musical tastes (such as 'Dalembert' or 'Mozart') and their technological fixations – in the early 1970s, one top player was called 'DC4' – (ibid.: 418). Today, as Nkwi and Vidacs recognize, football continues to reflect the incomplete projects of modernization and nation-building within the state of Cameroon.

In Sierra Leone, football also affords the possibility that the violence and social dissolution induced by military conflict may be set in reverse through the integrative experiences of play. During and after the end of British colonial rule in April 1961, Sierra Leone has been beset by the threat and realization of political turmoil and social violence. Economically, its mineral wealth in diamonds and iron ore have proven attractive to coup plotters and rebel armies, while a weak State infrastructure has struggled to arrest the financial haemorrhage of smuggling (Fyfe 1979: 157). Less than two centuries ago, the fledgling 'nation' was characterized by immense cultural pluralism, illustrated by over two-hundred major living languages, pointing to the problem of formulating a 'viable, tolerant society' in the face of such diversity (Last and Richards 1987: 408). Yet, the fragile social order that was constructed provides some objective testimony to the attainment of a new public amity, in spite of a rather Machiavellian war initiated in 1991 by a US economics graduate, Charles Taylor. The protagonists have engaged in the capture and enforced conscription of young people and the deliberate undermining of everyday contractual and affectual trusts. In comparison, where social accords are tenuously retained, football provides one avenue for resocializing the adolescents of war. Drawing upon his extensive ethnography, Paul Richards, arguably the world's leading expert on Sierra Leone, explains that football is one highly popular social practice which is organized to preserve the welfare of its young citizens. In doing so, he offers a reflective deconstruction of the football–violence metonym, which has filled Western political agendas and media commentaries.

Within African sport, witchcraft is often employed to serve less altruistic ends, namely the winning of the game, although its usage reflects the wider cultural tensions of tradition and modernization. In a classic paper, Fox (1961) examined how baseball became a 'competitive intrusion' into the societies of Pueblo Indians. Superstitions over the role of witchcraft abounded when the peace was disturbed and the villagers were divided. The new sport of baseball, and the fresh form of conflict to which it gave rise, thus came to induce new discourses on the intrusive role of sorcery. Similarly, reports have emerged from black Africa, of crowd disorder at football fixtures, induced by the belief that *juju* has been harnessed by rival players and spectators against those resorting to riot (Igbinovia 1985: 142–3). Scotch (1961) argues that while football serves to curb anomic tensions through the expression of aggression in a modern and acceptable form, the game still galvanizes disruptive fears and hostilities through beliefs in sorcery and witchcraft.

Anne Leseth's research into body culture in Tanzania drew her also into the study of football sorcery and witchcraft. While the institutions of modernity may seek to demonstrate the empirical irrationality of belief in *juju*, the Tanzanians may marshall more compelling legitimations for its ceremonial practice. All football cultures utilize some form of witchcraft, disguised by the discursive science of 'superstition', 'lucky' attire or 'pre-match routine'. The Tanzanians may simply be said to be employing their own, more elaborate techniques for awakening the supernatural. Their sorcery is even organized and deployed by a bureaucratic method, through forming various football club committees to discuss, measure and prepare the requisite level of *juju* which each match may merit.

The concluding section of the book centres upon the English-speaking developed world, including those nations which possess a colonial historical link to the United Kingdom. It begins with three chapters on football culture in England and Scotland, before examining two locations to which the game prima facie does not belong (Australia and the United States). The opening chapter by Gary Armstrong and Malcolm Young discusses the perennial issue of football hooliganism, but with particular reference to its juridico-political underpinning. Borrowing from the eponymous text by Bauman (1987), the authors endeavour to deconstruct the institutional control wrought on those fans engaged in essentially ritualized performances of competitive masculinity (see Marsh, Rosser and Harré 1978). In the past thirty years since 1966, English football fans have attracted intensifying levels of social control, commencing with segregation inside the ground and culminating most recently with the pilot usage of video phonelines. The authors represent an exceptionally informed combination of writers on the subject, as they make use of their previous work on both sides of the fieldwork fence: Armstrong has undertaken over a decade's research with English football hooligans, and Young has spent more than thirty years in the police force. Subsequently, they draw implicitly from the critical epistemologies advanced through the structural anthropology of Mary Douglas (1987) and the post-structuralist historiography of Michel Foucault (1977). Previously, John Fiske (1993: 82) had argued that sport is popular because it inverts the logic of surveillance found in the Foucaultian panopticon: 'Instead of the one in the centre monitoring the bodies and behaviours of hundreds around the perimeter, the thousands around the perimeter monitor the behaviour of the few in the centre.' However, Fiske has clearly failed to survey the CCTV and other forms of panoptical monitoring which the authorities exercise within and without football grounds. In the 1990s, UK policing of large football crowds has entered what Jean Baudrillard has termed the 'hyperreal', where virtual and actual realities become indistinguishable. Police control strategies are written in telematic centres that project the 'worst case scenarios', such as underground disasters, bombs inside stadiums or rooftop snipers. The excess of surveillance enables the agency of control to 'simulate a space of control, project an indefinite number of courses of action, train for each possibility, and react immediately with preprogrammed responses to the "actual" course of events' (Bogard 1996: 76).

The contributions on Scottish football come from Hans Hognestad and Richard Giulianotti, which respectively explore the culture of fandom surrounding two top clubs, Heart of Midlothian (Hearts) and Aberdeen. Historically, Scotland played a major role in the early development of football's playing techniques and social organization. In the late nineteenth century the Scots humiliated their English rivals into learning the benefits of a 'passing game' (Baker 1988: 125). Meanwhile, the Scots' migratory tradition ensured that many expatriates came to introduce football and to found clubs overseas, throughout Europe, the Americas and Asia particularly (see Forsyth 1991: 31–2).

In the 1990s, Scottish football does retain some important executive powers within football's governing bodies.[4] However, Scotland's international team has never gone beyond the first round of the World Cup Finals; nor do its club teams pose much threat at European level. Additionally, Scotland's national stadium does not possess the facilities or grandeur expected of a premier football force; and it continues to lack a genuinely 'world class' national player to grace its turf. In Raymond William's terms, Scottish football's international status is now more distant and 'archaic' rather than material or 'residual' (Ingham and Loy 1993: 3–4). The arrested evolution of the Scottish game is persistently commemorated by team results, routinely witnessed by playing 'styles', and lampooned or bemoaned by football pundits, comedians and supporters nationally.

These self-critical, dominant narratives on Scottish football are often further expressed through the cultures of support that can emerge at club level. Scottish club fans have to contend with the further unsocial fact, that the domestic game is dominated by Glasgow's top two teams, Rangers (especially) and Celtic (now potentially). Accordingly, as Hans Hognestad shows, a club such as Hearts fosters a practical, if fatalistic, outlook among its supporters to explain its distinctive lack of trophy-winning success. The game's innate serendipity is thus conceived of as conspiring with more intractable, economic forces to overshadow the playing side's potency on the pitch. In these unpromising circumstances, players and supporters attach great significance to the invention of a tradition around the club, and to the collective pride that is found in wearing or celebrating the Hearts colours and motifs.

Whereas Hognestad explores the diffuse and generalized aspects of Hearts fan identity, the chapter by Richard Giulianotti examines the particular culture of fandom which emerges from the 'fanzines' of another Scottish football club, Aberdeen. Since the late 1980s, UK football fanzines have been the most important and colourful vehicles for disseminating and disporting football fans' outlook on their respective teams, players, opponents and authorities. As with other cultural forms of football fandom, that which is prevalent at national and global levels is translated into a more local context for its everyday engagement to be meaningful (see Duke and Crolley 1996). Thus, though the format of football fanzines tends to be commonly shared, their content is highly varied, reflecting the meaning of the club for its supporters, and the wider cultural mores of the locality. Accordingly, Aberdeen fanzines carry a classic variety of cartoons, spoof stories and measured invective; their editors and writers also derive from the social strata found elsewhere among fanzine writers. Yet, these fanzines still crystallize the local ambivalence towards militant/ irrational support of the team; the North-East's amorphous distrust of the more powerful Scottish regions (whether in football, media or politics); and the parodic scepticism which the supporters routinely target at the club's leading officials.

Australia's male sporting practices tend to draw their history and social prevalence from the nation's colonial relationship to the United Kingdom. The two rugby codes (union and league) and cricket are imperial sports which Australians (especially the hegemonic Anglo-Australians) play to the highest international standards. However, football is the single major sport which owes its development in Australia to the immigrant communities from the Mediterranean. Whereas typified 'Aussie sports' become vehicles for the expression of an Australian cultural nationalism (Holt 1989: 230), Australian football often actuates prejudicial discourses and mores from its indigenous detractors. The game is popularly referred to as 'Wogball' by Anglo-Australians (Vamplew 1994), and prone to processes of 'Aussification', most notably by banning 'ethnic' names (Hughson 1992). The latter step was provoked by concern among Australian football's controlling body that the ethnic affiliation of its member clubs was encouraging the Balkan conflict to be played out vicariously inside Australian football grounds (Mosely 1994).

John Hughson's paper examines how the ethnicity of one Australian football team, Sydney United (formerly known as Sydney Croatia), underpins the support afforded it by its fan sub-culture, known as the 'Bad Blue Boys' (see Hughson 1995). These fans are generally second generation Australians of Croatian extraction and are fiercely nationalistic. Their culture of support is inspired by the hooligan fan groups which follow clubs in Croatia. Football in Croatia is a site of intense political and cultural nationalism. International fixtures in Zagreb have become a kind of public ceremony in which the new Croatian state receives its emotional validation; the national football team literally wears the national flag as a football strip; the origins of Croatia's secession from the former Yugoslavia may even be traced to a Croat–Serb club fixture in 1991, at which over sixty fans were injured in rioting and Croatian players fought with Serbian police officers (*The Guardian*, 7 October 1995). Hughson's study explores how the Bad Blue Boys in Sydney resource this nationalism, in tandem with other, more established Croatian properties, such as shared cultural values and social practices, or the general culture of football hooliganism in Croatia (see Vrcan 1992).

Like Australia, the United States has proved infertile territory for germinating a mass football culture. Famously, the separate development of American sporting culture is dominated by the modification of British colonial games to produce baseball and American football (Gorn and Goldstein 1993). The global game of football is thus *only* known as 'soccer' in the United States, to save confusion with the indigenous sport. American soccer has enjoyed moments of international interest, notably a historical victory over England in 1950, and the 1970s NASL competition which attracted faded overseas superstars to play in empty stadiums (Williams and Giulianotti 1994: 4). The American game's survival has relied upon its continuing engagement by European and Hispanic immigrant communities in new urban areas, between and after the world wars; yet even within these communities, the collective desire to engender a new American identity commonly entailed the abandonment of this alien sport (Riess 1991: 106; Sugden 1994: 239). Indeed, subsequent American social research concluded that the 'club policies of ethnic football clubs inhibit the structural assimilation of members' (Pooley 1976: 491), an analysis later lent support by Canadian research (Walter, Brown and Grabb 1991).

Nevertheless, as the chapter by Andrews, Pitter, Zwick and Ambrose demonstrates, the successful allocation of the 1994 World Cup Finals has two underlying social causes. Firstly, FIFA remains convinced that the United States is a vast, untapped, and peerlessly enriched market for football's further commodification. USA '94 pulled in a profit of some $25 million, and has been used as a marketing springboard to launch the delayed MLS (Major League Soccer). The new league shares the corporate managerial vogue for 'downsizing'; it opened with only ten teams playing in stadiums of a maximum 28,000 capacity, and within wage caps of $1.3 million (*World Soccer*, April 1996). Secondly, the future of MLS is reliant upon successfully transferring the 16 million registered US soccer players into spectators and dedicated consumers of soccer merchandise. Since the mid-1970s, the game has been cultivated by the young, white middle class, alienated by the expense, physicality and gender segregation of more 'traditional' American sports, particularly the native version of football (Guttman 1988: 161; Sage 1990: 151–4). As indicated by this case study of football in Memphis the future of the game's American genesis rests on the question of whether its engagement merely represents a contemporarily convenient form of cultural 'distinction', for marking off this privileged social caste in class and ethnic terms.

Future Research Locations

In the fullness of time, this collection will seem to have marked out for itself an almost natural niche, within the overall historical configuration of academic texts on football. The matter of whether the book's disciplinary and methodological precepts are professionally worthwhile, may only be resolved within future debates on football cultures. We would like to conclude, therefore, by indicating some areas in which future research might be directed profitably.

Locations of future research are often easily identified. Major international tournaments within the changing world of top-flight football are certainly of interest. The World Cup hosted by France in 1998 will bring thirty-two finalists from a starting line-up of 173 nations, double the number of finalists who went to Argentina in 1978, and a third as many again since the last *mondiale* of USA '94. The tournament then makes its first exploration in the Asian continent, when Japan and South Korea become co-hosts in 2002. If the rapidity of change over the previous decade is any form of barometer, then the pressures of advanced modernization will sweep further across the world of football. We may expect to see more national sides representing peoples formerly without a nation, as we have recently witnessed in Europe's former Eastern Bloc countries. We may also see nations with diasporic histories experiencing heightened levels of support at fixtures played on what would otherwise be termed as 'foreign soil'. Ireland have led the way here, particularly through its expatriate support during USA '94 (Giulianotti 1996, 1997); Turkey is following suit at European club and international matches (see Kozanoglu 1996).

A further tournament worth close scrutiny is the Olympic Games' football competition. The prestige accorded this tournament within the sport is reflective of football's greater institutional globalization, as well as shifting power balances within the game, in favour of those disadvantaged within traditional competition. At Atlanta '96, the power blocs of the USA and China were represented in the women's final in front of a crowd of 76,000, whilst Nigeria in beating Argentina in front of 85,000 spectators became the second African team to win a major world tournament following Ghana's success in the Junior World Cup of 1991. As some of the chapters within this collection suggest, the increasingly frequent prominence of black African successes at a global level, is underpinned by a rich tapestry of social processes and conflicts that merit further research.

The dynamics of the free market may be behind football's expansion into territories such as those mentioned above, although the political role of nation-states is at least as significant. For example, European football is coming to terms with the 'Bosman case', in which out-of-contract EC players may move free of charge to any club in a different EC nation. Moreover, just as it has been in the democratic and totalitarian states of Europe and Latin America, football may still become a special public space, in which popular and violent protests against symbols of the politically dominant serve to bring into view the hidden scale of the authorities' might. In June 1996, over fifty fans were shot dead in Libya when the referee allowed a dubious goal to stand in favour of a team patronized by the son of Colonel Gaddafi. At the same time as the massacre in Tripoli, the European Championships were being hosted by England, televised in 194 nations, and sponsored to the tune of £200 million. A £20 million security operation was put into action, producing a proportionate ratio of over 1,000 arrests, but only a handful of convictions for genuinely serious offences. (For such a sum, a nation such as Libya might 'civilize' its security arrangements, though trade embargos might preclude their bankrolling by McDonalds, Coca-Cola and other agents of Americanization.) Advertised as a success by the organizers, the tournament's stadiums were frequently half empty, as sporting performances and mercantile expos merged into one. Twenty per cent of tickets to the Wembley final were handed to corporate rather than core supporters.

Further transformations within the game may be expected, with the social uses of new technology paving the way. The vexed question of goal size may be settled finally in favour of securing a higher scoring 'spectacle' for transient television audiences. Controversy and enduring beliefs in injustices could be banished if referees are to be assisted by touchline officials, literally replaying on television monitors those borderline moments of action. Growing numbers of European football fans have access to daily live football, broadcast on satellite or cable television. The impending ubiquity of screened football inspired one media impresario, Silvio Berlusconi, the owner of AC Milan and former prime minister of Italy, to formulate an apocalyptic vision of the game's public dimension. Echoing the worst prophecies of the sociologist and seer Jean Baudrillard (1993: 79–80), Berlusconi predicted a post-modern time when spectators would be admitted free of charge to football stadiums, since the 'hyperreal' event at home on family television would be more entertaining. The trend was perhaps highlighted in the United Kingdom where, as the European Championships attracted a record UK television audience of 26 million for one fixture, two top clubs, Arsenal and Manchester United, were reduced to inventing reserved 'singing sections' in a bid to re-create the match-day 'atmosphere' which has been destroyed by all-seater stadiums. If television (and vicarious fandom) is to play the dominant commercial role within Europe's top club tournaments, clubs will still maximize the revenue-raising potential available to that market segment seeking the sensational authenticity of cheering players in the flesh. The leading Dutch club Ajax have shown the way at their state-of-the-art Amsterdam Arena, inside which entering fans may only purchase club merchandise with the official club currency.

To those of classic Marxist persuasion, this commodification of football's material culture must threaten to inculcate alienation among supporters. Yet, the wider process of modernization figures strongly throughout the game, and cannot abolish *in toto* the public pleasures which it actuates. Drawing upon the concepts of Roland Barthes (1975), the distinction between the pleasures of *plaisir* and *jouissance* goes some way to theorizing these developments. *Jouissance* is the (increasingly outmoded) form of pleasure that is more harmful to the interests of capital, within football or any other area of social life, as it may challenge the bourgeois social order, such as through violent or intoxicated behaviour off the field, or ignoring professional tactics while on it. Reducing the public manifestation of *jouissance* entails squeezing the pleasures of football into *plaisir*, where the interests of the prevailing social order are accommodated and occasionally modified in a bid to develop particular forms of identity. *Plaisir* is therefore to be found in those who support successful teams, usually through the medium of television, or who adopt efficient playing and coaching styles. Importantly, *jouissance* is the realm of the natural and corporeal, and provides irreductive energy and numinous senses of empowerment; *plaisir* belongs to a more cultural and reflective universe, providing meaning and social contextualization. *Jouissance* is found in the magical play of Maradona, or the faith in the powers of football *juju*. *Plaisir* is found respectively in the defensive systems that attempt to eliminate him, or the pro-science incantations of the authorities in black Africa. While this collection may seem to be restricted to the language of *plaisir*, its contributors unanimously seek to hint at the *jouissance* afforded by their specific venues of research.

This irreducible appeal of football seems to lend itself to a

Parsonian lexicon. For just as players and teams adapt themselves when confronted by difficult opponents to improve their goal attainment, so the system of the game itself continues to modify its shape and form, to survive and thrive in new natural and cultural circumstances. Yet, while we may say that football operates efficiently within its own domains, the human needs that it nourishes are less easily explained. As one South American novelist has written: 'Cultured or uncultured, rich or poor, capitalist or socialist, every society feels this irrational need to enhance idols of flesh and blood, and burn incense to them . . . Footballers are the most inoffensive people on which one can confer this idolatrous function' (Varga Llosa 1996).

Perhaps, to explain the human prerequisites that football satisfies, we can only begin by returning to comparative studies of fieldwork research, to the discipline of ethnology. Part of the game's fascination is the anthropological diversity of cultural meanings and body styles through which it is played and watched, understood and discussed, throughout the world. Ethnological enquiries like this one that examine football in its different cultural contexts, provide striking illustrations of the heterodox moral and existential issues, which envelop a seemingly frivolous contest between opposing groups of players. Undertaking research at the World Cup Finals or the Olympic Games is one common strategy for garnering ethnological data. These tournaments appear to provide ready-made (if ultimately selective) arenas for observing the intra- and inter-active cultures of different footballing identities, and their exact periodicity fits neatly with the academic calendar. Nevertheless, these national supermarkets are sited in ultimately unsatisfying research locations; superior studies follow from fieldwork carried out in the genuine host context of these disparate football cultures.

As we noted at the outset, the academic field within which football is examined has tended to omit anthropology, particularly in the UK. Since the late 1980s, a network of football researchers has been spun and respun. Rather often, the intellectual and explanatory value of the resulting work is questionable, and seems to offer little to those not *au fait* with the game's minutiae. It is a frustrating experience indeed to be neatly compartmentalized, by peers and public alike, solely into the 'football studies' locker. It would be a bigger and more worthwhile challenge to the often charmed circle of football academics, to bolt out of this discursive detention, and demonstrate to the uninitiated and the uninterested how the game provides a crucial venue for many kinds of social organization. The game distils and plays out fundamental social questions, relating not only to class, gender, ethnicity and age, but also to moral, existential and ontological dilemmas, within delimited times and spaces. Anthropologists such as those contributing to this collection are taking up the challenge. No anthropologist worth professional accreditation can ignore games such as football, if a fuller understanding is to be contributed to the social and cultural life in most societies.[5] We would therefore encourage and cajole any researcher within an industrial or non-industrial setting to look at football or the dominant sport, in order to embellish at least the meanings of that society which are already at hand.

Notes

1. For the benefit of North American readers particularly, we recognize that the game is more generally known as 'soccer' there. Hence, the chapters in this book move between these two forms of nomenclature, although in this introductory chapter we shall retain the more traditional term of 'football'.
2. Although Korr is based in the United States, his cited work is on the social history of a classic English football club, West Ham United.
3. An example of this kind of 'research' is provided by one sociology of sport textbooks. In his discussion of football hooliganism in England, Cashmore (1996: 214–15) follows simplistic newspaper coverage of the phenomenon. He repeats common-sense assumptions about the effectiveness of the police in tackling fan violence, and draws special attention to the role played by one group of political extremists in stoking up hooliganism. Sociological fieldwork into the subject, which calls into question both of these popular assumptions, is inexplicably ignored.
4. Off the field, Scottish football officials include UEFA's Technical Director (Andy Roxburgh), the Vice-President of FIFA (David

Will), and the Chairman of UEFA's Stadium Committee (Ernie Walker); Scotland also has a major role in safeguarding the laws of football, as it has one of eight seats on the International Football Association Board (Finn and Giulianotti 1996).

5. For example, we look forward to seeing the completed work by Mark Nuttall on the centrality of football to the everyday cosmology of the Inuit in Greenland.

Chapter 2

'And Give Joy to my Heart'. Ideology and Emotions in the Argentinian Cult of Maradona[1]

Eduardo P. Archetti

At the end of October 1994, four months after the Maradona doping scandal at the USA World Cup, a long march of protest against the economic policies of the national government reached Buenos Aires, the capital city of Argentina. Thousands of exhausted and enthusiastic provincial State employees were joined by thousands of university students and political sympathizers of different opposition parties in a tumultuous and noisy rally in the city centre. This political demonstration, as is usual in Argentina, began with the national anthem being sung vehemently by the crowd. The second song surprised me. With even more energy, the participants chanted the popular rock song 'And Give Joy to my Heart' by Fito Paéz, perhaps the most popular contemporary Argentinian rock composer and singer. The text reads:

> And give joy, joy to my heart
> it is the only thing I ask you today,
> and give joy, joy to my heart
> and out of me will go the grief and the pain.
>
> And you will see,
> the shadows that were here
> will not be,
> and you will see,
> we will drink and the city will be drunk.
>
> And give joy to my heart,
> it is the only thing I ask you today,

and give joy, joy to my heart
and turn on the lights of my love.

And you will see
how the air of this place is transformed,
and you will see
that you don't need anything more.

And give joy, joy to my heart
please, that yesterday I did not have a good day,
and give joy, joy to my heart
because if you give me joy better I will be.

Fito Paéz supposedly composed this song in honour of Maradona in 1986, during his glorious performance at the Mexico World Cup.[2] According to the composer, the lyrics were motivated by an acute psychological depression; they had nothing to do with the exploits of Maradona on the Estadio Azteca pitch, and the eventual joy Paéz experienced watching him dribble round the world's most resolute defenders. However, during the 1990s, and after Argentina's defeat in the World Cup final in Italy and after the first doping scandal involving Maradona over cocaine use in the Italian league, the Argentinian fans interpreted the song as evoking warm support for their football hero, and expressing the joy they had experienced watching him play. Hence, the song was seen as offering an optimistic view and anticipating the joy of Maradona's comeback. Fito Paéz accepted this reading as legitimate, arguing that in Argentina rock and football go together because they are able to stimulate profound emotional states (*El País*, 6 July 1995: 34).

At the political rally of 1994, the Maradona song conveyed a sense of criticism as well as hope for better days to come. In the context of the demonstration, one can claim, the troubled provincial employees and the suspended great idol were on the same side: the side of the maltreated and humiliated.[3]

I asked a provincial employee, whom I think was from the province of Salta, about the meaning of this song and his steady response was:

yes, this song is the song of Maradona and of course of all of us today. Did you recognize who the singer was? I mean the record played through the loudspeakers . . . Well, she is Mercedes Sosa, the 'black', our greatest artist. There is hope in the song and there is hope today. We will win this struggle and all the strikes that will come in the future and, of course, Maradona will be back, next year, no doubt. FIFA will not crush him and the national government will not suppress our voices. You see this song unites us in the present, now, in this moment. It is our song because we have decided this way . . . What does the song mean? Hope, confidence and faith.

In this chapter, I will analyse the cult of Maradona in Argentina. My observations are based on fieldwork carried out in Buenos Aires from October to December 1994, during the time Maradona was suspended for doping by FIFA. The suspension lasted fifteen months, from July 1994 to October 1995. My informants were at different stages in their lifecycles: the youngest was thirty-seven and the oldest sixty. I have had intermittent exchanges and dialogues with them since 1984 on the meaning of football in Argentinian masculine culture. They constitute the 'hard core' of the oral history component of my research, which also includes historical documentation; books, magazines, newspapers, biographies and pamphlets of all kind (see Archetti 1994a, 1995, 1996a). The majority of my informants belong to the well-educated Argentinian middle class, but some of them are lower-class, service workers and unskilled State employees.

My partial and limited findings can be seen as a contribution to a better understanding of the relationship between the perceptions of the complex character of Maradona and some recurrent topics in the imagery of Argentinian football. Maradona is concrete and contemporary, but the frame within which he is placed by my informants is more abstract, integrating the lived and imagined past as well as the perceived traditions of Argentinian football. In this frame, Maradona is represented and talked about in social discourses belonging to the realm of ideology. Ideologies are themselves products as well as producers of social reality. Without entering into a long discussion on the concept of ideology, I am simply alluding to a process of constructing a given other (in our case Maradona) against which is imagined an individually and collectively created 'player' or 'Argentinian-style player' possessing archetypical qualities (see Sangren 1995). Maradona is paradoxically constituted by this process as a kind of abstract and ahistorical person. I will argue that, given this ideological device, Maradona is regarded as neither reasonable nor responsible, as a *pibe* (a young boy), and in this way a particular cultural construction of maleness is presented and publicly discussed.

Ideologies are embodied in emotions which are asserted in various contexts, formal or informal, at home or in public (see Abu-Lughod and Lutz 1990). Emotions like pride, shame, joy or grief are fundamental in the lite and discourses of football supporters (see Dal Lago and De Biasi 1994; Bromberger 1995a; Hognestad 1995; Archetti 1996b). After all, Fito Paéz composed a song on the importance of joy and its connections with Maradona's life. This was made relevant to me by many Argentinians of different backgrounds who attended the October political rally. In this chapter, I will maintain that the choice and the importance of joy in the lyrics and discourses of the supporters and political activists is not arbitrary. Joy is of course an inner feeling which is impossible to deny. However, anthropological analysis must transcend the domain of individual psychological feelings, and examine the role of emotional discourses in social interactions. The focus is on a special kind of symbolic interaction: the performances of Maradona and their impact on the football public. This impact is not only an instantaneous one at the time of a labyrinthine dribble, a perfect pass or a marvellous goal. For my informants, these moments are part of an embodied memory, a certain emotional reservoir that can function like a replay on the television screen: the visual image (the concrete achievements of Maradona as a player) triggers particular experiences and emotions which can be re-enacted in a continuous movement from the present to the past and vice versa. Maradona's performances were remembered in a kind of ritualized, commemorative bodily communion and as a genuine expression of joy (or happiness as some of my informants preferred to say). Juancho, one of my main informants, a very articulate and critical observer of Argentinian football, presented this idea clearly:

> I cannot hide from you some of my profound inclinations: football is (and if it's not it should be) an artistic expression, but an art that is not the product of something rational. Football is the artistic expression of the unexpected, of something that is created in an improvised manner. Only the artists can do it this way, spontaneously. Maradona is an artist, and like him there are very few, very few, I assure you . . . You see him, you watch him on television, and you admire him, you feel an aesthetic pleasure, something you sensed,

something you will always remember. The things he is able to do are so unexpected, so extraordinary, and then you always remember, because he is not like the others, because he will always try to do something unmatched.

Maradona: the *Pibe* and the *Potrero*

In the dominant Argentinian football imagery, the *pibe* and the *potrero* (an open and irregular field in an urban context used to play football) are powerful concepts and symbols of what is considered the *criollo* style (*la nuestra*) (Archetti 1995, 1996a). The imagery of *pibe* emphasizes that there is an infantile beginning in football, as in every game, but also stresses the importance of freshness, spontaneity and freedom which is associated with childhood and which is usually lost with the advent of maturity and its resultant responsibilities. Maradona is still called *el pibe de oro* (the golden young boy), hence the other great *pibes* of Argentinian football history are eventually made of silver or bronze, less prestigious metals. Moreover, Maradona was discovered to be a prodigious player already at the age of ten; at the age of twelve, the media declared that Argentinian football had never had such a talent. At fifteen he played his first match for Argentinos Juniors in the first division. At sixteen he was admired as a precious gift to the nation. At seventeen he played his first international match with the Argentinian national team. At eighteen, as captain, he won the first gold medal for Argentina in the Junior World Cup in Tokyo. His precocity and, of course, his ability were confirmation of his quality as a *pibe*.

Childhood is, as we know, a culturally defined transitional period in the life of individuals. Tomás explained to me that:

to be a *pibe* is not only to be liberated from several responsibilities. To be a *pibe* is to feel the pressure from the authority of the family, the parents, the school. But also to be a *pibe* implies that it is easier to see the positive aspects and to forgive the imperfections. It is common to say here, in Argentina, and perhaps in a lot of other places too, 'but he is a *pibe*, just a *pibe*, let him be a *pibe*'. Maradona is a *pibe* and will remain a *pibe*. He represents this state of perfection and freedom when we disregard the most negative traits of an individual. Spontaneity, to be fresh and to do things just right away without thinking on the negative consequences are qualities that we appreciate. A great football player must have these qualities.

For many years, and without any doubt for most of my informants, Maradona looked like a *pibe*. They would say that he really looked like a happy *pibe* when he received the World Cup trophy in Mexico in 1986. This image is perhaps the most perfect symbol of his achievements and global fame. Moreover, he seemed like a 'naughty child', and for that reason, he had not yet lost his freshness. This paradox, a mature young man (twenty-six years old) at the top of his career being defined as a *pibe*, is significant: an important virtue for the best Argentinian players is then to preserve as far as possible, this pure, childlike style. Through this image it is conveyed that football is a game and, as such, can only be fully enjoyed when one has total freedom. Football is ideally perceived as an ideal game for children.

Another forceful image emerged in the memory of my informants. When he was twelve years old, Pipo Mancera, at that time a famous television entertainer, showed Maradona juggling with a ball, doing incredible things that even a worshipped professional player would have enormous difficulty in imitating. After a minute of juggling, 'a minute that was eternal' according to Sergio, Mancera asked Maradona what his dreams, as a football player, were and he, without hesitation, answered that he had three dreams: to play in the first division, to wear the shirt of the Argentinian national team in a World Cup and to win it. Sergio explained to me:

> it was like in the famous tango *El sueño del pibe* (The *pibe*'s dream), do you remember? But Maradona was more aspiring and conscious of his capacity. Well, the lyrics narrate the story of a talented *pibe* that, while crying of joy, shows to his mother a letter from his club telling him he has been accepted as a player in the Fifth Division. During that night, he dreams that, like so many crack Argentinian players, he will reach the First Division and that on his debut he will score the winning goal. Look, in this tango the *pibe* is a forward and he scores after dribbling past all the defenders of the opposing team. It is difficult to be a real *pibe* and to be a defender. Defenders ought to look and perform like real men, not forwards.

These images have been used hundreds of times in Argentinian and international television programmes devoted to the life of Maradona. The perfect synchronicity of the performance, the age of the performer and his future career, matches real life with the flavour of a soap-opera. Nothing is better for committed football supporters than when fiction is transformed into strong reality, as in this case. It is possible to argue that it is destiny, fate, almost a natural development, or that it 'was written', as many would say. I would like to add that in the case of Maradona, he knew the tango very well and was able to sing it in a television programme in 1994. Sergio, Tomás and Amílcar reminisced distinctively about this occasion.

Maradona has the benefit of the shape of his body. It is easier to associate his status of *pibe* with his height, his roundness, his tendency to be fat, his sudden acceleration, his theatrical exaggeration, his way of walking with short movements, and his constant struggle against rude and aggressive defenders. Maradona has looked casual, unkempt, unfit for long periods of his career, and, in many ways, inelegant. My informants compared Maradona's body with the bodies of other great international heroes of Argentinian football: Di Stéfano, the legendary player of Real Madrid in the 1950s, and Sivori, the skilful 'angel with a dirty face' (and then a *pibe*) who captivated the supporters of Juventus in the 1960s. Both were forwards, and Sivori was, like Maradona, a typical inside-left. In comparison, Sivori comes close owing to his dribbling style and ability but he was a more disciplined and hard player. Di Stéfano was blond, almost a Scandinavian type, his figure was stylized and he had premature baldness. Energetic, he was a real leader, even a fighter, and very elegant. Di Stéfano was defined as a mature, hard man. Of course, in our conversations, we found a lot of players that could be described as *pibes*, such as René Houseman, the right-winger of the Argentinian team which won the 1978 World Cup, the one who was perceived as a 'brother', as a cultural and almost genetical associate of Maradona, but with the opposite body. Houseman was short, nonchalant, bony, nonconformist and daring. We agreed that there are different bodies, or figures, that can represent the ideal image of the *pibe*. The imagery of the *pibe* is plural and full of ambiguities.

The meaning of *pibe* is related to a cluster of features that promote and limit the social construction of the stereotype. One such feature is the small body, particularly in terms of height. In addition to body shape, the content of bodily performances seems to be another important feature. The image of a typical *pibe* player is based on an exuberance of skill, cunning, individual creativity, artistic feeling and improvisation. In this sense it is easy to understand that the image of a powerful, disciplined and perfect athletic body is absent. A third related feature is the kind of daily life *pibes* carry on. In the case of a *pibe*, a lot of disorder is expected. Chaotic behaviour is the norm. There is a tendency to disregard boundaries, to play games even in private life (life is experienced as a permanent game or gamble if necessary); additionally, there is a capacity to recompense, penalize or forgive others in an exaggerated way; to convey arbitrary judgments and choices; to display stupid and irrational heroism, and a capacity to 'die' (by being imprisoned, a drug-addict or an alcoholic) and to be resurrected; and a special talent in critical games to make the unexpected move, ensuring victory for the team. Thus, a *pibe* is creative, free of strong feelings of guilt, self-destructive and, eventually, a bad moral example to other players. In the global moral evaluation of this kind of player the ultimate criterion is the creativity of their bodies. My informants, and I imagine the supporters in general, tend to forgive the lack of moral and social responsibility of the *pibes*. Explicitly, the amount of joy given by the *pibes* is more important than any consistent moral evaluation. We will explore this issue later.

We can classify the *pibes* as liminal individuals, as being on a threshold, a state 'betwixt and between', in a kind of trans-formative period. My informants, however, put the stress on the fact that in football 'once a *pibe*, always a *pibe*'. I hope that it is clear that the category *pibe* is marked by ambiguity, ambivalence and contradictions, because the model of interpretation is based on a potential disorder: *pibes* will not become mature men. The recognition of liminality makes possible the differentiation of players and particular bodies and performances. Liminal individuals provide an object of identification that appeals to the subjects establishing the differences (see Norton 1993: 51–93). Identifying a typical *pibe* in the cultural construction of football has the power of evocation. My informants recognize the 'eternal *pibe*' condition in some men (even among themselves) through identification with players like Maradona. This process involves the differentiation of qualities proper to an established dominant ideal of masculinity, based on reason and responsibility, from those alien to it: the *pibes*. The *pibes* serve as mirrors and, at the same time, operate as models defining the ideal of a style, a way of playing. The image of Maradona contains these two aspects.

The fact that a liminal condition does not entail a future transformation is of theoretical interest. This means that the liminality of the *pibes* transcends the accepted notion of rites of passage. Bourdieu has raised a relevant question in relation to Van Gennep's 1960 theory: what are the social functions of boundaries or limits which rites of passage allow one to pass or transgress in a lawful way? He is right to point out that by stressing the temporal transition (e.g. from childhood to adulthood) some important questions are not asked. He states:

> this theory does not conceal one of the essential effect of rites, namely that of separating those who have undergone it, not from those who have not yet undergone it, but from those who will not undergo in any sense, and thereby instituting a lasting difference between those to whom the rite pertains and those to whom it does not pertain.

> (Bourdieu 1991: 117)

He suggests a redefinition of the rites of passage as 'rites of institution'. The central function of 'rites of institution' is to establish arbitrary boundaries (ibid.: 118). Maradona belongs to the world of *pibes*-players which adult-players will not enter. The stress is on the boundary between childhood and adulthood, not on the transition from one condition to the other. In the ideal construction of football which many of my informants dream of, a perfect universe is created by *pibes* – players from which disciplined, powerful and cynical men (adult-players) have been excluded. In this context, Maradona is thought of as the most archetypical player helping to fix the fundamental line separating them and the others. Maradona is perceived by my informants as a key figure in a rite of institution that consecrates the crucial difference between kinds of players.

The ideological impact of a rite of institution is related to the way the different individual and social attributes of a *pibe*, and of *pibes* in general, are transformed into properties of 'natural nature'. Maradona as a *pibe* is a natural product and the historical fulfilment of an idea of football based on the naturalization of some playing qualities. Tomás enunciated this in the following way:

> Maradona is like a gift from God or from nature if you are not a believer. In Argentina there is a mythical style of playing football that has at last been realised in the body and the performances of Maradona. Thus, to be a *pibe* is something that cannot be explained, it is like this and that is all. We must accept it.

What Tomás is telling us is that a *pibe* is a *pibe*, a natural condition that must be known and recognized by himself and the rest of us. The first consequence is that in front of the *pibes* we must be indulgent. We, adult men, must transform our conduct, we must adapt to them. The second consequence is that the *pibes* are themselves obliged to behave in a subtle way that reproduces this representation. Maradona, the ideal *pibe*, is neither reasonable nor responsible in real life and it is not expected that he will be any different. Maradona creates himself as potently as others create him. The social rite of institution is an act of communication. Bourdieu (1991: 121) writes:

> it *signifies* to someone what his identity is, but in a way that both expresses it to him and imposes it on him by expressing it in front of everyone (*kategorien*, meaning originally, to accuse publicly) and thus informing him in an authoritative manner of what he is and what he must be.

Should the Maradona that is defined (and dreamed of) as a *pibe* abandon his true nature? If for a moment we imagine that he did, how would his supporters react? In the dramatic theatre of football, mirrors and models are created and reproduced. In this process, social and personal identifications fuse in a pervasive and, perhaps, perverse way. Maradona is himself a concrete individual and, at the same time, a kind of archetypical person representing a style and mythical condition. Tomás clearly expressed this idea:

> you imagine the *pibes* as the best players, as being a part of our style, our way of playing, and then, suddenly, the most perfect one appears. It is perfect. You have been dreaming along with thousands and thousands of football fanatics, and one day your dream is transformed into a reality.

The assurance of Tomás and other informants, without one single exception, made me feel that an entire nation had been waiting for this occasion to materialize. The figure and the performances of Maradona can be seen not only as the continuation of *el mito del pibe* (the myth of the *pibe*) but also as its most perfect historical realization.

To be and to remain a *pibe* is a powerful image because in football the most creative period for some players is associated with immaturity. My informants do not deny the role of experience and the passing of the years (*el paso de los años*) in the development of physical automatization and tactical sense. These qualities are considered important for expected performances. But a *pibe* is by definition an unpredictable player finding unexpected solutions in the most difficult moments of a game. The magic of Maradona is always understood as a performing skill – for producing inexplicable effects and illusions paralysing opposing players and charming his audience. This is defined as a powerful bewitching quality. This is even more astonishing when it is associated with a *pibe*.

The imagery of Maradona is even more complete as he is the product of one of Buenos Aires' poorest neighbourhoods, where *potreros* still existed. A *potrero* is a patch of waste ground in the city which has not yet been cemented over. In Argentinian football mythology the meaning of *pibe* is accompanied with the representation of the arena of his first public performances and victories: the *potrero*. It is easy to presume that in Villa Fiorito, Maradona's neighbourhood, the streets lacked asphalt and there was a plethora of *potreros*. The most original Argentinian players come from the *potrero*. They do not come from the playgrounds of primary or secondary schools, or from the clubs, the spaces controlled by teachers and trainers. The *potrero* is an exclusively male child space, where neither adult males nor women are ever present. The *potrero* is a world of naughty, wilful and crafty boys. Consequently, the great players are the pure products of a freedom that allows them to improvise and create, without the norms and rules imposed by experts or pedagogues. The *potrero* is thus opposed to the formal school and the trainer's blackboard. What has not been learnt in the *potrero* cannot be taught elsewhere. Carlos explained to me:

> Maradona is pure *potrero* even when he is not playing football. Well, I can put it this way: he still lacks civilized manners and he has obvious problems in accepting boundaries and control. In *potrero* life you learn how to be free and to improvise. Later in life you realize that this situation is temporary, then you change and adapt to society. This even happens in a football club and this is the role of managers and trainers. In addition, trainers will try hard to teach players new tricks, to be better technically and to think in tactical terms. Thus, you will hear some players saying that they are thankful to a given coach because he taught them many things or because they became accomplished players due to his knowledge and advice. Well, you never heard Maradona say that someone taught him anything. I

believe that is true. His knowledge and skills were developed in the freedom of the *potrero*. His ability and capacity for inventing new tricks is something that is impossible to learn from a coach. On the contrary, I will postulate that his creativity is a victory against discipline and training. You can write, if you want, that his accomplishment is the victory of the *potrero*. I assure you that I am not exaggerating.

In several discussions with my informants, they insisted on the importance of situating Carlos's arguments historically. It was emphasized that Maradona appeared as a player at a moment when national and international football was dominated by ideas of the superiority of elaborate tactical systems, based on an integrated, machine-like team. The international dominance of Dutch and German football in the 1970s was related to these aspects. Franz Beckenbauer and Johan Cruyff were perceived as emblematic players representing this style. They were, it was stated, technical and intelligent players but they were great because they had the quality to intensify the performance of their team-mates. In other words, their influence in the teams they played for was above their own ability. They were the main component in a complex and well-lubricated engine. Maradona, however, will always impregnate the teams for which he plays with his solitary and unique style. One of my informants uses the metaphor of the aroma of the *potrero*:

> the teams which Diego played for were transformed by his aroma. His aroma was in a way the aroma of the *potrero* of Villa Fiorito. I mean, an aroma that you cannot resist and that will follow him all his life. I do not like it when people say that he has the *potrero* in his blood. Well, this is perhaps true but I prefer to imagine the *potrero* and its aroma.

He also argued that the teams which Beckenbauer and Cruyff played for will always be recalled with their names: Bayern Munich or Ajax. He pointed out that the impact of Ajax was perceived as 'Ajax's revolution' and the Dutch national team's playing style was defined as *la naranja mecanica* (the mechanical orange). He finished his argument saying:

> the teams where Maradona was victorious will each be remembered as *el equipo de Maradona* (Maradona's team). I will try to explain this better to you. You see, he was not successful at the World Cup in

Spain in 1982. The Argentinian team had many stars competing for top status and Maradona was defined as one player like the rest. In this team, Argentina had Passarella, Ardiles, Tarantini, Kempes and Díaz. The same happened when he went to Barcelona. In Argentina when he played for Boca Juniors before leaving for Europe we talked about Boca as Maradona's team. But this was much more clear during the 1986 World Cup. In Mexico, Argentina, our national team, was without any doubt Maradona's team. Who will remember the other players 25 years from now? Nobody, I assure you nobody. He won alone. In Italy too twice he won the League single-handedly, playing for the average Napoli team.

The Emotional Contract of Joy

Some of my youngest informants are almost the same age as Maradona. They have been socialized within a historical context that is monopolized by his figure. The oldest experienced the 'golden age' of Argentinian football in the 1940s when the national team dominated South American football and the best first division teams toured Europe undefeated. It was the time when the forwards of the 1947 national team were chosen by public opinion. The Argentinian coach had previously admitted that with so many good players available, he could not make up his mind. It was also the year which saw the beginning of the impressive exodus of great players to Europe, Colombia, and the rest of Latin America. But, in spite of differences of what is remembered, experiences and, of course, personal preference, all of them agreed on one thing: the emotional contract (*el contrato emocional*) between Maradona and the Argentinian public is unequalled. Many reasons were given. Let me briefly present some of them.

The early public discovery of his talent, in an age when television had become the central vehicle for creating popular idols, was mentioned. By comparison, Di Stéfano and Sivori, the other two great Argentinian forwards with an international fame, belonged to an epoch when radio and newspapers dominated. Maradona's exploits could be simultaneously watched in Buenos Aires, Manila and Lagos. He was more easily transformed into a world sports hero and into a kind of universal Argentinian commodity. It was stated, moreover, that his debut in the national team at the age of seventeen and his long international career (16 years) transformed him into a symbol of Argentinian football. It was mentioned that Di Stéfano and Sivori had played more matches with the national teams of Spain and Italy than with Argentina. Maradona was also perceived as a true romantic, almost as an extreme nationalist (*un chovinista*) and defender of national pride and honour in international arenas. Images of him crying when defeat occurred or being euphoric when victory was achieved were touched upon in our discussions. But, above all, full agreement was attained on the fact that being the most skilful and successful contemporary player born in Argentina was a sufficient reason for his stature as a national symbol.

We must accept that his skills and accomplishments are, after all, key aspects in fixing a distinctive individual and collective memory over time. This memory is shared with Napoli supporters, where he was almost cultivated as a God while he played for this club, and with thousands and thousands of football enthusiasts all over the world. The fond remembrance of his achievements however does not explain his almost sacred status and cult in Argentina. I began this article with the song of Fito Paéz and believe that such an emotional dimension of the relationship with the image of Maradona is decisive. His possession of the human gift of producing and giving joy lies behind his incomparable cult. Being the cause of individual feelings of joy and enabling a collective expression is Maradona's precious secret, a very simple one indeed. Carlos told me:

> when we were told that he was taken for doping in the World Cup, I just could not believe it, I said to myself that it was impossible. It was painful. Maradona and drugs was difficult to accept for many Argentinians in spite of evidence about his consumption in the past. This relation was clear, at least for me and many of my friends. After a week I accepted that this could have happened in reality. I was still sad and felt pity for him. Then I realized that I was very selfish and my sadness was related to the breaking of an unwritten contract I had with the *pibe*, a contract of which he was unaware. This contract I called the contract of joy (*el contrato de la alegría*). My wife still protests when I, always jokingly, refer to this contract. But I had a contract, an unsigned contract. For me it was evident, so evident . . . so many times I was full of joy (*pipón de alegría*) from watching him play. It was not only at times when he did something stunning, it was more than that. He produced a state of joy which persisted for days and even weeks. In addition, each time I recalled the image in my mind, I could share it with friends and colleagues. But now, suddenly I was alone, without him, without his dribbles and his art. Then, my pity was changed

into fury and I thought, like millions of Argentinians, 'If this is true he cannot do this to us, to me, ever again'. I felt that he was unjust, he did not have the right to do this to us. He was killing something that was important for me. I was in pain.

Carlos describes an emotional state which is dependent upon a kind of symbolic contract which compels the two parties, Maradona and the supporters, not only to agree on the meaning of joy but also to share it.[4] Maradona has always been explicit in pointing out the existence of this contract. In an interview in 1994, after the suspension was made effective, Maradona developed two main ideas that confirm Carlos's argument. He emphasized that he has an everlasting contract with the people, based on experiencing a common joy and sharing dreams of success and victory with the national team (*El Clarín Revista*, 30 October 1994: 17–34).

Carlos expanded his idea on the meaning of joy by pointing out to me that joy, as well as pain, operates in what he terms *el puro corazón* (the pure heart). He also said that the intensity of his feelings, the way he could change from joy to pain in the space of seconds implied that a football supporter is made of *pura pasión y puro corazón* (pure passion and pure heart). I then asked if we can say that being a football supporter means being in a condition of emotional disorder. He agreed in principle to this, but explained to me that these 'irrational reactions' are in his case selective and are related to the quite special status of Maradona. He said:

The joy you feel with Maradona is unique and it has been lengthy. There have been many, many years of enjoying him as a football player. He left Argentina, he went to Spain and to Italy. I followed him. I watched him scoring in Madrid or Seville, in Naples or in Rome, and I supported Barcelona and Napoli because he was playing in these teams. But I knew that if we needed him he was going to play with the national team. He was the entire national team. We played badly in 1993 and were eliminated by Colombia. Qualification for the USA World Cup depended on the play-offs against Australia. He was retired and then he decided to come back in order to ensure we qualified. He did it. You see in his life all the ups and downs of your life, your country, and thus you learn of the importance of duty and sacrifice at particular times. Joy or pain is what you feel as a supporter. The pain or joy of training is something that belongs to Maradona himself. You are certain that he will give his last breath to his country and then to me and millions like me. Out of this reality grew what you can call my irrationality.

Carlos advances here a potent idea: his irrationality, his potential emotional disorder is more than a representation. Football is a game, a theatre, a ritual, and as such we can imagine that it is pure fiction. Football is transformed into a reality when supporters transform this fiction into a weekly profound emotional experience. The doping crisis permitted this reflection on fiction and reality, on joy and pain. In many ways Carlos experienced doping as fiction because he could not believe that it had happened. But once he accepted it, the reality of the real Maradona transcended this event, as his life was like the life of everyone else.

Carlos's pain was not exceptional. The day after the doping announcement the front page of *Página 12*, an Argentinian newspaper with a subtle intellectual style and clear centre-left political inclinations, gave Carlos's words a powerful image. The title, huge and dramatic, was *Dolor* (pain) and below it a touching picture of a boy aged between ten and twelve with a sad and tearful face holding an Argentinian flag in a gesture of mourning. The impact of a *pibe* suffering from the punishment of the greatest Argentinian *pibe* was reinforced by a series of articles written by prestigious writers and journalists. Osvaldo Soriano, a very popular novelist, defined Argentinians as *huérfanos* (orphans), meaning that the God (Maradona) was lost and the team was reduced to an impotent human condition (*Página 12*, 1 July 1994: 32). Juan José Panno conveyed an intense state of pain through a careful description of a cold and grey winter day in the city of Buenos Aires, and in the bodily sensations of the people: pain in the stomach, in the bitter mouth, in the eyes closed to reality, and in millions of hearts. He ended his article pointing out that very few things can produce real pain among common people in Argentina in the manner of this episode (*Página 12*, 1 July 1994: 2). Eduardo Galeano, the Uruguayan essayist, stated that the World Cup is finished because:

> Maradona is gone. The World Cup will not be the same. Nobody enjoys himself so much and amuses so many as he does by talking with the ball. Nobody gives so much joy as this magician that dances and flies and defines matches with an impossible pass or an explosive shot. In the frigid football at the end of this century, which decrees victory and forbids pleasure, the man who is able to demonstrate that fantasy can also be efficient is leaving. We are left alone.
>
> (*Página 12*, 1 July 1994: 12)

The next day Martín Caparrós recalled that he had seen a front page with the same title on the occasion of President Juan Perón's death, the mythological Argentinian politician. He compared a pain that can change our lives, like the death of Perón, compelling actors to political action and existential changes, to the pain produced by Maradona's doping, that is related to an event that will not transform our lives. He was inclined to think that the extreme pain of losing his best player for an illegal act is a clear indication of the nation's turbulent and chaotic emotional situation (*Página 12*, 2 July 1994: 8). Tomás, one of my informants, with a typical phrase from the popular press, condensed what Carlos and millions of Argentinians felt that morning:

> It was like at the end of the Falklands War. At that time until the very end we believed in victory, we were in a nationalistic mood where everything was possible, even the impossible. Maradona created this feeling after the two clear victories against Greece and Nigeria. We thought that we were in the finals, that Maradona would bring us the World Cup. And then the shock, the surprise, the hidden truth. If I say to you that for millions of Argentinians it was like the Second Falklands War, I am not exaggerating. The same sadness, fury, impotence, pain, you could feel it, it was everywhere.

By Way of Conclusion

Maradona is a controversial cult figure, almost on a par with Argentinian political idols. Many Argentinians will deny or, at least, argue against the fact that he exemplifies an image of Argentina, that he must be amalgamated with a modern and responsible State that is more than football, meat and tango. Interpretations will fluctuate between strong moral criticisms because he is not a model of sportsmanship to the denial that football is a cultural phenomenon shaping Argentinian national identity. Class-based statements will also be advanced, with Maradona representing bad taste and manners, amoral sexuality or a lack of social discernment. My informants know very well this field of symbolic discourse and popular (and psychoanalytic) interpretation. Since the World Cup scandal the Argentinian media has been daily concerned with Maradona's life, future and opinions. Maradona talks about everything: rock, religion, politics, football, friendship, drugs, modernity, love, family, football authorities and managers, capitalism, poverty, money, women, men and children. He is a kind of erratic oracle: arbitrary, enraged, irrational, offensive, charming, but above all unpredictable.[5] In addition, authoritative figures in political studies, literature, philosophy, journalism and psychoanalysis have presented the most divergent pictures of the real and the mythical Maradona in the media. One feels that nobody in Argentina escapes his performances, extravagances and magic. But what kind of magic?

My informants, in an honest attempt to interpret their own and other's cult of Maradona, are caught between two kinds of accounts that, in many ways, complement each other.[6] The cultural logic of the *pibe* and the *potrero* is ideological and functions as an ahistorical frame of interpretation. It is a mythical account in the sense that a concrete person is the product of essentialized features of Argentinian football. When history and comparison are used, differences in styles and individual bodily performances are recognized but they are systematically related to a fixed model. In other words, they are functional to the reproduction of myths and have a central role in the myth of Maradona. Valdano, a team-mate of Maradona at the Mexico World Cup in 1986, greeting his second comeback at the end of 1993, perfectly summarized this way of thinking:

> Diego is our national treasure, one of the most important, because he has touched the most sensitive nature of our culture, that is our love for football. Moreover, Diego is something of a genetic miracle, a perfect synthesis, and an accomplished result of the dream of Argentinian football.
>
> (*Página 12*, 14 September 1993: 3)

All the elements are combined: the nature of Argentinian football culture is related to the genetics (the body) of Maradona. The player is a kind of miracle, a religious phenomenon, a divine gift to a privileged nation. And finally, he realizes *the dream* of Argentinian football, not the dreams in plural. A dream transformed into reality illustrates the power of ideological accounts. New Maradonas would appear only in the world of *pibes* and *potreros*. This rationality is not instrumentalist and it is difficult to explain. The 'facts' of the creative *pibes* and the freedom endured in the *potreros* belong to a local interpretive community. These 'facts' can hardly be modelled more clearly than in this case. My informants are more interpretative than descriptive in the attempt to place Maradona in a holistic perspective. They talk about Maradona and at the same time they reaffirm the 'natural' existence of a local football tradition.[7]

This ideological rationality is fused with an empirical account. Joy as well as pain are what individuals feel. My informants give a concrete description of what they experience and name the different emotions and feelings. It is empirical in the sense that you just need to pass through the concrete events in order to be able to find the words. The words for emotions are publicly displayed. They belong to a cultural reservoir that is activated in specific circumstances. The confluence of individual pain with the front page and the analysis of experts in *Página 12* is a clear example of the intermixing of levels, the individual and the collective. Without this confluence, imagined by my informants in a Durkheimian way, the worship of Maradona would not exist.[8] The idea of an emotional contract based on joy (and of course pain) is even acknowledged by Maradona himself. In this context, the public performances of the idol fuse with the individual feelings of the supporters in creating a collective flow.

It is important to keep in mind that the empirical account is encompassed by ideological arguments. The meaning of emotions is dependent on the holistic perspective conditioned by ideological interpretation. Maradona is the perfect product of a mythical tradition and is put historically into motion through the emotional contract with the worshippers. The cult of Maradona is the worship of a tradition.

Notes

1. My thanks to Richard Giulianotti, Gary Armstrong and Marit Melhuus for their critical suggestions on an earlier version of this chapter.
2. Fito Paéz is not the only Argentinian composer to write a song for Maradona. There is a long list of popular contemporary composers, representing styles as different as folk, ballad and rock, writing songs for Maradona: Peteco Carabajal's 'Canción

del brujito' ('Little sorcerer's song'), Juan Carlos Baglietto's
'Vengan a ver' ('Come to see'), Julio Lacra's 'Dale, diez' ('Go
on, number ten'), Charly García's 'Maradona blues', and
recently Riky Maravilla's 'El baile del rey' ('the King's dance').
In France, the popular rock group Mano Negra wrote a hit
called 'Santa Maradona' ('Saint Maradona'). In the history of
Argentinian football this veneration is unique. Maradona's close
relationship with rock composers like Fito Páez, Charly García
and Andrés Calamaro is also very special.

3. In 1994 Maradona was still identified with left-wing political
   positions. He protested not only against Havelange and other
   FIFA leaders and Argentinian football bureaucrats, he was also
   a professed opponent of the Argentinian President Menem and
   of the Vatican. He supported Fidel Castro, visited Cuba several
   times and was against the economic boycott of the island. He
   was what many people imagined a political rebel to be. My
   informants, however, were divided on this judgment, as many
   Argentinians are. For many, Maradona is not a political rebel
   with an explicit radical ideology. This side of Maradona I will
   not discuss here. However, I would like to point out that since
   that time, Maradona has changed his opinions and he is now a
   strong supporter of President Menem. I am quite sure my
   informants would tend to explain this transformation as
   something related to his personality, of being a *pibe* (a young
   boy).

4. It is clear that Carlos's argument about the existence of an
   emotional contract has intrinsic moral significance (see Oakley
   1993). I will not explore here the complex relationship between
   football, morality and emotions which I have developed
   elsewhere (see Archetti 1996b).

5. Throughout 1994 and 1995 Maradona denied all charges of drug
   use during the USA World Cup. He presented himself as a
   victim of FIFA's manipulation, as revenge for his open criticism
   of President Havelange and other authorities. In January 1996,
   unexpectedly, he admitted taking drugs from 1982 onwards,
   defining himself as a drug-addict (see *Gente*, 1589, 5 January
   1996, *El Gráfico*, 9 January 1996 and *Noticias*, 7 January 1996).
   The Foucaultian argument on the importance of 'telling the
   truth' has been used by Maradona himself and the general
   reaction of Argentinian public opinion and the media has been
   positive. It has been emphasized that telling the truth is the

beginning of a real curing process. Analysis of the social impact of his declarations lies outside the scope of this chapter.

6. I have been inspired by the way Evens (1995) distinguishes instrumental and mythical rationality in his study of an Israeli kibbutz.

7. Maradona has refused to be identified with a national tradition. His talent is an individual and 'divine gift'. He has often declared that he is touched by the magic of God and not by the power of his Argentinian football ancestors (see *Corriere della Sera*, 11 November 1985). However, he usually accepts that he learned everything as a *pibe* in the Argentinian *potreros*. In his lecture at the Oxford Union Debating Chamber on 6 November 1995 he clearly stated that he is a *pibe*, a pure product of *potreros*. Maradona's account, at this level, is empirical and entirely related to his lived experience. My informants move further, making the connection between individual cases and a football tradition. They thus take part in the production (and reproduction) of an ideological account.

8. On the meaning of Maradona in Europe see Dini and Nicolaus (1991); Dujovne Ortiz (1992); Paoletti (1993) and Bromberger (1995a: 142, 303, 341–2).

Chapter 3

Successes and Contradictions in 'Multiracial' Brazilian Football

José Sergio Leite Lopes[1]

Introduction

One way of understanding the peculiarities of the rapid dissemination of football in Brazil is to analyse how early and to what degree blacks and mestizos entered the upper echelons of this sport. Football's spread among the Brazilian population was related to the sport's appropriation by the various classes and social groups, but this was not independent of skin colour or 'ethnicity'. The speed with which football achieved popularity (apparently a widespread phenomenon, hitting England in the latter half of the nineteenth century and many other countries in the twentieth) was characterized in Brazil both by a greater gap between the élite and the popular classes (a major portion of whom were descendents of slaves[2]) and a greater mixture between the classes as a result of this sport.

The British pattern of rapid spread and professionalization was repeated by several countries – and Brazil was outstanding in this regard – but the repetition of this British phenomenon was not immediate, rather it occurred in Brazil approximately half a century later. Football was transplanted from England to other countries by the local élites: at the very moment that the sport was spreading and professionalizing in England, the élite were those who provided the resources for its spread within other countries.[3]

In this chapter I seek to analyse the social contradictions between the consequences of football's predominantly aristocratic beginnings in Brazil and the potentialities of the appropriation of this practice by social groups from below, leading progressively to the transition from amateur to professional football. This transition fostered a huge growth of entry and success in the game by players from the working classes in general and blacks and mulattos in particular. Just a few years after professional play had begun, the main national idols for the burgeoning football public were blacks like Leônidas da Silva and Domingos da Guia, yet in the sporting world there persisted racist beliefs and practices which took new forms and gained strength after the defeats Brazil suffered in the 1950 and 1954 World Cups. Even when Brazil won in 1958 and 1962 – temporarily reversing these racist stereotypes, taking previously stigmatizing bodily attributes and turning them into an internationally consecrated 'Brazilian style' – after the defeat in 1966 many football analysts and coaches considered this style outdated as compared to the new European 'power football' (*futebol-força*).[4] There was thus a recurrent discussion in the period between the 1974 and 1994 World Cups concerning the offensive type of 'art football' (*futebol-arte*) and the defensive 'pragmatic football' (*futebol de resultados*); among coaches and managers only a minority trusted in a reappropriation (for the current context of football) of the 'Brazilian style' consolidated in the 1958, 1962 and 1970 World Cups.

While professionalization which began in 1933 led to a considerable promotion of players from working-class backgrounds, learning the implicit rules of professional sport and assimilating the requirements of a career with new peculiarities were not easy tasks for such players: their difficulties in professional career management were thus repeated by succeeding generations of athletes. If the very characteristics of the 'Brazilian style' of football implied skill, acrobatics and having fun while competing, then such traits displayed a structural homology with the hedonistic lifestyle of a portion of the working classes. Incorporating this style and simultaneously making it compatible with the asceticism and discipline needed to pursue a successful career was an achievement that few players managed. Players such as Domingos da Guia and Pelé (or even Nilton Santos and Zico), reached a level of classicism that romantic and baroque players like Leônidas da Silva and above all Garrincha, both of whom were revolutionaries in the 'style', had difficulty in maintaining, much to the detriment of their own professional careers.[5]

The Football of the Brazilian Élites

While football became increasingly popular in Great Britain with the competition for the FA Cup/League Title and the acceptance of professional play within national borders, early internationalization of the sport followed the network of contacts stimulated indirectly by previously established and spontaneous relations between local élites and English élites and their institutions. This was the case for the early spread of football in Brazil: the first football games on record in Brazil were played by English sailors (material witnesses to the degree of the sport's popularization in its country of origin) and more sporadically amongst employees of English firms. Yet the games played as the outcome of the missionary effort by the local British colony to convince Brazilians (and later by the young élite Brazilians – former students in England, Switzerland, or Germany – upon their return to Brazil), were those that resulted in the founding of permanent teams in pre-existing clubs or the *de novo* founding of football clubs themselves. Outstanding examples of such initiative include Charles Miller, the son of an English father and a Brazilian mother, a student in Southampton, who returned to São Paulo in 1894 with two leather balls and a complete football outfit in his baggage; Oscar Cox, the son of an English family that had settled in Rio de Janeiro two generations earlier and who returned to Brazil in 1897 from Lausanne, where he had played football in secondary school; and Hans Nobiling, who that same year arrived in Brazil from Hamburg, where he had belonged to the Germania Club. Miller convinced members of the cricket team from the São Paulo Athletic Club to practise football, and, having achieved fame as a player in São Paulo, he is credited with introducing the sport into Brazil. Cox took three years to set up a team of Brazilians in the Rio Cricket Athletic Association, founded by his father, and later helped found the Fluminense Football Club in Rio de Janeiro in 1902, the first football club in Brazil. Nobiling founded the Germania Club in São Paulo and recruited top business employees from that city to play against the teams of British players which were springing up in clubs and colleges. Although some football initiatives appeared inside companies, their top employees soon met in clubs in order to socialize more freely.

Thus, many of the major football clubs ended up reproducing (both on the field and in the stands) the social selection practised by élite families from Rio and São Paulo. The clubs turned into places for urban socializing; by providing participation in, or attendance at, physical and sporting activities, they prolonged the receptions and soirées bringing together the dominant families from early twentieth-century *sobrados* (town mansions) in those two cities. In addition to cricket, played by the British, until the 1920s the clubs were organized around men's rowing. The rowing contests in Rio attracted the city's population to the beaches and shoreline along Guanabara Bay and were the main source of attraction for the city's budding sports press. A regatta club like Flamengo (founded in 1895), which afterwards became Brazil's most popular football club from the 1930s, had initially refused to have a football team in the first decade of the century and later resisted incorporating a dissident team from the Fluminense Club after 1912. Those who practised rowing felt that football was not a very masculine sport, with what they viewed as chasing and 'prancing' around the field. Still, the Fluminense Football Club gradually became the game's benchmark for the *carioca* élites, attracting an elegant public to its stadium, including men in suits, ties and hats, and smartly dressed young girls and women, wearing hats decked with flowers and clothes which made clear that they belonged to the finest families in Rio. A little hat band in the team's colours, imported from England and worn by the men, was a discreet detail which indicated the club's coded, select membership (see Filho 1964: chap. 1). The cry from the stands when the team entered the field, 'Hip, hip, hurrah!', an English inter-jection, and the team's solemn sideline bow to the fans (especially to the young ladies), were also signs both of refinement, through the imported details from the world metropolises, and the kind of social belonging that was common to both players and fans. Such common belonging was manifested by the players' frequent visits to the stands during half-time and after the game, when they met up with their own families and those of their peers.

Players also frequented dances at the club: playing football regularly was one of several characteristics of an élite lifestyle. Several football clubs were made up of university students, and access to law, medicine and to a lesser extent, engineering was a form of social reconversion (via schooling) for the declining

Brazilian rural aristocracy, or an expanded reproduction of the new scholarized urban élites. Thus, while the original Fluminense team was made up of young businessmen, top employees of factories and major stores, and *rentiers* – the sons of moneyed parents, educated in Europe – from 1910 on it was forced primarily to recruit university students, who were younger, had more time for the game and who were competing with Fluminense in successful rival teams. The Botafogo Futebol e Regatas team, made up originally of secondary-school students who had been admirers of the adult players at Fluminense, was by now successful with a generation of university players. The America Futebol Club from the city's northern zone was also made up of university students, the Flamengo team meanwhile consisted almost entirely of medical students.

Thus, the original football players from Rio de Janeiro's élite society in the early twentieth century were *university football majors* as compared to the *primary* players of the working classes, according to a school metaphor used by Mário Filho. Although the equipment needed to play the game was comparatively unsophisticated and not exclusive, at that time the leather ball had to be imported from England, as did the football boots. The grass-covered field was also an attribute of players with greater financial resources. Yet the popular substitutes for imitating this leisurely practice were not at all expensive: stocking balls served the purpose for the sandlot games hotly disputed by barefoot players, with goalposts easily improvised from any variety of possible materials. Children and teenagers from the working classes could watch the football matches between the big élite teams (in the neighbourhoods frequented by the élites) either by working as ballboys or watching from the cheapest, ground-level places in the stadium, an area used as a ploy to recruit cheering sections for decisive matches. There were no restrictions, like having to get into clubs or stadiums, to watch the Flamengo team, which had split off from Fluminense in 1911 who for the years to follow (having no field of its own) practised in a park, attracting crowds of working-class fans in a non-confined space. And there was also the opportunity to see games in the working-class suburbs and neighbourhoods: more and more factories and companies were promoting football as a form of leisure and integration between administrative employees and manual workers.

Factory Football and Company Towns

The year 1904 witnessed the founding of The Bangú Athletic Club, where football was played by English managers, overseers, mechanics and employees at the textile factory called *Companhia Progresso Industrial*, located in the Rio suburb of Bangú.[6] There, contrary to other clubs in Rio, where the original English nuclei were capable of attracting other Englishmen to make up the respective teams, Bangú's geographical isolation from the city proper meant that the English had to include Brazilian supervisors, overlookers and administrative employees and those of other nationalities, and even shop-floor workers. Thus, Bangú's first line-ups included one or two Brazilians amongst five Englishmen, three Italians, and two Portuguese. The number of Brazilians and factory workers increased over time: the workers stayed at the factory longer, and learning football was a continuous process for them, while managers and overseers tended to return to their native countries or change jobs, and their replacements were not always good at the sport. As the number of workers increased on the team, so did the number of black and mulatto players. In the Bangú stadium there was no distinction between the *gerais* (literally 'general area', the ground-level area with no seating) and stands or reserved seating. The community of workers, their families, and other people from the neighbourhood made up the team's working-class supporters, which later grew tremendously when Bangú was incorporated into the Rio de Janeiro football league, the first division in the Carioca championship. The Bangú team was soon more famous than the factory itself and ended up serving as a positive marketing image for the latter.

Bangú inaugurated the figure of the worker–player: a worker known less for his work inside the factory and more for his performance as a football player in the factory team. This justified certain relative privileges in the company: time off from the factory for training and games; assignment to *light* work, perhaps in the 'cloth room' (for quality inspection and recording of each worker's fabric productivity). While football was originally introduced by the English for their own enjoyment and socializing, the company was soon to realize that the sport fitted well with the activities and the use of time in a company town, up to date as it was with international practice by other European companies, who promoted football as a stimulus to workers, to increase their sense of belonging to the company community (see Rosenfeld 1993 [1956]: 82).

The board of directors at the Bangú factory were quick to discover what would soon lead to one of the watersheds for the spread of football among the various social classes in Brazil, as it already had in other countries in Europe and South America. That is, adopting football as a pedagogical and disciplinary technique for 'total institutions'; a technique invented by élite English boarding-schools but applicable to disciplining (morally and symbolically shaping) working-class youth in various types of institutions (see Bourdieu 1980b). Thus, it was not only schools (catering to the élite in a country with little schooling available to the general population) but also companies which helped to disseminate both the playing of, and direct access to, football among the working classes.

Several factories (especially in the textile industry) started encouraging this sport among their administrative employees and factory workers, founding teams in great numbers all over Brazil in the first three decades of the twentieth century and quickly taking up the Bangú factory and team as their point of reference. Prime examples of such factories were the so-called 'company towns' (or factories practising the 'cottage-system'), where football complemented other recreational activities aimed at maintaining discipline.[7] Thus, in 1908 the English managers of the *América Fabril* company founded the Sport Club Pau Grande in the rural village of Pau Grande, in the county of Magé, some ninety kilometres from Rio de Janeiro, importing balls, seeding the field with grass, and providing access to administrative employees and workers to the equipment and teaching of the rules as practised by the big-league clubs. Forty years later this factory boasted an outstanding team in the championships between textile factory teams in the Petrópolis region and routinely beat visiting company teams from Rio. The Pau Grande team even outstripped factory teams sponsored by the same company in the city of Rio de Janeiro. Garrincha, one of the players on this team, who was already playing the same basic style that fans would come to love in the future, became a world champion ten years later, in 1958 (see Leite Lopes and Maresca 1989).

In addition to Bangú, another textile factory club participating in Rio's first division championship was Andaraí, located in the northern zone neighbourhood by the same name. Yet Bangú survived even after the transition to professional football, and in retrospect it became more important. As an isolated company town, the Bangú factory formed its team from the little leagues and junior teams such as *Esperança* (meaning hope), where famous players like Domingos da Guia started their careers. Outstanding young players from these teams could hope to be hired as worker–players in the factory and be guaranteed a stable job, even beyond the age at which competetive football could be played. In addition, both Bangú and Andaraí allowed players from the working classes – poor whites, mulattos, and blacks – to measure their strength and skills against those of players from the major élite clubs (who had introduced and mastered football in Brazil), an opportunity denied to the small teams springing up in the main working-class suburban towns, both inside companies and at the initiative of small groups of neighbours, sponsored to a greater or lesser extent by local institutions. Yet while Bangú was feared when it played on its own field, backed by the home supporters, it was no real competitor for the city title: more available time and resources and greater knowledge of the tactics and training, spreading directly from Europe or via Argentina and Uruguay, gave the élite amateurs from the big clubs the upper hand when compared to the limited resources available to the worker–players who (albeit on 'light' work schedules) had to subordinate football to factory production needs.

Social Tension and Crisis in Amateur Football

The élite clubs' hegemony, as expressed by victories in every previous Rio de Janeiro city championship, was only broken in 1923, when Vasco da Gama, which belonged to the populous colony of Portuguese immigrants, competed for the title for the first time and won. The Vasco team, second division champions in 1922, had a secret: it recruited the best players from the working-class suburbs, whether they were white, black or mulatto, and kept them in a regimen of semi-confinement, financed by the club, so that the athletes were available to play football full time (see Filho 1964: chap. 2). Vasco was a sign of football's growing popularity, the sport was being played in all the working-class neighbourhoods and with a burgeoning public audience. This allowed for two simultaneous processes of embourgeoisement and proletarianization, much as they had occurred in England. In fact, unlike the aristocratic clubs dominating the first division championship, the Clube de Regatas Vasco da Gama had no athletes from the same social extraction as its members. In the aristocratic clubs, athletes and member fans socialized during half-time and after the match, just like they did in the daily life and dance parties of the club itself – as family members, family friends, acquaintances and suitors. The Portuguese club, on the other hand, apparently had no athletes from the same social origins as its members. One possible explanation was the lack of free time for youth of Portuguese extraction, who were directly involved in learning and tending business for the bourgeoisie and petit bourgeoisie of their compatriot colony, practising a type of family continuation that excluded a long period of formal schooling in élite secondary schools or universities. This way of life, immersed in work and tending the family business, was quite different from that of the sons of the Brazilian aristocracy, which was modelled after élite European schooling, where a long formal education and the playing of sports represented not only a transition period, separating one from work and intensive business management, but also an educational process preparing one to exercise top-level economic and political domination. The bourgeois and petit bourgeois sons of the Portuguese colony, with their hands-on approach to family business, played an improvised, haphazard kind of football in neighbourhoods that included working-class youth. The only possible way for Vasco da Gama to compete was to 'proletarianize' its team by unrestricted recruitment of the best players from the working-class suburbs and simultaneously to both make it bourgeois and monetarize it by supporting these players (who had no resources of their own for continuous leisure activity) in a situation of semi-confinement where they were fed, given material support, and encouraged to train at least as much as the athletes from the major clubs. Vasco's 1923 championship team consisted of white, black and mulatto players who had already been part of a *de facto* scratch team in the suburbs, with a taxi driver in goal and several former factory workers from Bangú and Andaraí and other minor league teams.

Vasco's victory in the 1923 Carioca championship fuelled the defensive ideological stance taken by amateur football *vis-à-vis* the rise of subordinate social groups in quality football. As Dunning (1994) has pointed out *vis-à-vis* a similar process that had already occurred in England. From the moral qualities associated with the essence of modern football, which in turn was seen as an important part of the way of life which characterizes and distinguishes social groups who classify themselves as select, the precepts and practices of amateur play now turned to excluding the 'outsiders'.[8]

The big clubs were quick to react: they set up a new football league which Vasco was not invited to join, allegedly because it had no stadium of its own. In response, the Portuguese colony organized and funded construction of the city's largest stadium (until the construction of Maracanã in 1950), with a capacity of 50,000, inaugurated in 1927. Fluminense's stadium could hold no more than 20,000 spectators. Yet the Vasco stadium's unusually large blueprint was not only based only on a logic of honour in response to the discrimination the club had suffered: the team played top-quality football, the supporters grew in the wake of mobilization by the Portuguese colony, opposition from other teams' supporters increased, and all the while the fans flocked to watch the matches. So much so that the big clubs relented (for economic reasons), allowing Vasco to join the first division even before its stadium was completed.

Yet other measures were taken. The Rio all-star team competing for the national championship had not a single player from Vasco's championship team. The new league set up a commission to investigate players' means of survival, to determine to what extent they were actually playing as amateurs. The very substance and procedures of this investigation expressed a number of class distinctions and prejudices. In fact, in addition to keeping the team in semi-confinement, paying for food, lodging, uniforms and training equipment, Vasco had a policy of paying them the so-called *bicho*,[9] a bonus based on one's performance in the match, in addition to a 'travel allowance' for train fares. The extent of this coverage of athletes' expenses, which assumed they had no resources of their own, appeared to be incompatible with the naturalized notion of players' social quality as conceived by the managers and athletes who had introduced football into Brazil. On the contrary, the latter purchased their own sports gear, financed their own free time, and covered their own expenses when the team went to play outside of Rio or outside of Brazil: when the teams travelled to São Paulo, Montevideo, or Buenos Aires, the players never failed to take their dinner-jackets along for the hotels and receptions. Aware of the new league's investigation into the means of financial support for athletes, Vasco's bourgeois members offered to give the players make-believe jobs, generally in their own stores, where they would have many more perks than the worker–players in the factories. Meanwhile, the latter were welcomed by proponents of amateur play, as if the moral shaping provided by the factory and the fact that a worker–player simultaneously worked and kept up his athletic performance (and indirectly lacked the time to compete on equal footing with other athletes in the big clubs) were sufficient legitimation, with the additional merit of not totally excluding the poor from amateur sport. However, some occupations and professions like stevedores, soldiers, and those who habitually received tips, for example, waiters, taxi drivers, and barbers, were arbitrarily mentioned in writing as prohibited from playing in the first division.[10]

Another step by the new league was to require that players know how to read and write properly: when they entered the field, they had to be able to sign their names on the scorepad and to fill in quickly an 'enrollment form' with several items. This implicit test of schooling is very characteristic of the indirect, euphemistic exercise of class and colour prejudice in Brazil. As they entered a game, under the eagle eye of the league representatives, athletes had to fill in the questionnaire with the following required information: full name, both parents' names, nationality, place of birth, date of birth, and place of study and work (see Caldas 1990: 84). Vasco da Gama and São Cristóvão, another club recruiting players from the suburbs, had their athletes attend specially organized literacy crash-courses and remedial primary-school tutoring. Their players from working-class origins, and who for this very reason were almost invariably illiterate or functionally illiterate, managed to scrape by this apparently neutral writing trap, albeit with great difficulty.

The most famous cases of racial prejudice were also indirect attempts to block access to first division football by working-class players. The most famous cases of racial prejudice were also indirect. Such was the case for the myth behind the origin of the term *pó de arroz* (rice powder) for members and supporters of the Fluminense Futebol Clube, the oldest football club in Brazil and the one with the most aristocratic origins. The mulatto player Carlos Alberto, son of a photographer (who took university graduation portraits), was playing in the second team for the

América Futebol Clube, where he was friends with a number of university student players. In 1916 he was called up to the Fluminense first team. Before entering the field, when the players were posing along the sidelines to greet the select public in the stands, Carlos Alberto was reported to have been seen in the dressing-room spreading rice powder on his face to lighten his complexion. In a game against América, the supporters from his former home team standing in the cheapest area of the stadium refused to forgive their former star athlete and shouted out, 'pó de arroz!' Since Carlos Alberto paid no heed to their heckling (although probably mortified inside), the stigma of pretentiousness and self-whitening ended up sticking, quite appropriately not only for the entire team but for the aristocratic club as a whole. This episode, which is supposed to have occurred in the 1910s, was further publicized and immortalized in the chronicles by sports writer Mário Filho in the 1930s, to stimulate rivalry between supporters and attract bigger crowds to budding professional football. So, when Flamengo was becoming the city's most popular club in the late 1930s, the Fluminense fans counter-attacked by heckling the Flamengo supporters with 'pó de carvão' ('coal dust') (see Rodrigues and Filho 1987: 57–62). Launched at the time as rival offences, both cheering sections ended up assimilating them as self-designating, and the nicknames have survived to this day.

This episode, with its mythical overtones, denotes not only how mulattos and blacks internalized their inferior social situation, but the joking effect and conciliatory outcome also expresses much of the ambiguity around racial stereotypes and prejudices in Brazil.[11] An exemplary case occurred with black and mulatto players in the Brazilian team travelling to Montevideo in 1923. During the formal dinner served on the ship, a white player from Fluminense pretended to drink the lavender water placed on the table after dinner for washing one's fingers: the working-class players, who had never witnessed such a thing, attempted to drink the lavender, making them the butt of a joke which ended up serving the purposes of managers who were in favour of vetoing blacks on international team delegations for reasons of etiquette (Filho 1964: 152). Of the examples cited by Mário Filho, the only case of overt racial prejudice was committed against the player nicknamed *Manteiga*. In 1923, the managers of the América team, motivated by the same spirit of competition that had led Vasco to base its team on players recruited from the working classes, set out on a more timid recruiting mission in the docks area of Rio. They recruited a successful local player, a sailor playing right-wing and nicknamed *Manteiga* (Butter), because of his slick passes. They proposed that he leave the Navy and take a job at a business owned by one of the club's board members. But Manteiga was black: when he was getting ready to enter the field for his first game, other players from the team walked out of the dressing-room in a blatant display of prejudice. Next, nine players from the club's first and second teams resigned in protest against the inclusion of this new player. These dissidents were later absorbed by Fluminense. The board members kept Manteiga on despite the crisis, but he felt extremely uncomfortable. When he left his distress had a greater effect on the club in general than on the playing field itself. During a tour by América to Salvador (Manteiga's home town where there is a higher concentration of blacks than in Rio), he stayed behind, abandoning the team (Filho 1964: 54–55).

One can thus easily understand the big clubs' reaction to Vasco da Gama's successful entry in 1923, with a team made up of poor whites, mestizos and blacks. Having excluded Vasco from the club league in 1924 and 1925, Fluminense and Flamengo won these two titles respectively, and proper order appeared to have returned to the league: even though 'little' São Cristóvão won in 1926 and Vasco (back in the league) took the title in 1929; the 1927, 1928, 1930, 1931 and 1932 titles went to the traditional clubs. Yet the crisis in amateur football, which was already appearing as 'yellow amateurism', fuelled the various factions of players, sports writers and even board members of clubs in favour of adopting professional sport.

Not only blacks but also white players from outside the élites who had introduced football into Brazil were uncomfortable with their daily experience of amateur football. Such was the story told by Floriano Peixoto Corrêa – a player from the 1920s and 1930s – in a rare instance of a book written by a player himself and motivated by his own experience in this crisis. Floriano was born in 1903 in the interior of the State of Minas Gerais, the son of local small farmers. At the age of thirteen he entered the military academy in Barbacena in his home state and ended up better known for his football than his studies. He later transferred to the military academy in Porto Alegre, in the State of Rio Grande do Sul, where he continued to play football, not only at school but also for local clubs. He came to Rio in 1924 to compete in the national military football tournament and was invited to play for Fluminense at the strategic position of centre-half. This club, harried by competition from other teams, was quietly attempting to imitate Vasco da Gama by recruiting players and supporting them fully at the club's expense. The difference was that while the Portuguese club was doing this with working-class players from Rio's poor suburbs, Fluminense was attempting the same strategy with white, middle-class players from the Brazilian hinterlands. Floriano was soon incorporated into Fluminense's first team, whose board members provided him with lodging in the club headquarters itself and an allowance which enabled him to frequent it, which meant that he had to spend a considerable amount on clothing. Since Floriano was white and from a 'good family' from the Brazilian interior, he was considered socially acceptable enough to frequent the club's headquarters and parties, something rather more complicated for a player like Manteiga, for example, even at a less aristocratic club. Since the new league was investigating 'false amateurs' with fake jobs, the board members at Fluminense, having taken Floriano out of the Army, postponed their promises to give the player a job and kept him with loans that he was unable to pay back. Tired of having to ask for such loans periodically, Floriano began to make money on the side by scalping tickets to important matches. He would obtain numbered seats from the box-office treasurer and sell them through touts, on the eve of the games, at trumped-up prices. When the league's inquisitional impetus over 'false amateurs' waned, Floriano was given an administrative job at a financial newspaper in the city. In 1927, when he was going through a bad phase with regard to football (skipping practice regularly) because of the bohemian lifestyle not uncommon among football players, and plagued by problems in his love life, Floriano played poorly against América during the final game of the city championship and was accused of having accepted a bribe from the rival team's fans. These rumours made it impossible for him to remain at Fluminense. After going for a time without playing, Floriano was invited to play with América, a gesture seen as a vote of trust in him and proof of his innocence regarding the bribing accusation. He played for América in 1928 and 1929, but just before the final championship game between América and Vasco, a man came to him with two indirect offers (and then a direct one) of a bribe to play poorly against Vasco, all of which Floriano refused. América lost to Vasco anyway, and the bribe rumours involving Floriano gained further momentum, forcing him to leave América. He finally went on in 1932 to São Paulo, where he played for by now professional Santos Futebol Clube, (see Corrêa 1933). Presumably, his situation as a poor white in an aristocratic club like Fluminense, his attempts to make money scalping tickets, and his 'professionalist' concern over the money to be won or lost with the sport made him the prime target for bribery charges, commonplace in amateur football, a highly valued practise by a growing and moneyed public. When América lost, he was chosen again as the scapegoat, supposedly as a repeat offender. In 1933, the charges at Fluminense and América led him to publish one of the few books written in Brazil by a football player, telling of his experience in the crisis in amateur football as a middle-class, white athlete.[12] Later on, with professional football in place, suspicion of taking bribes was aimed mainly at black players (see Filho 1964: 277).

Black Players and the Formation of a Brazilian Style of Football

The internal crisis in Brazilian amateur football was getting worse, and it finally became unbearable owing to the outside pressure exerted by football practised on an international scale. With the beginning of the World Cup, players who felt 'enslaved' by the traps of amateurism found a way out in the 1930s, as European clubs, particularly the Italians, raised a demand for South American players. Soon after the first World Cup, won by Uruguay, and in light of preparations for the second World Cup, to be held in Italy, Mussolini began to promote Italian football by promising to build a stadium for the winning team in the Italian Cup. Rivalry amongst teams ended up sparking a race for the best players from South America, which in the context of Mussolini's Italy meant the best players of Italian ancestry in Argentina, Uruguay, and Brazil (especially São Paulo). Argentina's football was threatened the most by this recruitment: the solution for the Buenos Aires teams was to adopt professionalism; they were followed soon after by the Montevideo teams.[13] Professional football would be coming soon to São Paulo and Rio. In both these cities there were cases of white players who were not *oriundi* (of Italian ancestry) who adopted Italian names, altering their identification papers with the acquiescence of clubs from Italy. Faced with such an exodus of players, factions favouring the implementation of professional football gained momentum.

White players were exported to Europe, while black players, blocked from entering the most significant importing country, Mussolini's Italy, and with little stimulus to remain for long in countries where blacks were the exception, became virtually non-exportable.[14] Such was the case of the black player Fausto, a centre-half and a contemporary of Floriano, who was highlighted by international sports coverage in the 1930 World Cup. Rising in the ranks from the Bangú company town club, recruited into what became Vasco's 1929 championship team, highly rated for his performance in the 1930 World Cup, and someone who wanted to live full time off football, Fausto had difficulty putting up with the false amateurism in the big Brazilian clubs. During a tour with Vasco to Spain in 1931, Barcelona made him an offer and he remained there. Yet his experience with professional football abroad led him to break his contract, an episode that he repeated in Switzerland. When professional football was implemented in Brazil, he returned to Vasco in 1933. The same occurred with Vasco's black goalkeeper, Jaguaré. Recruited by Barcelona along with Fausto, he came back in 1932, even before professional football began in Brazil, offering to play again for his old team. The same happened with Domingos da Guia and Leônidas da Silva, who had led a victory by the Brazilian all-star team in 1932, beating the world-champion Uruguayans on their home turf in Montevideo. Both players stayed abroad for only a short while. Domingos was hired by Nacional of Montevideo and Leônidas by Peñarol: the former was successful in Uruguay (and later in Argentina) while the latter was not. Both rejoined Brazilian football in 1934, after professional play had begun. Meanwhile, many white Brazilian players who had gone to Italy ended up integrating into that society, encouraged by the Italian colony in São Paulo, who considered a triumphant return to Italy an ideal to be achieved by Brazilian-born descendents of Italians. Blacks, in turn, appeared to be 'condemned' to 'local' success, to be great local players, to be Brazil's greatest players. In this sense they were identified as the great initiators of Brazilian national football. Football thus could not have the same meaning for both black and white players. Between them there was a difference separating 'good professionals', prone to exercising their talents on the international football scene, and talented players, who – through their athletic success – were seeking their ethnic emancipation but condemned to succeed exclusively in their own homeland.[15] Professional football became a means of emancipation for black athletes, a necessary condition to establish football as a 'national' sport. This undertaking was not just a business strategy (involving money); it established an identity between players and the public, united in their adherence to a common project of social emancipation through sport (see Leite Lopes 1994; Leite Lopes and Faguer 1994).

This identity between players and the public was tested soon after the move to professionalism. When Flamengo hired players like Fausto, Domingos da Guia and Leônidas da Silva, the team, which had had an amateur policy until then, became the most popular one in the city. By heavily recruiting working-class players as Vasco da Gama had done since 1923, Flamengo, twelve years later, had the advantage of being identified as the prime example of a universally 'mixed-race' Brazilian club, as opposed to the nucleus of Portuguese-colony board members and supporters from the equally popular rival club. Flamengo's football club head-quarters and field were also moved, in 1935, from a traditionally élite neighbourhood to one characterized at that time by its proximity to factories, company compounds, and a shanty town (which have since disappeared, giving way to a middle-class neighbourhood). Domingos' and Leônidas' tremendous popul-arity, which had increased with the return of the all-star team competing for the World Cup in 1938, was transferred to and assimilated by Flamengo.[16] Meanwhile, Fluminense, which had begun decisively supporting the implementation of professionalism in 1932, aimed at a policy of separating the athlete-as-professional-employee from the exclusive club membership, expanded its practice of recruiting white players from São Paulo and the interior of Brazil. Symptomatically, Bangú was able to free its worker–players from their factory jobs and hire a coach who had worked for the big clubs, and in 1933 it was the city's first championship team under professionalism.

The 1930s were thus marked by progress in a process of democratization within football, for both the professional defin-ition of players, coaches and trainers, and the incorporation of a broader, mass public.[17] This process continued into the 1940s: even when Leônidas and Domingos left Flamengo,[18] the team's popularity continued to grow as it won three straight city titles, in 1942, 1943 and 1944. The popularity of some charismatic players who had moved to São Paulo (i.e. Leônidas and Domingos) was transferred to the team as a whole (where mulattos and blacks were in the majority) and to the team's shirt, consolidating its universalist image of mixture.[19] Little by little, the young mulatto Zizinho occupied the place left by Leônidas. Yet even when he was transferred to Bangú in 1950, the team pulled together without any charismatic players and won three straight city titles again, in 1952, 1953 and 1954. Still, in the late 1940s the big team was Vasco da Gama, the core for the all-star team competing in the 1950 World Cup, bringing this club great popularity, splitting the preference of Rio's lower classes with Flamengo.

The Resurgence of Racist Stereotypes After the 1950 World Cup Defeat

While such progress in the democratization of football did in fact occur, ambiguous, dissimulated stereotypes and prejudices present in Brazilian society as a whole were also active throughout sport. Thus, the flow of young, poor, black athletic candidates meant that the greater or lesser faults and threats hovering over the players' careers, like lack of discipline, drinking, and taking bribes, were attributed more readily to blacks, albeit sometimes unconsciously (see Filho 1964: chap. 5). There was also an ambiguous split between the adoption and idolatry of black athletes by the home fans and the stigmatizing of black athletes from other teams, an expression of the kind of 'cordial racism' permeating Brazilian society and orientated by one's own personal relations.

According to this logic, Brazil's defeat by Uruguay in the final game of the 1950 World Cup, held in Brazil, sparked a barrage of accusations focused upon the colour of several black footballers on Brazil's defence who were targeted as the scapegoats for the tragedy. These racial insults and simplistic stereotypes were backed by a pretence at erudite justification in the evolutionist and social-Darwinist theories produced by physical anthropologists and essayists from various professional backgrounds, and were widely accepted by the Brazilian élites.[20] One result of the confrontation between such internationally drafted evolutionist racial theories – proposing a hierarchy in the various human 'races' and belittling racial mixture – and the reality of widespread Brazilian mis-cegenation was the prediction of a gradual 'whitening' of the Brazilian population. This prediction was based on policies introduced to encourage European immigration, and prognoses that the trend in miscegenation in Brazil would result in the predominance of the white 'race'. According to the theories of racial hierarchy, the less 'civilized' black and mestizo Brazilians were prone to greater emotional instability with regard to achieve-ments and decisions. Although such theories admitted the existence of bodily qualities and skills in blacks and mulattos, such as those associated with music and dance, in sports such skills were allegedly linked to the counter-trait of instability in the realm of achievements and decisions. The result of the 1950 World Cup Final thus appeared to illustrate adequately these erudite sup-positions; and a number of sports directors subscribed to them: the best team in the championship, displaying great beauty and skill in its footballing technique, had succumbed by a score of 2–1 in its own stadium, the biggest in the world with the largest cheering section, to a technically inferior yet determined team.

Again, when Brazil was eliminated from the 1954 World Cup in Switzerland by the Hungarian team (the score was 4–2, and the match ended in a free-for-all), it gave the head of the Brazilian delegation the opportunity to publish a report on the team's tour, turning to the above theories to justify Brazil's defeat on the basis of the alleged emotional instability resulting from Brazilian miscegenation.[21]

The Reversal of Social Stigmas in a New Style of Excellence in Brazilian Football

The Brazilian all-star team's victory in the 1958 World Cup in Sweden, drawing with the English in the second game and beating the Austrians, Russians, Welsh, French and Swedes, belied the erudite theories and racist stereotypes concerning the alleged weaknesses of mestizo Brazilian football. And to contradict that 'only by chance or contingency might we become world football champions and establish hegemony in this sport' (see text in the above footnote), virtually the same team won again in the 1962 World Cup in Chile, beating the Mexicans, Spanish, English, Chileans and Czechoslovakians. It was the first mestizo team (blacks, whites and mulattos) to win a World Cup, at a time when the skin colour of European players was universally white. Indeed, after the defeat in 1950, suffered by the Brazilian population as a national tragedy, and the experience in 1954, the 1958 team had a more seasoned group of managers, the teamwork of a 'technical commission' in charge of organizing the entire tour, and above all a group of extraordinary players, combining the experience of left-back Nilton Santos and midfielder Didi with the youth and unnerving style of others like Pelé and Garrincha. The latter three helped turn disadvantages and bodily stigmata like skin colour into embodiments of excellence in football. Didi was a craftsman of sagacity and elegance, making long-distance, curved passes, taking penalty-shots with his famous *folha seca* (dry leaf) kick (where the ball took an elliptical, semi-boomerang flight, tricking the goalkeeper). Pelé was a teenage prodigy at seventeen, son of a former football player, aware of the virtues of asceticism to avoid the pitfalls of a professional football career, and heir to the synthesis of qualities of his father's generation, which had included Leônidas. Garrincha was the prime example of the transformation of bodily and social stigmata into physical and athletic capital. He was born and raised in a textile-factory company town in the rural village of Pau Grande, some ninety kilometres from Rio, where he lived until the eve of the 1962 World Cup. Garrincha embodied the *habitus* of a factory worker deriving the utmost pleasure from the marginal activities of a company town, like hunting, fishing, and playing as a worker–player for the factory team, shirking around the work routine and transferring this hedonistic pleasure to the professional football context. With his crooked legs and total detachment from all things professional in his career (and thus from the nervousness characterizing decisive games), the mestizo Garrincha, who bore all the marks and stigmata of the Brazilian lower classes, became a potent illustration of how one could turn such disadvantages into an unusual, unnerving style – as indicated by his dribble down the right-wing which was so fatal to the opposition's defence (see Leite Lopes and Maresca 1989).

The 1958 World Cup may be used as a yardstick in order to compare Brazilian football with what was going on in Argentinian football, since it brought this country's all-star team back into international competition after a period of isolation in South America, where it maintained hegemony until the 1950s. Football had spread amongst the Argentinian working classes ever since the 1920s, and the country's all-star team beat the Uruguayans in the 1921 and 1927 South American Cups, but it lost when competing for world football domination against Uruguay in the 1928 Olympics and the 1930 World Cup. Such defeats fuelled the Argentinian supporters' image of their football as 'generous', more concerned with art than winning, unlike Uruguayan football. This image was reinforced when Argentina exported a large number of players to Italy in the 1930s, lending a new, more imaginative style, to the tough football style then present in Italy, and helping Italy win the world championships in 1934 and 1938; and later in the 1950s, when it gave strength to the major Spanish teams (considered the best in Europe), the most notorious case in point being Di Stéfano with Real Madrid and the Spanish all-star team. The Argentinians thus maintained high self-esteem in their football, even though they did not enjoy favourable enough conditions to win in the 1920s and 1930s. Excluded from the World Cup for several years, Argentina's return in 1958 deflated this self-esteem, with a 6–1 defeat to Czechoslovakia which caused a sense of national frustration comparable to that experienced by Brazil in the 1950 World Cup.[22]

Meanwhile, Brazil, who took Argentinian football as its model between the 1920s and 1950s and who failed to achieve outstanding international results until then, did not suffer the same exodus of players to Italian and Spanish football. Brazil's great black and mulatto players, as we have already seen, were 'condemned', so to speak, to exercise their talents in their own country, while certain other players would spend short periods abroad, generally in Argentina or Uruguay. They succeeded in making a major contribution to the creation of a national style of football in their own country, beginning in the 1930s. On the other hand, although football had spread throughout Brazil from the 1930s on and the public wanted to see exhibition, style, and 'art football', there was still a strong belief in the inferiority of Brazilian football as compared to that of Europe (especially England) and Argentina. Factors contributing to this belief were the aforementioned stereotypes and erudite racist theories, considered natural by the majority of the population and even internalized by blacks and mestizos themselves. The latter, in turn, appropriated a certain 'functional democratization' (in the sense proposed by Elias and Dunning 1994) in Brazilian society through football, silently constructing their 'ethnic' and social liberation through this sport, giving it a style through bodily techniques and *habitus*. Brazil's World Cup title in 1958 – which had been so close in 1950 in Maracanã but which had turned into a national tragedy – thus in a sense came as a surprise to the country. It took Brazil's international adoration in Sweden to reinforce a positive self-assessment of Brazilian football, finally reversing the people's sense of inferiority.

As we have seen, that sense of inferiority was linked to the internalization of racial stereotypes. The victory of 1958 (and its consolidation in 1962 and 1970), with its 'multi-racial' team, established a new style of excellence in football. The 'Brazilian style' of football is associated with bodily techniques (in the sense described by Mauss 1968) applied to the practice of this sport, which resemble those physical activities which have ethnic Afro-Brazilian origins. One can look, for instance, to those occasioning features of Afro-Brazilian dances of different kinds (like *samba*) or of those manifest in Afro-religions, or in martial arts such as *capoeira*. These footballing bodily techniques, largely subconscious as most bodily *hexis* and bodily *habitus* appear to be, were probably developed after the massive influx of blacks and mulattos into the first division, which accompanied the process of demo-cratization of Brazilian football. However, the social and ethnic origins and composition of this style is not something which can be pointed out as a substance with an underlying nature. It is rather a historical process with unplanned issues and contradictions. It is a process that begins with football as an aristocratic practice, but which turns out to be a popular practice, with its early 'multi-ethnic' and 'multi-racial' teams. Its style can be related to other Afro-Brazilian practices and bodily techniques, but ones which are exercised as such by 'whites'. The style can be seen as an outcome of diverse factors such as the investments of 'industrial paternalism' in workers' leisure and sports; and in the early recruitment of working-class players by the Portuguese immi-grants' club in Rio. These players filled the gaps left by the dearth of amateur athletes from élite backgrounds who were common to the aristocratic clubs; and by the export of many star white players to Italy in the early 1930s. The permanence and relative stability of black and mulatto players in the country was solidified further by the appearance of new generations of non-white players in the late 1950s (the generation of Didi, Garrincha and Pelé), who were aware of the lessons to be learnt from previous defeats. But if this style is now already socially invented and legitimized, it will reproduce itself among all kinds of athletes with their diverse social origins; and amongst them will be white athletes too. The style is reproduced and re-created in the less common sandlots in urban working-class neighbourhoods; and in the growing numbers of social programmes in slums and poor parts of the great cities. But it is also at play in the indoor football frequently practised in middle-class schools, clubs and neighbourhoods. The rapid diffusion of football from the aristocracy to the working classes is probably linked to its capacity to be appropriated in different ways by different social classes and groups. To put it another way, Brazil's social élites finally adopted the successful 'black' style of football. Football style is socially regarded as invented by players with working-class origins; and so, as in most Brazilian social contexts, it has become nationally dominant. As part of the national sentiment and identity associated with football, the incorporated 'black' style, inverts social and 'racial' stigmatization. As something that is embodied, it is certainly a phenomenon that acts frequently in a non-conscious and understated way. Indeed, perhaps the reasons for the power and frequent re-creation of the 'Brazilian style' rest in this successful reversal of social prejudices which still remain in society as a whole.

From Hedonism to Discipline: Difficulties in Professional Career Management

This national style incorporating the bodily techniques of blacks and mestizos had been consolidating since the 1930s, owing to its widespread practice by young lower-class males who, in addition to the sandlot games or *peladas*,[23] had the opportunity to use available fields in factories and companies, schools and military institutions, empty lots in neighbourhoods and dry riverbeds. The autobiography written by Zizinho, from the 1950 all-star team, clearly describes this availability of football fields in the city of Niterói, across Guanabara Bay from Rio de Janeiro. The biography of Mário Américo, the black masseur for the Brazilian all-stars from 1950 onwards, describes the riverbed fields in São Paulo that disappeared with the urban sprawl which began in the 1960s. The 1970 World Cup generation started playing football on these amateurish, working-class neighbourhood fields, but for those from the 1974 World Cup generation, opportunities to play spontaneous football on makeshift (yet eleven-player-sized) fields became scarcer. Changes also occurred in the paternalist relations maintained by companies, who until then had sponsored non-factory activities including football. The demise of Garrincha's style of football and the impossibility of the emergence of another player like him was also related to the disappearance of both a specific class of workers (belonging to the paternalistic company towns) and those benefiting from the expansion of social rights, which began to disappear during the military regime installed in 1964. There was a certain amount of upward shift in the social groups practising football, with a relative increase in participation by middle-class players, who were initiated through court football or beach football.[24] Some of the latter were behind the foundation of the first footballers' trade union in the early 1980s, when a redemocratization of Brazil's political life occurred, which struggled for better conditions in professional football (see Benzaquem de Araújo 1981). Indeed, long after professional football began in Brazil (i.e. well into the 1960s), there persisted a standard and substance of living which resulted from the combination of monetary and non-monetary income characteristic of 'yellow amateurism', and the players' heavy dependence on club managers.

After the 1970s, Brazilian players were coveted by European clubs and frequently moved abroad (by now mestizo and black players went too) to participate in a more 'globalized' European football, which included players of colour from Portuguese, French, Dutch, Belgian and English colonies and former colonies, who also began to circulate around the clubs of Italy and Spain. In the 1970s, Brazilian players, including Pelé, played football in the USA, but in the 1980s Japan became the major importer. There was an enormous increase both in the amounts paid in transfer fees and as players' salaries.[25]

Before the 1970s, when the living standard of most good Brazilian players was not very far above that of 'yellow amateurism', there were already great difficulties in reconciling the working-classes' innate hedonism (see Hoggart 1969), which was internalized in the players' bodily techniques and characteristic of the 'Brazilian style', and the implicit discipline and sacrifice needed in athletes' lives.[26] Once again, Garrincha took this working-class hedonism to an extreme: on the one hand it helped to distil his style of game to the utmost; but on the other hand it accelerated his career's demise and jeopardized his subsequent, post-football retirement on the other. He exemplified an enormous group of players who enjoyed the simple pleasures of the working classes – drinking, sex and a bohemian lifestyle – described in great detail by witnesses like the masseur Mário Américo (Matteucci 1986). This masseur had functions beyond massaging which included assisting the coach in keeping watch over the players' discipline in the full-time institutions known as *concentrações* (confined training camps). Nevertheless, today's players who come originally from the working classes or lower-middle classes encounter a consumer hedonism in which they can participate owing to their high salaries and high standards of living. They can afford houses and apartments in new, chic neighbourhoods, as well as imported cars,[27] thereby increasing the possibility of a bohemian lifestyle or tumultuous matrimonial relations. Career-management problems are no less complicated than they used to be, given the rapid leap in athletes' living standards and their harassment by the media and fans. The equilibrium achieved by ascetic athletes like Pelé[28] and Zico is not often repeated.

It was no coincidence that in the early 1980s an evangelical movement called 'Athletes for Christ' was founded, first in the State of Minas Gerais, then in Rio in 1984, and the following year in São Paulo. By 1985 this specialized evangelical group already had 300 members, the majority of whom were football players. All-star players like Jorginho and César Sampaio belonged to the group. Through Bible readings and religious meetings, the group stressed the qualities of discipline and asceticism which are needed in an athletic career. Thus they dealt with the dilemmas and tensions of professional football players, aggravated by the sport's increased commercialization and the pressures of consumer hedonism, which hinder the management of what is already a structurally unstable kind of career, traversed by uncontrollable, short-term factors.

Along with the phenomenon of the specialized evangelization of football players, the clubs' cheering sections kept expanding their groups and sub-groups. Unlike the tenuous supporters' groups of the 1940s, 1950s and 1960s which were predominantly made up of mostly male (with a few female) adult factory and office workers, supporters' organizations of the 1970s, 1980s and

1990s have consisted primarily of young people. While the traditional carnivalization of the stands is still present, through the adaptation of old *sambas* or songs from the *escolas de samba* clubs, contemporary cheering sections have concentrated on the music and body language of funk, which has spread all over the slums and working-class suburbs in Rio and São Paulo.[29]

From the 1970s onwards, one notes a trend towards relatively greater participation by players from higher social origins, a certain sense of regret over the demise of the sandlot football fields of yester-year, and a nostalgia for a greater presence of blacks on the Brazilian all-star team (seen as more authentic representatives of the 'Brazilian style'), but in the 1990s one observes considerable effort and initiative in promoting football among the working classes in Brazil's large cities. While previously there had been a spontaneous process of 'functional democratization' through football by which the working classes could achieve real participation and success, there now began an educational process aimed at creating the conditions for social skills and discipline among children and youth in these social classes. These young people, in addition to no longer having the same access to sandlot or factory football fields, have now often found themselves in neighbourhoods where unemployment, a deteriorating school system, the committal of misdemeanours and felonies have become the prospects for a generation of youth no longer incorporated by the productive system as manual or factory labour. Even so, in smaller towns in various parts of the country and in the poor suburbs where opportunities still appear for working-class youth to practise football, skilled young players continue to emerge.

Mestizo football in Brazil thus survives, with its traditions of success and more or less silent conflicts relating to access by and the continued presence of working-class (and thus mulatto and black) footballers in an area of activity highly prized by Brazilian national identity, even when the legitimized hierarchy of professions ascribes priority to more dominant activities in economic, political and intellectual life. With the vast majority of spectators and footballers originating from the working classes, both can still take interest in an activity joining the various classes together in a common language, even though living conditions for the lower classes are aggravated by the persistent lack of social sensitivity by the majority of the country's political and economic élite, who combine the traditional old-fashioned kind of 'master and slave' domination with modern, exclusive neo-liberalism. By using a unique body language and inventing an original style for a quasi-universal sport, these working-class athletes have succeeded in making a silent contribution to their relative social ascent, while providing an important domain for Brazilian national identity, wherein they have contributed to a reversal of the élite's racist stereotypes and ethnocentrism internalized by society as a whole.

Notes

1. Social anthropologist of the Museu Nacional, Universidade Federal do Rio de Janeiro.
2. Slavery was not abolished in Brazil until 1888.
3. The local élite's appropriation of football as played by the English ruling class occurred in the following ways: a) by the local élite's frequenting and mingling at prestigious English schools (or schools from other European countries where football had already spread, for example Switzerland); b) through access to sports practice organized by English companies abroad, or at local companies where the presence of English advisors promoted this form of leisure among company employees; or c) through the founding of the originally élite form of English conviviality – the clubs – whether those devoted to other sports like rowing, cricket, or athletics and which later added football, or those founded explicitly as football clubs. From this élite origin, with emphasis on belonging to a community of students or alumni of prestigious schools or colleges, to the subsequent popularization of the sport, there occurred a process of dissemination with historical local specificities from country to country. (See, for example, Filho 1964; Walvin 1975: chap. 5; Wahl 1990; Rosenfeld 1993; Elias and Dunning 1994. See also Mason (1995: chaps 1 and 2) – a book I only had access to whilst completing this chapter.)
4. See, for example, Vários Autores (1968). This interesting book gives the opinions of football coaches on the eve of the 1970 World Cup. It also offers succinct information about the coaches' careers: many of them are ex-players and have a university degree in Physical Education.

5. For further information, see Leite Lopes and Maresca 1989; Leite Lopes 1994; Leite Lopes and Faguer 1994.
6. The name Bangú supposedly came from the term *bangüê*, a type of rural mill where sugar was made (see Oliveira 1991). The name indicates the homology between the isolated 'company towns' and labour conditions in the Brazilian sugar mills.
7. See Leite Lopes (1976: chap. 4, 1988: chaps 4 to 7) for a description of these activities in the context of the sugar mills in Brazil's *Nordeste*, where a regional championship was played between teams of different mills and even a small labour market of worker–players existed.
8. See Mason (1989: 147–8) for the less well-known persistence of amateur football in England and its conflicts with professional football from the end of the last century until the 1970s.
9. The term *bicho*, the bonus paid to a player which varied according to his performance, referred to the actual amount of money. The figure corresponded to a number in a clandestine lottery known as *jogo do bicho* (literally the 'animal game', and still in existence), where each number is associated with an animal. The semi-clandestine language of the 'animal game' was thus appropriate as a metaphorical, coded reference to the semi-clandestine payment of bonuses to amateur athletes.
10. The reference to professions associated with tips appears to be an indirect warning against semi-clandestine bonuses (the *bicho*) for amateur athletes.
11. See Seyferth (1993).
12. Floriano's book includes written testimony in his support from several players and former players as well as sports reporters. Such testimony was used as a weapon by the movement in favour of professional football at the peak of this campaign. Among such players defending Floriano was the mestizo Arthur Friedenreich, son of a German father (a member of the Germânia Club in São Paulo who introduced his son to the game at this club) and a black Brazilian mother. Friedenreich was the hero of the first Brazilian victory in international competition, against Uruguay in 1919. Having scored the winning goal, he became one of the first idols in Brazilian football.

13. Football had reached Argentina and Uruguay early. Argentina was one of the first countries outside England to practise the sport: ever since 1865, when a group of Englishmen living in Argentina founded the Buenos Aires Football Club. Uruguay were already twice Olympic football champions when the government proposed to host the first World Cup in 1930 (which Uruguay won). Argentina was runner-up in the 1928 Olympics in Amsterdam and runner-up in the 1930 World Cup. The first continental football confederation to be founded in the world, after FIFA was founded in 1904, was in South America in 1916. See the entry on 'Futebol' in *Enciclopédia Mirador* (vol. X, p. 5036–5038) and Archetti (1994a: 235).

14. We find here on a Brazilian national scale a kind of repro-duction of the closed world experienced by these players' ancestors and contemporaries on the large sugar or coffee plantation operations or in the company towns of the large factories. See R. Alvim (1985); J.S. Leite Lopes (1988); R. Alvim and J.S. Leite Lopes (1990) for an analysis of the confined situation in the company towns. See A. Garcia Jr. (1989: chap. 1) and J.S. Leite Lopes (1976) for an analysis of the closed world of the sugar mills in Brazil.

15. A good example is the comparison with (and extension to) what happened with the black midfielder Didi in the early 1960s, at Real Madrid. Like other great players, including Domingos da Guia and Garrincha, who were player–workers for textile factory teams, Didi started his career in teams like the Industrial Juniors, a textile factory club in his home town of Campos in the State of Rio de Janeiro, where he was preparing to be a skilled worker by studying at the 'apprentices' school'. As with Pelé, Didi's father, mother, grandmother and siblings played an important role in his life as a young pre-professional player. Something of the trad-itional folk medicine practised by his grandmother and which cured Didi of a bruised knee that was threatening to knock him out of football early appears to have rubbed off on him and was incorporated into his 'magic' repertoire of kicks, passes, dribbles and attitudes on the field (like his famous determined march, with the ball under his arm, from the Brazilian goal to the midfield line, after Sweden scored the opening goal in the final game of the 1958 World Cup, thus transmitting self-confidence to his team-mates). Like

Domingos and Garrincha, Didi started as a worker in a textile factory and (like Pelé, who worked occasionally in a factory in Baurú, São Paulo) in a machine shop in Campos, until he and a brother were hired by Madureira in Rio in 1947. During the 1950s he played for two clubs of aristocratic vintage, Fluminense and Botafogo, who at the time were finally giving in to the imperative of recruiting the best black and mestizo players in the competition between clubs which had been sparked by professional play. After the 1958 World Cup, where international sports journalists picked him out as the most valuable player, he was hired by Real Madrid, where he was unable to adjust to overcome the explicit sabotage by Di Stefano and other less explicit forms of discrimination. He thus repeated the same story as that of Fausto, Domingos and Leônidas, condemned to success in his own country: returning to Brazil, he became a world champion again in 1962. As a football coach, Didi was more successful abroad than in Brazil. In countries like Mexico, Peru and Turkey, Brazilian players and coaches joined foreign teams beginning in the late 1970s and early 1980s. Didi's biographical data are in Ribeiro (1994: chap. 3); Pelé's are in Filho (1963); Domingos' are in Filho (1964); Garrincha's are in Leite Lopes and Maresca (1989).

16. Flamengo has the country's most devoted and largest group of supporters, according to public opinion polls the club has 25 to 30 million followers in Brazil; followed in popularity by Coríntians (in São Paulo) and Vasco.

17. All this was happening in parallel with a process of regulated, controlled citizenship, with initiatives by a central State (which was consolidating itself at the same time), with the aim of regulating urban labour relations. This policy of incorporating large urban masses was a parallel to the large internal migration from the country towards the great industrializing cities. See Santos (1979) and Leite Lopes (1991).

18. Leônidas transferred to the São Paulo Futebol Clube in 1942, taking his popularity with him to the city of São Paulo, which had a larger white population than that of Rio. When he had returned from the World Cup in 1938, his popularity was greater than that of Flamengo itself and his contract was supposed to last for several more years; over time, however, his conflicts with Flamengo's board of directors led to his transfer, and the move was diplomatic in that it was easier for

the fans to accept him moving to a different city. His début was marked by a record crowd in the São Paulo municipal stadium.

In 1943, Domingos also decided (for financial reasons) to transfer to Esporte Clube Coríntians, São Paulo's most popular club. Despite the rivalry between the two cities – Rio with its political power as national capital until 1960 and São Paulo with its economic clout – and which the football matches helped bolster and consolidate, Leônidas' and Domingos' transfer to São Paulo contributed to the 'nationalization' of the Carioca football style, where the presence of bodily techniques, in the sense proposed by Mauss (1968), and black culture had developed since the beginning of the century (through the music and dance which would later produce a revolution in Carnival with samba and through the Afro-Brazilian martial art/dance known as *capoeira*).

19. Identification of this club with blacks and the poor began when Fluminense supporters responded to their own epithet of 'rice powder!' by heckling Flamengo fans with 'coal dust!', referring to heavy manual labour and the colour black, and the process has continued to this day, with symbols like the *favela*, or hillside shanty town (when Flamengo suffers a goal, the opposing fans goad the sad fans with *'Ela, ela, ela, silêncio na favela!!'*, translating loosely as 'Tum, tum, tum, silence in the slums!!'), and the black *urubu*, or buzzard (a symbol that has been fully assimilated by the Flamengo supporters). Their fervour and fanaticism, associated with grass-roots culture, and their plentiful presence and antics in the stadium, have made them a veritable institution in constant change, attracting youth from all social classes.

20. See Seyferth (1989, 1991, 1993). See also Da Matta (1981).

21. 'The Brazilian players lacked what is lacking for the Brazilian people in general . . . The causes . . . touch on the foundations of social science in the comparative study of races, environment, climate, eating habits, spirit, culture, and individual and common living processes . . . The ills are deeper [than the length of the cleats on football boots, the game's tactical system, etc.] and lead from the cultural *stage* to the football *stadium* [a play on words with *estádio*, meaning both *stage* and *stadium* in Portuguese]. They go back to genetics itself. It is undeniable that Hungary has a better predisposition, like so

many other countries, arming its respective all-star team with the best positive attributes. Our people's psychosocial state is still *green* [i.e. immature or unripe], and the athletes emerging from amongst the people cannot improvise the conditions and tools for overcoming [such immaturity] in athletic contests, requiring the mobilization of greater organic resources and reserves . . . The melancholic conclusions are thus laid bare, in a simple comparison between the average cultural level of Brazilian players and that of the Hungarian all-stars. In fact, rarely can Brazilian players read and write correctly or display basic revelations of spiritual life . . . This blatant state of organic and functional insufficiency is not limited to Brazilian ballplayers; it is widespread in most layers of the national population. Thus Brazil continues to be a country with a people, but with no opinion. The people are not enlightened by the culture of the soul, nor of the spirit, and still experience the primary outburst of their instincts . . . Such is the cause of the lack of control over [our] nerves, or our psychic impropriety in relation to playing football . . . Given the state of the Brazilian people, only by chance or contingency might we become world football champions and establish hegemony in this sport . . . In Brazilian football, flashy trim lends artistic expression to the match, to the detriment of yield and results. *Exhibition* jeopardizes *competition*. It would be easy to compare the physiognomy of a Brazilian all-star team, made up mostly of blacks and mulattos, with that of Argentine, German, Hungarian, or English football. Brazilian football goes to great lengths with the flashy surface of effects (exhibition), while outstanding players [must] develop the profitable depth of results (competition) . . . The study of Brazilian football has still not been dissociated from the knowledge applied to [the Afro-Brazilian martial art/dance] of *capoeira*. *Capoeira* displays a cultural state, the survival of which is diluted in the psychosocial life of blacks and mulattos. Sport brings revel-ations to life that relate to establishing the portrait of Brazil and are cultivated as the wealth of the human masses tied to the social basement; it does not meet up with the *Olympic aristocracy*, destined to remark itself periodically' (Lyra Filho 1954: 49–64). For an interesting, pioneering analysis of this text, see Guedes (1993).

22. I am basing this on the important analyses by Archetti (1994a and 1994c) concerning Argentinian football. Argentina's World Cup defeat in 1958 was partially compensated for in the 1978 and 1986 World Cups. Even so, Argentina's victory at home in 1978 at the height of a military dictatorship failed to produce the same sense of satisfaction as the 'art football' of the 1920s through to the 1950s, nor did the victory in 1986, when only Maradona embodied such virtues from football's past. In this sense, Brazil's victory over Italy in 1994, decided by penalties, also failed to have the same impact on the Brazilian people as the victories in 1958, 1962 and 1970, when the Brazilian team played a kind of football that was compatible with the 'Brazilian style' consolidated in 1958, 1962 and 1970.

23. The popular term *pelada* to designate spontaneous football played on the street or on empty lots, with an improvised ball and goalposts, and which is purported to have bolstered the development of skill and acrobatics among poor Brazilian youth, appears to be related to both the players' bare feet (*pelado*: bare, naked) and the field with no grass, thus bare, naked, bald.

24. Court football (*futebol de salão*), which is very widespread in Brazil, is played with five players on a basketball-sized court, with a smaller, heavier ball than that used for regular football. Beach football is another Brazilian variation, played with eleven, seven, or five barefoot players, with a ball similar to that of field football (but a little lighter).

25. In 1993, Brazilian players were distributed as follows in various countries of the world: 126 in Portugal, 11 in Spain, 2 in Italy, 12 in Switzerland, 14 in Finland, 4 in France, 25 in Mexico, 12 in Argentina, 9 in Uruguay, 5 each in Bolivia, Peru, and Venezuela, 19 in Saudi Arabia, and 32 in Japan, in addition to other countries on all of the continents. See the special edition of the magazine *Placar*, no. 1092, March 1994, 'Os Brasileiros no Mundo' (Brazilians Around the World).

26. See the important analysis by Wacquant (1995) on the extreme case of discipline and sacrifice for boxers (these were innate qualities for the group of boxers from black ghettos in Chicago that he researched).

27. Black footballers owning imported or luxury cars are stopped intentionally by the Brazilian police in routine traffic raids, since a black person driving a fancy car is considered suspect.

Frisked rudely or even violently, they are free to go as soon as they state that they are professional football players. See *Folha de São Paulo*, 14 January 1996.

28. Pelé who has recently been preoccupied, as Minister of Sports, in promoting sports and football in working-class neighbourhoods, has also been concerned by colour discrimination and racial inequalities. As he got back in touch with his ethnic origins he declared his desire to know the meaning of the nickname he didn't initially like. An intellectual of the black movement informed by newspaper that in yorubá language it would be 'rapid boy'. Another one disagreed with this meaning, but despite the mysteries of lost meanings, *Pelé* is now unequivocally associated with his person and his social biography.

29. Lever (1983) grasped the beginning of the changes in the cheering sections in the 1970s. In Brazil, it would be important to perform in-depth and focused ethnographic studies such as those done by Bromberger et al. (1995) in Marseilles, Turin and Naples.

Chapter 4

The Importance of Difference: Football Identities in Italy

Rocco De Biasi and *Pierre Lanfranchi*

Although the importance of football in Italian society is unquestionable, the interest of social scientists in the game is scarce, and over-focused on events related to violence and hooliganism. In fact, although the football industry is one of the most important economic sections in Italy, even this financial issue is ignored by academics.[1] In his two-volume monograph of post-war Italy the English historian, Paul Ginsborg (1989), did not have a single word to say about football. Perhaps his problem was one stated by the Brazilian sociologist, Roberto da Matta (1982), who noted how the presence of the game is so rooted in Latin societies that some analysts have difficulties seeing its implications. Finding reference to the game over the past fifty years in works that describe the transformation of Italy from a rural to an urbanized society is nearly impossible. Even in the 1990s historians and social scientists are reluctant to include passions for both football and *Totocalcio* (the Italian 'football pools') in their analysis of the country.

In the opinions of journalist Oliviero Beha and sociologist Franco Ferrarotti, 'Italy is a Republic based on Football'.[2] This definition is applicable and relevant but also paradoxical. The fact that the Italian football industry is the biggest in Europe could lead to excessive emphasis being given to the notion of Italian fans as 'consumers' in a manipulated form of consumption. Three national daily sports newspapers[3] offer Italian football fans not only news, but abstract and complex reflections upon matches and surrounding events. The Italian football spectator is thus often a sort of 'theorist' on his favourite sport, equipped with a sophisticated lexicon, exercised at a high level of abstraction. This fanatical culture involves the whole country so that the recent developments of the football system in Italy have occurred on fertile and cerebral land. This chapter, written by a historian and a social scientist, combines social and oral history with ethnography, and seeks to analyse the development of football in Italy. After presenting the historical and historiographic complexities of that evolution, we endeavour to analyse the styles of fandom in Italy, in particular those of the *ultras*. The symbiosis of club, team and followers is, in Italy, one which is fragile, regional in its chauvinism and dismissive of the idea of national unity.

Italian football differs further from expressions of the game which are played elsewhere in Europe. Firstly, local patriotism – *campanilismo* – is forever present in a country unified only a century ago. In a manner similar to politics and the arts, football continues to create and diffuse tensions in the nation and offers endless possibilities to display local pride and chauvinism. In nineteenth-century Italy, games were played in various local forms; one was known as *giuoco del pallone* which is similar to tennis and relevant to an understanding of the specific development of a football culture throughout twentieth-century Italy (Pivato 1992). Secondly, while being strongly anchored in the habits and customs of the nation, Italian football has never referred to social class or religious discrimination. Thirdly, the game's status as a global social phenomenon has developed in the cultural and political sphere since the First World War, and is now an essential component of Italian society. We may begin to examine these historical phen-omena by reference to the game that Italians call *calcio*.

What is 'Calcio all'Italiana'?

The Italian word *calcio* is not a literal or phonetic translation of the English word 'football'. Instead, it originates from a game played in Florence from the thirteenth to the eighteenth century (Artusi and Gabrielli 1986; Bredekamp 1995). In choosing this word to define a game imported from Britain, the Italian Football Federation in 1909 reassumed a characteristic of pre-modern ball games in Italy: the importance of difference. In local chauvinism, the differences could be small but significant. Florentine *calcio* proclaimed itself to be 'a *specific* and *ancient* game of the city of Florence'. Yet fifteen miles away, the textile city of Prato had played its own game of *calcio*; for its citizens the differences were fundamental, since their game 'differs a lot from the florentine game, because our ball is smaller, our public place different'. This somewhat contradictory pursuit of establishing a direct link with local traditions and the need for displaying difference has been a constant logic in Italian football throughout the century (Lanfranchi 1995).

A further distinction between Italian football and the English original emerged in the 1930s. The style of 'kick and rush' which monopolized English football was criticized by managers and journalists. Italian clubs began to enrol vast numbers of trainers from Central Europe, particularly Austria and Hungary, whose conceptions of the game adapted well to the contemporary nationalistic and fascistic view about the game's role. A new style known as *Il Metodo* (The Method) appeared. This emphasized the political ideology that players were warriors for the nation (Marri 1983), and closely related to the climactic and morphological situation of Italy. By focusing on the tactical skills of the players, rather than their fighting spirit and physical strength, trainers in Italy created the idea of a specific way of understanding and performing the game across this Peninsula. In November 1934, when Italy travelled to play England, the 'Battle of Highbury' was presented by the Italian media as a contest between the guardians of the temple and the iconoclastic world champions; as the opposition between two games, two cultures, and as the metaphoric representation of a *Kulturkampf* (culture struggle). The very idea of universality in the rules of football was, from that point on, over. Football was displayed as the metaphoric opposition between the old capitalist democracy (England) and the new vigour of fascist Italy. And football offered during the 'golden decade of the Fascist regime' two World Cup victories (1934 and 1938) and an Olympic gold medal at Berlin (1936). Abroad, it allowed the possibility of displaying itself as the antithesis of England and Englishness. This opposition was not only visible in how the game was played; it also assumed various forms in the different understandings of fair competition, supporter culture, news coverage, citizenship within football, the impact of football stars, the concept of what stadiums are, and the symbolic values of the game. Further differences are reflected through the Italians' collective understanding of the history of their club football.

Internal Differences, Unequal Partners

Since the creation of the Italian national championship in 1929, football clubs have been classified into three unequal categories: *le grande* (the big clubs), *le provinciali* (the small provincial clubs) and the others. The big clubs are the two sides of Milan (Inter and AC) and Juventus of Turin. At the start of each season they are all the favourites to win the championship. Having more money than the rest, they can buy the best players. They are favoured by referees; they are influential in the football federation and in political circles. More than any other club, Juventus exemplifies this category, being part of the Agnelli empire which owns FIAT. The club recruits supporters from all regions of the country, and is a symbol of immigration from the South to Turin to work in the car factories. After winning the league in 1982 following a long battle with Fiorentina, the latter's supporters claimed the victory had been unfair: Juventus had received too much help from the football federation and referees. Offensive slogans appeared on Florentine city walls, declaring 'Better second than bent' or, more famously, 'If *Juve* is magic then Cicciolina[4] is a virgin'. Over a decade later, this strong anti-Juventus sentiment retains the same power and vitality.

This hierarchy within Italian football has changed little over time. Some clubs, such as Fiorentina, Roma or Napoli, have managed for a few years to compete at the highest level, but *le grande* quickly re-establish their supremacy. Only two clubs, Inter and Juventus, have never been relegated in the 66-year-old history of Italy's first division, *Serie A*. The second category of clubs, *le provinciali*, will never win the League. As they compete for a place in the UEFA Cup, their managers usually state that staying in the top division is like winning the title for them. From Atalanta, Ascoli, Udinese to Catania or Vicenza, these teams are obliged to sell their best players and successful managers to the bigger clubs every season, and benefit only from their local support.

The third category, the others, is more complex. Fiorentina, Napoli, Roma, Lazio, Sampdoria, Genoa, Bologna and Torino make up this group. They enjoy plentiful popular support all over the nation, have big stadiums and have each won the league title at least once. Genoa and Torino are considered to be 'the big dismissed' (*le grande decadute*); they enjoy a large but rather resigned support. In the 1920s, Genoa was Italy's major club but never really adapted to professionalism. Torino's history is more tragic. In May 1949 all the players and staff were killed in a plane crash over the church of Superga, north of the city. They had won the last three league championships and had in Valentino Mazzola the captain of the Italian national side. Unlike Manchester United, sportingly they never recovered from this disaster. In 1967, Gigi Meroni, their most talented player, was killed by a car when crossing a Turin street, only three hours after playing his last match for the club. He was only twenty-four (see dalla Chiesa 1995).

All these 'other' clubs have experienced high points followed by major crises, and do not wear the exclusive gold star on their shirts (the symbol of ten league titles). They can keep their best players, like Antognoni (Fiorentina), Mancini (Sampdoria), Bruno Conti and Falcão (Roma), but are often not able to compete with *le grande* in the *Calcio-mercato* (football supermarket) held every summer in a big Milan hotel. Here, the ethics of competition are diametrically opposed to the American model. Every year, as always, the most expensive players on the market go to the best professional clubs. Such a lack of flexible mobility on the football scene is comparable to other Latin countries, such as Spain, Portugal or Greece, and reproduces in the sporting sphere the very idea of power and local or regional oppositions. Football is not open to big surprises.

In Italy, the aphorism that football is more than a game is especially true. In addition to the ubiquitous football media, the game's words and terms are major vectors in political and economic discourses. The former prime minister, Giulio Andreotti, a long-standing and influential Roma supporter, used to say that he never liked to sit on the bench. One of the major questions asked in the press during the last decade was, 'Is the Italian economy relegated to *Serie B*?' In recent years, this link has been emphasized by Silvio Berlusconi, first when he used football to develop his private television network in 1981, then upon becoming chairman of AC Milan in 1986, and then in his use of a football slogan to christen his political party as *Forza Italia!* (Come on Italy!) in 1993. Radio and the Sunday afternoon transmission *Il calcio minuto per minuto* play an important role in this liturgy. In the stadium, the majority of supporters bring a radio to learn of developments at other matches; in the cities, people everywhere listen to the voice of Sandro Ciotti to suffer with their team, and to know if they have won the *Totocalcio*. A Sunday afternoon may well change your life . . .

Sunday Afternoon 'Lay Religion'

Eric Hobsbawm has used the term 'lay religion' to define the
football culture (Hobsbawm and Ranger 1981), and the editor of a
book on football culture in Europe entitled an article one of the
authors wrote on Italian football 'Cathedrals in Concrete' (Lanfranchi 1995a). Thus, football matches could be understood as
perfect rituals with their own fixed rules. In a number of other
European countries, religious conflicts played a major role in the
dynamics of the development of the game through opposition
between religious communities. The catholic predominance in the
peninsula (at 90 per cent of the total population) excludes any kind
of religious football war. However, and this aspect has been
generally underestimated, the church and the parish organizations
play a central role in the structure of Italian football. As in Italian
sport generally, the Italian football association (FIGC) is only
organized for the élite. The infrastructure and numbers of qualified
trainers and organized competitions are insufficient, particularly
at youth level. Since the 1920s, the *oratorio* has been the natural
place for young boys to meet and learn football together after
school, under the supervision of the local priest. Initially, the strong
Italian socialist movement was steadfastly opposed to sport, and
proclaimed: 'More libraries, less stadiums' (Pivato 1992). Conversely, at the end of the nineteenth century, catholic theorists such
as Semeria gave major attention to sport as they were more inclined
to the development of activities for young people than any political
movement (ibid.; Porro 1995). In his biography of Gigi Meroni,
dalla Chiesa underlines the continuing importance of the *oratorio*
for the young winger. More recently, players such as Cabrini have
focused on the early years of their autobiography, when the priest
was coach and referee, and the pitch devoid of grass.

The Italian Catholic Church's long-standing partiality towards
football has been epitomized very recently on television. Lazio's
most celebrated supporter is *Suor Paola*, a religious sister in her
fifties who appears on TV screens every Sunday afternoon in the
midst of a group of young *ultras* in the stadium. During the match
her language is partisan rather than reasoned, though she justifies
this by arguing, 'I like to be where the youngsters are, to understand their passions . . . and I enjoy it.' In the 1990s, other clubs
exhibit their priests: Atalanta's is a TV spokesman for the *ultras*,
Fiorentina's has recently published a book based on player

interviews reflecting their strong religious feelings and attachment to the church (Vagnuzzi 1992). Yet, in this religious context, there is no official link with the catholic hierarchy. No Italian club is analogous to Barcelona, with its chapel next to the dressing-room. Gianni Rivera and his team-mates of the 1960s were called *gli abattini* by the major sportswriter Gianni Brera, as they looked as cold and superior as a young *abbé* (Brera 1993: 211).

Hence, the message is one of everyday faith in a popular religion conversely. Paganist rituals are also appropriated, and chance remains as a major factor in the rhetoric of Italian football. Pisa's chairman, Romeo Anconetani, was renowned throughout Italy for throwing salt inside the goals before every home game, to prevent bad luck. Helenio Herrera, Inter's successful manager during the 1960s, was not appreciated for his tactical qualities: his nickname *il mago* (the wizard) derived from his ability to transform ordinary players into prize-fighters. According to the press, the reason for his successes had nothing to do with training skills, but was instead rooted in his considerable power in hypnotizing players before matches!

Although this religious presence in Italian football has remained, since the 1940s young men have deserted churches but continued to attend matches on Sunday afternoons. Yet Italian football shows intense stoicism in celebrating itself on this most religious of days. Football in Italy is deeply attached to Sunday afternoons. The Federation has always been extremely reluctant to postpone matches. The relationship is reciprocated through the fact that football is also present in religious processions. In Naples in 1987, after Napoli's first league victory, images of Maradona were present at the popular procession of the Madonna dell'Arco, next to the images of San Gennaro (patron of the city) and the Madonna (Niola 1991). In addition, parodies of city processions, such as the wearing of bishops' dress by supporters, highlighted the religious impact of the club. In other settings, the trappings of religiosity find an expression in football. Obituary notices are placed to mourn the death of a rival team during a game, and circulated throughout the country. Significantly, only in their songs and lyrics do Italian supporters avoid using religious canticles. From the early 1990s, political songs, such as *Morti di Reggio Emilia*, the anti-fascist hymn from the 1970s, have been adapted on to the terraces. Yet, with the names of *ultra* groups referring to left-wing movements, like the red-black brigades of Milan or the face of

Che Guevara on the flags of Pisa supporters, the political aspect
has been manipulated to such an extent that it has become only a
generic symbol (Dal Lago 1991).

The Cultural Dimension of Italian Football: Politics and Social Research

As noted at the outset of this chapter, it is only recently in Italy's
post-war history that social scientists have come to appreciate the
significance of football in Italian society. It was not until the 1970s
that historians first dealt seriously with football, specifically
through their political interest in fascism. Even here, they were
concerned with applying previous work on Nazi Germany to
Mussolini's regime, focusing almost exclusively on institutions and
propaganda (Fabrizi 1973). The first innovative work appeared
about ten years ago. Stefano Pivato, who worked initially on
popular catholicism at the start of the twentieth century, dedicated
a book to the myth of Gino Bartali (Pivato 1987, 1996). In his
following work, he emphasized the importance of popular
catholicism as a catalyst in the development of a rural sporting
tradition. Cycling and football benefitted from the favours of the
public and the local clergy. The biographies of players have
reflected this rural tradition in Italian football. Ezio Pascutti,
Bologna's forward in the 1960s, embodied this tradition, coming
from a village of 450 inhabitants in Frioul which offered no future
except through emigration to America (Fiori 1996). Football was a
working-class game, belonging to the rural working class that
emigrated *en masse* to the major cities of the north (such as Milan,
Genoa and Turin), bringing with them rural values and catholic
faith. If historians did not pay much attention to football's
symbolization of changes in Italy, this theme was developed by
political scientists particularly with the growth of the post-1990's
Berlusconi phenomenon, though political involvement in football
had a longer history. During the Fascist period, football assumed
extraordinary importance. Giuseppe Meazza, captain of the
national team in the 1930s, was called *il Ballila*, the young soldier
of the regime. As Soldati (1964) records in his book *Le due città*,
'Juventus was a serious matter, it was, maybe, at that time the
most serious in life. We could not dedicate ourselves to politics
anymore, we were not allowed to think anymore, and it seemed

there was no hope Fascism could end.'

Biographies and studies describing the creation of sporting legends, like Maradona in Naples (Dini 1994), are essential to understand the cultural changes of the nation. Interestingly enough, the journal *Ossimori*, published by the Italian association of anthropologists, devoted its first issue to football in 1992. The influence of Christian Bromberger played an essential role in this choice but, as the editorial said, football passion may be considered as a legitimate and accurate object, through which the impact of modernity on rural society may be identified. Additionally, political association and supporter organization have direct connections. In the case of Naples, the journalist Antonio Ghirelli, whose history of Italian football is still the most valuable contribution to the field, wrote: 'People from Naples who emigrated to the North feel their football support as a transfer . . . .. They give to football matches a sense of their lives; it is a link with their origins, but also a way to fight against under-development' (Ghirelli 1978).

Participating in football remains the best way to express a form of genuine normality. Politicians and judges form their national team for charity matches in order to enhance their popularity. To name more famous cases of the football–politics connection, Gianni Rivera, football idol of the 1960s, has been a Christian Democrat MP for the past fifteen years; Giampiero Boniperti, former star then chairman of Juventus, is an MEP for *Forza Italia!*; the young Massimo Mauro, former Juventus and Naples midfielder, is representing the left-wing Olive Tree coalition, in the newly elected parliament. We doubt that any other Western democracy ever had such a large sporting tradition in politics. Artists are not absent from this 'footballization' of society. A book compiling all the publications of Pasolini, the writer and movie director, regarding football has been recently published and in the debate regarding Maradona some years ago, major cultural figures like Carmelo Bene expressed their opinion.

The Rituals and Differences of the *Ultras*

In order to analyse the relationship between politics and football in Italy more fully, we can consider the most discussed phenomenon linked to the game: spectator violence. This is an important looking-glass, through which we may examine different societies. In various countries football hooliganism involves the immersion of spectator violence in religious or ethnic conflicts, or has a cause instigated by extreme nationalist elements. In Italy, the influence of politics mainly relates to the particular forms of association which are transplanted into the stadium ends (the *curvas*). Deriving from the tradition of local associations, religious and political, which are deeply rooted in Italian culture, football supporters are organized, whether they are 'respectable' fans or *ultras*.[5]

Legacies of political commitment have influenced the *ultras* associations in the *curvas*. The political symbols displayed on the banners of each *curva* have lost their original reference point and assumed another meaning. There has occurred simultaneously a transposition of the firmly structured organizational dimension of some politically extremist youth associations. After the crisis of political commitment among young people in Italy during the late 1970s and early 1980s (Dal Lago and De Biasi 1994). The extreme left and right wing have created a form of association that presents itself in new contexts.

What we would emphasize is that *ultra* culture is an extreme culture towards which the expressions of the movements of the political margins are compelling. Thus, in the 1970s left-wing sentiment was manifest – to be replaced in the 1980s with those of the political right. But *ultras* do not simply mirror these marginal manifestations, they take what they want and recontextualize it into the football arena. The heterogeneous nature of today's *ultra* composition permits a variety of sub-cultural styles. The syllogism which equates the skinhead with the fascist and implicitly the manifestation of fascist sympathies has to be challenged. Political ideology is not the main issue in the *ultra* gatherings, the cognitive framework of the *curvas* is metaphorical and can assimilate young people of opposing ideologies.

Historical Changes in Organized Fandom in Italian Football

The birth of the *ultras* is linked to an historical change among spectators at football grounds. As Antonio Roversi argues, in Italy, spectator behaviour was always influenced by patriarchal and masculine values, and gave voice to feelings of local identity. This phenomenon was typical of spectators during the 1950s, from both the working class and petit bourgeoisie, and sometimes from the upper-middle class in the north of the country (Roversi 1990: 80). Football-related violence (in particular pitch invasions) was not regarded as rooted in any social problem; 'intemperance' was explained in terms of the inclinations of individuals or the 'contagions' within crowds.

During the 1960s, the greater professionalization of football and the televising of matches, watched nation-wide by broad, cross-class audiences, attenuated the relevance of local and municipal values, but damaged neither 'patriarchal' values, which still permeated society, nor the masculine mores visible in the attitudes of supporters and behaviour of players. At the same time, spectator violence moved outside football grounds, and involved police too, in common with the violent political demonstrations and riots of the time (see Roversi 1990: 91). Organized football supporters' clubs were also born, which later joined the Italian Federation of Supporters of Football Clubs (FISSC), founded in 1970. During the late 1960s, and on the fringes of these official supporters' clubs, new groups of young fans occupied the *curva* of Italian stadiums. A new era of football-related disorder began. As in the rest of Europe, and in Britain in particular, football hooliganism was now considered a social problem.

In the 1970s, the terrace supporters' associations, now named *ultras* (like the extreme political organizations of the same period), changed the atmosphere of the match event. The *curva* displayed a persistent form of collective support manifested in big banners and flags with the name and the symbol of the *ultras* group and, as on British terraces, new collective choruses and chants. The rise of this new generation of *ultras* involved various factors: autonomy from paternal tutelage (young fans went to the stadium with people of the same age); which combined with 'assimilation and imitation of the forms of the British hooligan style of support and aggression' and para-political patterns of group cohesion (Roversi 1990: 95).

Between the 1970s and 1980s press and public opinion focused upon the problem of football hooliganism as an issue of public order. Inside stadiums, the police began to segregate visiting *ultras*, allocating them the opposite end to that of the rival home supporters. In response the *ultras'* organization became more structured and hierarchical. The names adopted by some groups alluded to political extremism or terrorism and, crucially as police control increased inside the grounds, hooligans moved their confrontations outside it. Between 1983 and 1984 the frequency of violence increased, and the second generation of *ultras* arrived. Other small *ultras* groups were formed by gangs of punks and skinheads. There is now, in the 1990s, a fragmentation of *ultras* groups, and this organizational weakening makes their infiltration by extreme right-wing elements easier.

Roversi's description, summarized above, gives us some useful information about the birth and transformation of *ultras*, but his focus is mainly on the degeneration of supporter behaviour, and neglects other important aspects of the culture and form of organized supporters. We do not think that this is a mistake, but rather an issue of approach and our research, like other sociological and anthropological studies, is more focused on the *ultras'* rituals, symbols and culture (Dal Lago 1990; Bromberger 1995a). Moreover, the question of Italian *ultras'* 'assimilation and imitation of the forms of the British hooligan style of support and aggression' is misleading. British supporter culture has been influential, but it has not been a case of mere imitation. Compared with the British terrace model, the Italian *ultras* show at least two elements which are absent inside the British ends: the more sophisticated choreo-graphy of the *curva* and a strongly structured form of association among *ultras*. As Roversi (1992: 42) himself later argued, the *ultras* phenomenon represents 'an original "Italian way" of football hooliganism'.[6]

Rituals, Violence and the *Ultras*

It is appropriate to consider what actually goes on during a football match: describing these collective rituals is part of a 'frame analysis' (Goffman 1974) of the match event, within the overall *ecology* of the stadium.[7] Roversi argues that the *ultras'* rituals and expressive behaviour are part of the phenomenon of football hooliganism. By contrast, the anthropologists Dal Lago and Bromberger look at *ultras'* culture from a different perspective. According to Roversi, their chants and choruses (which he terms their 'autonomous modulation') intimate a lack of attention to the match itself: *ultras* prefer to celebrate themselves instead of the match. According to Dal Lago (1990), however, the collective rituals are linked to the match event. From this point of view, there is not necessarily a link between supporters' collective rituals and hooliganism. Since the dominant metaphor of *ultra* culture is war, Dal Lago argues that we can understand what takes place inside Italian stadiums every Sunday by introducing the political concept of 'opposition between friends and foes' (Schmidt 1927) to the realm of football. Dal Lago's approach is based on three assumptions:

1. As a *team sport (sport di squadra)* which allows identification with particular symbols (beyond specific loyalties), football splits the supporters' world into friends and foes. This split can, under some circumstances, according to predictable and ritualized forms, transform itself into physical fighting.
2. A *football match* is not only a competition between two football teams: for organized supporters it is the opportunity for ritual confrontation between friends and foes, which, under some circumstances, according to some predictable ritual forms, can transform itself into physical fighting.
3. A *stadium* is not only the physical environment for a football match: for organized supporters it is mainly the frame of the ritual celebration of the 'friends/foes' metaphor.

In this perspective the football 'war' is mainly (although not always) symbolic and theatrical.

Although Roversi states that this approach resembles the work of Marsh, Harré and Rosser (1978), Dal Lago does not seem to argue that 'ritual' and 'real' violence are mutually exclusive: his intention is to analyse the context of the behaviour of football fans in which violence is just one aspect of a wider cultural phenomenon. This point of view converges with the anthropological studies of Bromberger (1990) who states: 'There are few events which can be deemed to be "complete social phenomena", if this suggests – following Marcel Mauss rather than some of his commentators – phenomena which in some cases mobilize the totality of a society and its institutions.' Bromberger's fieldwork in Naples and Turin, focuses on the cultural dimensions of the phenomenon: symbols, rituals, rhetoric of choruses and chants, theatrical aspects of the match event and collective identification are all considered as anthropological issues. The football match is a sort of religious ritual, and 'for its symbolic plasticity, its contradictory properties and its ritual dimensions, the football match is, without doubt, one of the more enlightening viewpoints of contemporary life' (1995b: 137). In short, *ultras* can be analysed as a cultural phenomenon.

The Political Vulnerability of *Ultras*

As Roversi points out, Italian hooliganism on the terraces is increasingly vulnerable, in both a political and non-political sense. The *ultras'* organizations are undergoing a process of fragment-ation: born in the 1970s, and well established in the 1980s as highly structured organizations, they are now, in the 1990s, in a deep crisis. Symptoms of this crisis are the absence of a generational turnover of the old leadership; fragmentation into different groups; the emergence of violent 'non-official' groups that elude the control of recognized leaders; and the predominance of physical engage-ment with opponents, which is progressively less ritual and more 'acted' (De Biasi 1993). This aspect of the *ultras'* phenomenon is rising at the same time as the decline of other associative activities (like choreography, emotional involvement in the match, playful aspects of the stadium rituals, etc.). Consequently, *ultras'* organiz-ations risk becoming weaker and more changeable and, exactly for these reasons, more dangerous.

From this point of view *ultras* are without doubt a public order problem. Let us take, for example, the cost of policing football grounds: during the 1993–94 season, police reinforcements assigned to the *questure* (divisional police stations) amounted, on a national level, to over 88,000 officers (and more than 150,000 when counting *carabinieri*[8]). The total cost for one season is 70,000 million lira, at the expense of the State. In England, the price of maintaining public order is much lower and, for a large part, charged to the football clubs. In Italy, on the contrary, each day of the season costs the State 6,000 million lira (to which should be added the cost of the fuel for the means of transport and the cost of absences from work for the occasional injured policeman). Recent research on Italian police and public order (della Porta 1995; De Biasi 1995) shows that, although political tension and uncertainty are typical of the Italian situation, strictly speaking, public order problems seem to belong to another age. Especially for the *reparti mobili* (anti-riot police), the most frequent experiences of managing and violently engaging with crowds occur in football grounds, with the *ultras*. In truth, the *reparti mobili* also have to face new forms of disorder due, for instance, to the need to control large groups of *extracommunitari* immigrants in the major cities. This control function takes the place of more traditional tasks like the policing of protests; modern changes in the major cities now produce forms of disorder, the rules of which are still unknown.

Football hooliganism has also caused deaths (seven in 20 years), which no longer occur during mass political demonstrations. Football grounds provide the context in which the toughest equipment and most repressive techniques are still used by the Italian police and *carabinieri*, in a manner very similar to the policing of the political protests and riots typical of the 1970s. The opinion of interviewed police officers is that the *ultras* are the main precipitants of public disorder in the Italy of the 1990s. Nevertheless, police work has not improved qualitatively, but only quantitatively; hence, in some cases, 1,200 police officers may now be employed during a single football match. Quantity not quality seems to be their preferred method, combined with a degree of non-intervention. Surrounding the *curva* they permit the fans in it to behave in a way as if the *curva* were a zone of liminality. Such discretion points to a discrepancy between legal requisites and tolerated behaviour which is not manifested by the police in Britain.

The Absence of Nationalism

Although football hooliganism seems to be the main public order problem for Italian police (as reflected in workload and cost), the same phenomenon does not occur when Italian *ultras* travel abroad. There are no *ultras* following the national team – *ultras* travel abroad only when their favourite club is playing and not for the national team – and in such cases there has not been disorder or hooliganism. This is one of the main differences in comparison with the English situation. In Italy, nationalism, at least among football fans, became *ultra* in a municipal culture manifested in opposition to the national side. During Italia '90, the 'national team fever' coexisted with a critical detachment among ordinary spectators and with the competing loyalties of *ultras*, who often identified with foreign teams for which players of their favourite club were playing.[9] Hence, the match between Germany and Holland, played in Milan, became a sort of derby between Internazionale and AC Milan.[10] The semi-final between Italy and Argentina, played in Naples, split Neapolitan football fans, undecided between their national side and their city's favourite adopted son, Maradona. If the national team prefers to play in central or southern Italy, and finds hostility in northern cities like Turin, Milan or Florence, it is because supporters of these clubs (and *ultras* in particular) identify only with players who play for their club side. They often show contempt toward Italian players of rival clubs and oppose, with booing and chanting, the national team during the match. Moreover, if we take into account the fact that northern club sides are over-represented within *Serie A* (the Italian first division), the demand for international football at a high level is stronger in central and southern Italy, where spectators are more amenable to supporting the *azzurri*. Nevertheless, even when the national team plays in southern Italy, it is possible to observe giant banners with the symbol and the colours of the *ultras'* local team (and not the national one) adorning the stadium ends (De Biasi 1993). If we consider the separatist feelings which have recently found a *symbolic* space within the northern football fan sub-cultures (and in the South too: for instance, Naples *ultras* used to fly the old American confederate flag), it is easier to understand how nationalist feelings amongst football spectators, are now on the wane in the 1990s, and are not, for instance, comparable to the nationalism of English supporters.[11]

Playing Deep While Being Different

Football is a 'complete social phenomenon' which allows foreign observers to understand the 'otherness' of Italian culture. Football, to the whole country, is a form of 'deep play' as in the Balinese cockfight described by Geertz (1973). From this perspective (see Armstrong 1994) the behaviour which may seem useless or irrational to the unconverted owing to their lack of appreciation of the symbolic extent of the prize at stake, can be understood as a performance of a ritually dramatized self-portrait. Football fanaticism in Italy is not only about consumption. The actual relationship between football and economics or politics is not uni-directional: politics and economics do not invade the playful sphere of football any more than football culture floods into the domains of politics or the economy.

Notes

1. As noted by Caselli (1990: 32), 'It is hard, in Italy, to make a deep analysis of the economic structure of the industry of football because of the lack of official data about sport.' Marzola (1990) is the only monograph about the football industry.
2. See Ferrarotti and Beha (1983). This definition alludes to the first article of the Italian Constitution: 'Italy is a Republic based on work'.
3. These journals are *Gazzetta dello Sport*, *Tuttosport* and *Corriere dello Sport-Stadio*. Although they are general sports newspapers, 80 per cent of their coverage is on football.
4. The Hungarian born star of porn films known as Cicciolina successfully stood for political office in 1987. Elected on behalf of the Reform Party the actress never missed an opportunity to disrobe publicly to embarrass interviewers and political colleagues.
5. The distinction attempts to distinguish the *ultras* as the younger, boisterous, fanatical element drawn from a variety of class backgrounds, from the 'respectable' fan whose support is more sedate, who belongs to officially recognized supporters' clubs and tends to have middle-class, white-collar status. The basic characteristic of the official supporters' clubs is their formal recognition by the favoured football club. Usually, all the supporters' clubs linked to the same team are related to a 'Co-ordinating Centre', which is a member of the Italian Federation of Supporters of Football Clubs (FISSC). In the case of top clubs, the supporters' clubs can be situated in towns far from the location of the favoured team. In such cases, another federation co-ordinates the supporters' clubs: for instance, the Italian Association of Supporters' Clubs, founded in 1967, comprises 1,340 clubs, eleven of which are located abroad.
6. Moreover for Roversi (1992: 11), *ultras* groups 'are usually formed by youths who share common and unifying cultural

models instead of a common and disadvantaged material condition'.

7. According to Goffman (1961: 20), social situations 'place a "frame" around a space of immediate events, determining the type of "sense" that will be accorded everything within the frame'. According to Bateson (1972: 180), within the playful 'frame' messages assume the following tacit and paradoxical form: 'These actions in which we now engage do not denote what those actions for which they stand would denote.'

8. Small villages normally have only *Carabinieri*, while the *Polizia di Stato* (State Police) are present in larger towns or cities. For an analysis of the historical duality of the Italian police forces see Collin (1985).

9. I am not referring to the TV audience of the national team, but to organized supporters, both from official supporters' clubs and *ultras*. I do not intend to argue that the national team cannot involve other ordinary supporters, but the average spectator in the stadium prefers the football club's side to the national team.

10. The German team contained three players from Internazionale of Milan, and the Dutch had three players from their city rivals, AC Milan. The rival clubs' *ultras* were also in the habit of dressing in the colours of the German or Dutch national sides.

11. The national team represents a source of identification for television audiences, or for Italian immigrants living abroad, who are an important source of support at away matches. Italian immigrants in the USA were considered an important audience for the 1994 World Cup, in a country where football was still unknown to the native people.

Chapter 5

The Political Role of Football for Palestinians in Jordan

Dag Tuastad[1]

> *'One day when we had no voice, al-Wihdat was our voice'*
>
> (Yasser Arafat)

Introduction

Sobhi Ibrahim is the vice-director of the *al-Wihdat* football club at the *Wihdat* Palestinian refugee camp in Jordan. He remembers how once he was pelted with eggs and tomatoes outside the clubhouse in the camp after *Wihdat* had lost a match. He recalls that he received a phone call from an old woman:

> She was crying on the telephone. I told her – it was only a game. She said: 'Never play if you are going to lose. We have lost so many times, in 1948, 1967, 1970 and 1982. When you lose, you remind us of our losses.' I told her: 'to feel the happiness of winning, we have to lose sometimes.' 'No,' she replied, 'tell your boys – never lose!'

In 1970 Palestinians and Transjordanians (ethnic Jordanians) in Jordan fought a civil war. Today, when *Wihdat* is playing, it is as if the civil war is being fought again.

This chapter is about the political role football has come to play for Palestinian refugees living in Jordan. Ever since the PLO (Palestine Liberation Organization) left Jordan following the defeat in the civil war of 1970 to 1971, Palestinian national identity has been suppressed by the Jordanian authorities. However, football has remained an arena where Palestinian national identity is actively exposed. Football may be a way to restore or maintain honour (Hognestad 1995: 18) and the *Wihdat* club, in restoring

Palestinian honour, can, on the one hand, be seen as having become a symbol of Palestinian nationalism. The club may even be viewed as not only expressing Palestinian nationalism, but also as having an active political role – by way of representing Palestinians.

Wihdat v *Faisali*, Amman 1986

The Amman Stadium is packed as the match between the Palestinian *Wihdat* club and the Transjordanian *Faisali* team is to be played. *Wihdat* supporters are singing old songs from the time of the civil war. The stadium, however, is also packed with policemen. The supporters therefore only sing the first lines of their songs, not sharing with the police the rest of their chants – '*Wihdat* only the best for you' – they now sing. During the civil war in 1970, while Palestinians were under siege in their refugee camps, the song read: '*Wihdat* only the best for you in the battle of wars.' In 1986 they sing – 'The whole world applauds when *Wihdat* scores' – not continuing the rest of the old slogan – 'The whole world applauds when the commandos carry out an operation.' The *Faisali* supporters answer them, singing – 'all the people of *Wihdat* sell tomatoes' – hinting at Jordan's biggest vegetable market inside *Wihdat*, indirectly ridiculing camp residents for their poverty and thus insulting their honour. 'We are all Palestinians,' *Wihdat* supporters start singing, omitting what they had sung in the presence of considerably fewer police during their last match in Irbid – 'We are all *fedayiin* (guerilla soldiers).'

Fifteen minutes into the first half, *Faisali* have scored twice. *Wihdat* are in *Faisali*'s penalty area when one of the *Wihdat* attackers is brought down, but no penalty is given. *Wihdat* supporters scream, crazy with anger, at the referee. As their chanting gets higher and higher, armed policemen approach their corner.

'*Al hakam maniak, al hakam maniak* (the referee is an ass)', the chant goes. *Al hakam* (the referee) is an ambiguous term in Arabic. The roots of the words, *h k m*, have to do with the verb 'to rule' – *hakim* is a ruler, a king. The chant could thus be understood as referring as much to the Jordanian king as to the referee. As the *Wihdat* supporters chant, several supporters get involved in fights. Suddenly gunshots are heard, and teargas shells are shot into the *Wihdat* crowd. In the chaos that erupts, both *Wihdat* and *Faisali* supporters panic. The struggle round the arena continues with policemen entering the stands amidst fighting and chaos. By the end of the day, several supporters are arrested and injured. One *Faisali* supporter is dead.

It could be argued that football as an arena for the expression of political 'subversive' identities, might not contradict the interests of power holders. It may be counter-productive to suppress strong political identities. If the opportunities to extinguish ethnic or national identities are minimal, such suppression may lead to fierce reactions, as happened during the *intifada* (Palestinian uprising) which erupted in 1987 in the Occupied Territories. To avoid political uprisings like the *intifada,* the Jordanian regime can be considered to be using football as an arena where political aggression is externalized under controlled circumstances by the security apparatus of the State, permissable as a kind of cathartic ritual. These two perspectives on the political role of football will be illuminated throughout this chapter. To understand the various political roles that the football club *Wihdat* has come to play, it is necessary to know more about the situation of Palestinians in Jordan.

Palestinians in Jordan

The final results of Jordan's 1994 census, revealed on January 27 1996, show that the Jordanian population has increased sevenfold to nearly 4.2 million since 1952. The questionnaire asked for detailed information on Jordanians' places of birth, including former Palestinian refugees who have, since 1952, held Jordanian citizenship. These questions on place of birth aroused suspicion that the head-count had political motives. Was the Jordanian regime interested in finding out the percentage of former Palestinian refugees in order to be able to seek compensation in the current Middle East peace talks? However, no official numbers on the ratio of Palestinians to ethnic Transjordanians were published. 'The state decided that the classification of this data (displaced persons and refugees) is against the public interest and will not settle the issue. To the contrary, the classification will only create confusion.' Abdul-Hadi Alaween, head of Jordan's Department of Statistics, announced at a news conference: 'The street has its interpretations of that (who is a Palestinian and who is a Jordanian) and so does the political street. Therefore, the decision was not to process and finalise this data, now or later' (Mansaf 1996).[2]

The fragile political situation of two nations – ethnic Transjordanians and Palestinians – constituting the Jordanian nation-state, originates from the partition of Palestine in 1948. The population of Jordan was estimated at 340,000 prior to the 1948 war (Brand 1988: 150). King Abdallah succeeded in annexing the West Bank after the war, enlarging the kingdom with 900,000 new subjects, of which half were refugees (ibid.). Many of the Palestinian refugees, scattered around in tents and degraded as a people, obtained Jordanian citizenship as a result of the Jordanian annexation of the West Bank. They thus found it easier to identify themselves as Jordanians than Palestinians. The policy of the Hashemite Kingdom was to erase all references to Palestine, by force if necessary. But the 1967 war which resulted in Israel's occupation of the West Bank and Gaza, left the Palestinians trusting no one but themselves to fight their struggle. As a result of the Israeli occupation of the West Bank, Jordan lost territory, skilled labour, 45 per cent of her GNP, and Jerusalem – the kingdom's main source of tourism revenue. The complement of the loss was an additional 250,000 to 300,000 Palestinians taking refuge in the East Bank, requiring emergency outlets for food and shelter (Brand 1988: 157). While the war threw the Jordanian Army and the State into disarray, the decline in the power of the State following the war enabled Palestinian institutions to develop and expand in Jordan. As the PLO's power structure inside Jordan became more and more threatening for the Jordanian kingdom, the Jordanian Army was mobilized in September 1970 against the Palestinian guerillas. Estimates on the casualties of the ten-month-long civil war that followed vary from 700 to 20,000 killed (Shimoni 1987: 260; Tiltnes 1994: 65). After the war all Palestinian institutions were either closed or destroyed. Resistance fighters were gaoled or fled the country. Those who remained had either to abandon political activity or go underground (Brand 1988: 171).

'The Republic' of the Refugee Camp *Wihdat*

The Palestinian refugee camp *Wihdat* is located in what is now downtown Amman. Originally, the camp accommodated 5,000 refugees who lived in 1,400 shelters constructed by UNRWA

(United Nations Relief and Works Agency for Palestinian Refugees in the Near East). Over the years the camp has grown into an urban-like quarter and is surrounded by areas with a high population density. In 1995 there were 2,660 shelters accommodating the 38,000 persons registered by UNRWA as living in the camp (see map of UNRWA's area of operation 30 June 1994), and 32,000 Palestinians not registered by UNRWA (see UNRWA – Jordan Field Office, January 1994). The pressure on the infrastructure of the camp generated by a more than tenfold increase of the population living inside the camp since 1950, without any concomitant increase in the size of the camp, means that the capacity of the sewage, garbage and water systems, constructed for the original number of shelter-units, are overwhelmed and close to breaking down. *Wihdat* has a huge and busy market, including the well-known vegetable market.

The biggest factions in the PLO, Fatah with their leader Yasser Arafat, and PFLP (Popular Front for the Liberation of Palestine) with their leader, George Habash, had their headquarters in *Wihdat* prior to, and during, the civil war. During the civil war *Wihdat* was shelled by tanks. No camp in Jordan suffered more injuries, deaths and destruction (Brand 1988: 183). Before the civil war, Palestinians in Jordan used to refer to the *Wihdat* camp only as *al jumhuriyya* – the republic – implying that the authority of the king was not valid inside the borders of the camp. The political and military significance of the camp, and the suffering of camp residents during the civil war, have made *Wihdat* a symbol of Palestinian resistance and defiance of the Jordanian regime.

The Political History of the *Wihdat* Football Club

As part of its services in the realm of social affairs, UNRWA has established youth and activity centres in the refugee camps. The only condition for admission in the centres has been that people are Palestinian refugees. The centres are most often located inside schools built by UNRWA where, among other activities such as vocational training and sewing courses, the centres run sports leagues, using the space of the schoolyards as playing fields. The camps have leagues, with teams competing in organized annual championship tournaments in football, basketball, volleyball and boxing.

In 1975 *Wihdat* Football Club qualified for the national league in Jordan. As *Wihdat* climbed in the league tables, their games became very popular amongst the camp population. Wherever *Wihdat* played, Palestinian refugees rushed to see the match. While the supporters of some teams in the Jordanian league could be counted in hundreds, the matches of *Wihdat* at Amman Stadium rarely attracted less than 20,000 supporters. In 1980 *Wihdat* played against *Ramthla*, a Jordanian team. The match was disrupted by fighting between the supporters of the two teams. *Wihdat* won that match and eventually, the Jordanian league. The victory of *Wihdat* sparked off huge celebrations among Palestinians in Jordan. Even West Bank Palestinians living under Israeli occupation began to follow the fortunes of *Wihdat* with great enthusiasm. In the East Bank, insignia of *Wihdat* became more and more visible in the streets. At a time when Palestinian national symbols were being suppressed, supporters started wearing the green, red, black and white strip of *Wihdat*, which are, through no coincidence, the colours of the Palestinian flag. A special horn-honk from cars also came to be associated with support for *Wihdat*. As supporting *Wihdat* grew to be a statement of one's Palestinianness, so identity became commonly expressed along communal lines through football teams. Violence became commonplace at games involving *Wihdat* and Transjordanian teams (*Wihdat* supporters were arrested at nearly every game, following disturbances). As fights and brawls inevitably accompanied the matches, it was as if the civil war was being fought all over again when *Wihdat* played against Transjordanian teams (Brand 1988: 183).

From *Wihdat* to *al-Difftayn*, the Two Banks

Following the bloody disturbances at the Amman Stadium in 1986 during the game between *Faisali* and *Wihdat* referred to above, the Jordanian authorities decided to crack down on *Wihdat*. After the match UNRWA was asked to surrender its responsibility for the youth centres in Jordan. The leaderships of the clubs were then dissolved and new councils were formed. *Wihdat* was now to be called *Nadi al-Difftayn* (The Club of the Two Banks). The new club was to include both Palestinian and Transjordanian youth, and the new board of the club included highly ranked government officials. *Wihdat* was to be punished further by downgrading the team to the third division, and four players were to be banned from playing, accused of having encouraged supporters to get involved in the fighting at the stadium. The *Wihdat* leadership complained about the punishments to the Jordanian Prime Minister who reconsidered some of the suggested measures. The result was that no player was to be banned from playing, and the club was allowed to stay in the first division. Still, the new name, *al-Difftayn*, had to be kept. Voices from within *Wihdat* opposed changing the name of the club. It was after all a suggestion which did not come from inside the camp, and the change was commonly understood as an attempt to cut off relationships between the camp and the football club. Others reacted to the suggested name-change by ridiculing the Jordanian authorities. This ridicule is related to the fact that *al-Difftayn* is linguistically a much more pregnant name – it symbolizes Palestinian nationalism – whereas *Wihdat* means 'units', and refers simply to the shelters which formed the housing-units when the refugee camp was erected. For the refugees in *Wihdat*, the name *al-Difftayn* would have far more nationalistic connotations. The intended meaning of the name *al-Difftayn* (the two banks) was to symbolize a union between the Palestinians of the West Bank and the Transjordanians of the East Bank. But it could easily be interpreted as denoting a union between the Palestinians on the two banks. *Wihdat* supporters used to sing – '*shalit, shalit shalit – shilet, wihdati min stad Amman lil-daffa al gharbiye* (Take off! – move! – all the people will move with *Wihdat* from Amman Stadium to the West Bank)' implying a return to a Palestinian unity or a return to war, led by *Wihdat* fighters.

The new and 'imposed' administration at the club, *al-Difftayn*, did not enjoy much popularity in the *Wihdat* camp. The relationships between players, coaches and structures around the team, and the administration remained tense. The players and the supporters of *al-Difftayn* were still all Palestinians. However, *al-Difftayn* had great success in the sports arena. For the first time in the history of Jordanian football, a Jordanian team, *al-Difftayn*, qualified for the final round in the Asian Cup. During the 1988–89 season the club won its qualifying group, beating teams from Iraq, Lebanon and Qatar. The Asian Cup was to be completed with a tournament in Malaysia, consisting of the respective national champions. Although the qualification was the biggest achievement ever in the football history of Jordan, the new, imposed, club administration decided not to send the club to Malaysia, using the poor economic situation of the club as an excuse. In *Wihdat* this decision was understood as a political decision, as a token of suppression of Palestinians. This increased the tensions inside the club further. The antagonism eventually ceased when the Jordanian regime introduced democratic political measures and opened for elections in November 1989. The Jordanian Parliament had hardly gathered before it addressed the question of *Wihdat*. The new parliament, of which the Muslim Brotherhood constituted the largest block, promptly decided to let the refugees of *Wihdat* regain control over their football club, its board and its name.

Wihdat in the Era of Democracy and the Peace Process

The Oslo agreement, concluded in September 1993 between the PLO and Israel, paved the way for a peace treaty between Jordan and Israel. In the new political situation of the 1990s, the democratization process continues in Jordan, and is 'irreversible' according to King Hussein of Jordan (Tiltnes 1994: 110). Political parties are now being made legal, and the Middle East peace process is running on track.[3] One might ask if the opening of these political channels have lessened the political role of football. My impression from visiting a match at the Amman Stadium in the autumn of 1995 is that football in Jordan remains highly politicized.

29 September 1995, Jordan v Iraq

On September 29 1995, at Amman Stadium, Iraq is playing against Jordan whose team was recently ranked number 142 on FIFAs ranking. The game is a qualifying game for the 1996 Olympic Games in the USA. The sunny side of the stadium is filled with Iraqi supporters (Iraqi workers and long-term 'tourists' after the Gulf war), visible in their long white clothing (*jallabias*). In the shade on the other side of the stadium the corners are packed, while the centre is almost empty. '*Wihdat, yallah ya wihdat* (go, *Wihdat*, go)', *Faisali* supporters chant, fully aware that the match is between the Jordanian and Iraqi national teams. The *Faisali* supporters hence communicate, for reasons that shall be elaborated upon below, that they suspect *Wihdat* to represent Jordan, the *Faisali* supporters thus support Iraq. The supporters in the north corner, Palestinian refugees predominantly from the *Wihdat* refugee camp, enthusiastically clap their hands as Jordan attacks. Then Iraq breaks, attacks, and scores. The *Wihdat* corner quietens, while the *Faisali*, Transjordanian supporters in the south corner and the Iraqis on the sunny side, cheer. When Iraq increases its lead to 4–0, the *Faisali*, Transjordanian supporters are ecstatic, screaming: '*bir-roh, bid-damm, nafdika ya saddam* (with our soul and blood we sacrifice ourselves for you, Saddam)', alternated by '*yallah ya wihdat* (go *Wihdat*, go)'; and addressing the coach of the Jordanian team: 'Izat, where are your people?'. As the game ends the Iraqi supporters are celebrating on the sunny side of the stadium, accompanied by the *Faisali* supporters in the southern corner. While the winners leave the stadium, *Wihdat* supporters remain in the stand. When they leave, they gather outside the dressing-room. As the coach of the Jordanian team comes out, they start to sing: '*al raba'i, al raba'i, al shabab wihdat, koll fedayyi* (oh commander, oh commander, all the young in *Wihdat* are guerilla soldiers)'.

The role of the Jordanian coach as a known Palestinian activist in the *Wihdat* refugee camp, helps to explain the ostensibly contradictory chants at the match. The coach of the Olympic team of Jordan, Izat Hamza, has grown up with, played for, and coached *Wihdat*. In the camp he is a hero. In 1992, in the middle of the season, he suddenly quit his job as a coach for the Jordanian national team – 'to rescue *Wihdat*' – he told the author of this chapter, as *Wihdat* was positioned close to the bottom of the table. Hamza refused to meet the Jordanian Football Association to discuss the matter. The incident led the Ministry of Youth and Sport to intervene and request Hamza to continue as national coach, but he still refused. Hamza then took *Wihdat* to second place in the league that year. Despite being a known Palestinian political activist, in Jordan Hamza faces no competition in the acquisition of sporting merits. In 1994 he was again appointed coach for the Jordanian national team (the Olympic team). Among the first eleven of the Jordanian Olympic team, six are from *Wihdat*, not one is from *Faisali*. This explains the peculiar chants of *Faisali* and *Wihdat* supporters during the Olympic team match. For them, it is not an international match, it is a continuation of the struggle between the two teams – and nations – the Palestinian and Transjordanian. The Transjordanians do not accept that *Wihdat*, in the form of six players and their former Palestinian coach, represents them. The *'go Wihdat go'* chant of the *Faisali* supporters during the game against the Iraqis is ironic, and would not have been chanted if they were not sure Iraq would win the match. The *Faisali* supporters thus manage to humiliate the Palestinian side at the same time as they disassociate themselves from the Jordanian team which is playing. In their view it is not a Jordanian national team because there are no *Faisali* players in the team. *Faisali* supporters also repeat the slogans chanted in Palestinian refugee camps while they were surrounded by Jordanian army tanks in the beginning of the Gulf war: *'bir-roh bid-damm, nafdika ya saddam* (with our soul and blood we sacrifice ourselves for you, Saddam)'. *Faisali* supporters would rather sacrifice themselves for Saddam than for the Palestinians playing on the pitch. As *Faisali* supporters chant – 'Izat, where are your people?' – *Wihdat* supporters wait until the end of the match with their reply. Despite their defeat, they cheer their 'commander' as a hero when he appears. He is commander of their struggle for which they will sacrifice themselves, as they sing: *'al raba'i, al raba'i, shabab wihdat, kolluhum fedayyi* (oh commander, oh commander, all the young in *Wihdat* are guerilla soldiers)'. The match at the Amman stadium was not between Iraq and Jordan, but between the two nations constituting the Jordanian nation-state: *Wihdat* representing the Palestinians, versus *Faisali* representing the Transjordanians. Within the football ground, the civil war between these nations is still being re-created.

Protesting Over the Peace Process

The peace process paved the way for *Wihdat* to visit and play against teams from the West Bank and Gaza. Sobhi Ibrahim, vice-director of *Wihdat* recalls:

> When we arrived to play in Hebron, it was a magic moment. There were people everywhere; 40,000 must have been around, ten times the capacity of the ground. When our players entered the pitch, they gathered around the central circle. Then they kneeled. As they kissed the earth, people cried.

The experiences from the tour strengthened, rather than moderated, the fighting spirit of the club members and leaders. The peace process created a crisis for the Palestinian diaspora. Although political parties are now allowed in Jordan, they have to be Jordanian parties. Palestinian parties and organizations are still banned. As the PLO has returned to the autonomous areas, and Palestinian organizations in Jordan are prohibited – no one is representing the interests of the refugees in the Jordanian refugee camps.

The following article appeared in *The Star*, a Jordanian weekly, on 25 January 1996:

al-Wihdat soccer team won't play in Israel

For apparently political reasons, the Jordanian *al-Wihdat* football team refused to play against any Israeli-Arab team either in Israel or in Jordan. According to the Jerusalem Post, *al-Wihdat* declined to play against Hapoel or Maccabi teams from Kfar Kanna, near Nazareth, or against a combined squad from the village. They pointed out that these teams might include Jewish players. Mr Yousif Ali Taha, president of Hapoel Sports Club in Kfar Kanna, said that they have received information that *al-Wihdat* refused to play against the Israeli Arab Maccabi team – which is currently in Jordan – for the same reason. He added that if it is proven correct, it is strange and confusing as there should be no connection between politics and sports, especially in a time of peace. These words were also echoed by the Kfar Kanna Council's Chairman Wasil Taha, who hosted the Jordanian team last year, when he said that though *al-Wihdat* is mainly composed of Palestinian players, it refused to play against either of their teams during the stay.

(The Star)[4]

The *Wihdat* football club has thus come to represent Palestinian refugees in Jordan, not only to symbolize Palestinian national struggle. In May 1995 when the club toured the West Bank and Gaza, they were invited to meet the chairman of PLO, Yasser Arafat. Sobhi Ibrahim recalls: 'When Arafat received us, he said: "One day when we had no voice, *Wihdat* was our voice."' This statement was repeated to me several times, as I visited the *Wihdat* refugee camp in September 1995. In the camp, Arafat's statement is interpreted as a recognition by their leader, not only of the football club's historical political role, but of its current political role as a representative of Palestinian refugees in Jordan.

The Political Role of *Wihdat*

The football club *Wihdat* became the symbol of Palestinian national struggle in Jordan. As its symbolic value increased, the football club came to *represent* the refugees. The football club further enabled the possible reconstruction of the *Wihdat* refugee camp as a political centre for Palestinian national struggle. I believe the distinct political role that the club developed is founded on how it accumulated honour and thus provided camp refugees with pride.

The Arab code of honour is related to the collective responsibility of family members to protect the virginity of unmarried female members of their patrilineal descent groups (see Dodd 1973). Palestinian refugees are quoted as having said: *'shirridna bi-irdna* (we escaped with our honour, after being exiled)' (ibid.: 43). The Arab words for honour and land are quite similar in their pronunciation: *'ird* (honour) and *'ard* (land). As Palestinians fled to neighbouring countries of the new Jewish state, they were met with contempt by their Arab compatriots because they had lost their land, implying that they had simultaneously lost their honour. Sayigh describes how refugees in Lebanon were 'put in a category . . . of no respect, the lowest level of human beings' (1979: 126). He also describes the mockery endured by the refugees: 'When we left the camp they used to follow us pointing and laughing. Often we would return weeping. An early form of mockery, often shouted out, was "Where are your tails?" Lebanese children are reported to have asked their parents to buy them a Palestinian to play with' (ibid.: 125).

In the same way as in Lebanon, the Palestinian camp-refugees in Jordan were stigmatized. The political role of the *Wihdat* football club could be related to the club overcoming this stigma. When *Wihdat* played, their supporters sang: *'ma biddna thiin wa la sardin, bidna 'anabil* (we do not need wheat, or sardines, we need bombs)'.

The refugees in the camps have been provided with food rations from UNRWA, wheat and sardines, and this role as recipient has commonly been regarded as shameful for the refugees. At the *Wihdat* matches, as during the struggle of the Palestinian resistance movement, the supporters can communicate that material goods do not matter – they are willing to suffer economic vicissitudes to regain their land. Hence, the *Wihdat* football club creates honour at their games, and the supporters cheer and communicate what they are experiencing as they sing: *'suffu al karasi, suffu al karasi, al wihdat al akhdar, biyirfa al raasi* (arrange the chairs, arrange the chairs, the green *Wihdat* raise our heads)'.

When *Wihdat* players lift their heads, they lift the heads of the suffering refugee population. When *Wihdat* – their fighters – win, these victories are experienced as national and political victories, giving pride to the Palestinian nation. '*Wihdat*,' I was told in the camp, 'is something holy, something . . . high, it is Palestine. When *Wihdat* loses, Palestine loses.'

Football as Resistance

The repressive measures taken against the Palestinian opposition following the civil war in Jordan simply left no other arenas – but the football arena – open for the refugees to express themselves. In the football arena the militarism of the refugees can be expressed. Thus, football may be seen as a form of what Scott labels as ideological resistance (Scott 1990). At the football stadium the ideological resistance could be hidden, and at the same time expressed openly, albeit in a disguised form. The rumours, gossip, folktales, songs, gestures, jokes and theatre of the powerless are described by Scott as vehicles by which a critique of power is insinuated while the powerless are 'hiding behind anonymity or behind innocuous understandings of their conduct' (ibid.: xiii). Scott quotes George Orwell's observation of how the Burmese, colonized by the British, managed to insinuate contempt for the colonialists 'while being careful never to venture a more dangerous open defiance'. He writes:

> Anti European feeling was very bitter. No one had the guts to raise a riot but if a European woman went through the bazaars alone somebody would probably spit betel juice over her dress . . . When a nimble Burman tripped me up on the football field and the referee (another Burman) looked the other way, the crowd yelled with hideous laughter . . . In the end the sneering yellow faces of the young men that met me everywhere, the insults hooted after me when I was at a safe distance, got badly at my nerves. The young Buddhist priests were the worst of all.

> (from George Orwell *Inside the Whale*: 91, in Scott 1990)

The case in hand, Palestinians in Jordan, subordinated within the Jordanian nation-state since their loss following the civil war of 1970 to 1971, could be seen as having had the football arena as a vehicle of ideological resistance. Not only could patterns of disguised ideological insubordination be seen displayed on the football pitch. While the football arenas are packed with this form of ideological resistance, the arena can also become the location of 'those rare moments of political electricity when, often for the first time in memory, the hidden transcript is spoken directly and publicly in the teeth of power'. In the Palestinian instance football has provided an arena for ideological resistance – an opportunity for the subordinated Palestinian refugees to express forbidden attitudes in public, without being persecuted. What makes the football stadium suitable for ideological resistance is 'the "safe distance" that makes the insulter anonymous: the message is public but the messenger is hidden' (Scott 1990: 14–15). As the audience sings they do not simply express slogans, they also create collective experiences of national sentiments and emotions that contribute to the reproduction of their political identities. *Wihdat* is eventually transformed from a symbolic representation of the Palestinian refugees' national struggle, to an actual political representation of them.

I believe that if we are to analyse Palestinian nationalism in Jordan, the *Wihdat* football club may be seen as both expressive and instrumental in the reproduction of this nationalism. However, the role football has played for the Palestinians represents something different from what football represents for the Jordanian authorities. While football games serve as vehicles of ideological resistance for Palestinians, football matches represent to the authorities vehicles for political control which are at their disposal.

Football as Catharsis

Why did the Jordanian regime not exclude and forbid the football club *Wihdat* when they banned other expressions of Palestinian nationalism following the Civil War of 1970 to 1971? Since the late 1970s when *Wihdat* became the symbol of Palestinian nationalism, hardly a match finished without disorder, and between ten and fifteen *Wihdat* supporters getting arrested. Why did the regime not interfere with *Wihdat*, the symbol of Palestinian struggles during the civil war, until the death of the *Faisali* supporter in 1986? And if the Ministry of Youth and Sports were to repress and punish Palestinians expressing nationalism in the football arena, why did they provide Izat Hamza with the job as a coach for the Jordanian national team two years after he quit his job 'to save *Wihdat*'?

In his discussion of the political use of ritual, Kertzer regards football as an example of how rituals act to channel political tensions in relatively harmless directions. According to him, international football contests can be understood by supporters as battles between themselves and other nations, where supporters are able to vent their national chauvinism and their hostilities toward other nations (Kertzer 1988: 129). Within the football arena, the sentiments and emotions of supporters are externalized and communicated. The regular externalization of the energy of the supporters could be seen as *catharsis*. Catharsis means that aggression is ritualized and controlled. Cathartic rituals thus have the political function of substituting tensions engendered by conflicts inherent in the social order. Football matches can in this sense be viewed as cathartic rituals, where 'repressed emotions are evoked and then purified' (ibid.: 57). A political implication of the cathartic effect of football is that football can be used to control political turbulence, as the political energy, if any, of young men reaches its climax during the matches, under controlled circumstances and limited in time and space.

As we have seen, it is hardly the case that football in Jordan is allowed to divert young men's energies from politics. The Jordanian authorities are fully aware of the impossibility of denying the existence of Palestinian national identity. Nevertheless, the rulers of the Jordanian nation-state have national security interests at heart in controlling how Palestinian national identity is expressed. Brand (1988) puts forward the idea that it has been in Jordan's interests to maintain a medium level of tension between Palestinians and Transjordanians. If it is in the interest of the regime to have a tacit policy of preferential treatment towards the loyal Transjordanians, in the army and in government departments, the idea of the impossibility of complete co-operation and unity should be reinforced. As communal tension is maintained, intercommunal organization based on class, does not materialize. The football matches of *Wihdat* give the Jordanian authorities an arena in which Palestinian refugees are able to let off political emotions and attitudes, while they are under the control of the state's security apparatus. At the football stadium, a dynamic relationship involving a negotiation between Palestinian nationalists and the regime develops. The presence of the regime in the form of the police forces, tolerating exposure to criticism which is not tolerable elsewhere, implies the development of a mutual understanding regarding the limits of the rhetoric of Palestinian nationalism. At the same time, the regime can use as an excuse the militant display of Palestinian national rhetoric, to legitimize a discriminatory policy against Palestinians, or imposed limitations on democratic rule. The performance of the weekly ritual of the civil war at the stadiums always carries the risk that Palestinians exceed the limits of their tacit understanding with the Jordanian regime, as witnessed in 1986 at Amman Stadium when the King became the target of the chants of the *Wihdat* supporters. On the other hand, that occasion served as a way the regime could demonstrate the limits of Palestinian nationalism, and thus reinforce those limits. Demonstrations on the streets or inside the camps are more dangerous for the regime, as was the case during the beginning of the Gulf war in 1991 when tanks surrounded the refugee camps, than the controlled externalization of aggression at the football stadium. According to Brand, 'communal tensions and the ability to manipulate them constitute one of Hussein's greatest strengths' (Brand 1988: 185). Football is also a beautifully constructed ritual for such a policy.

Postscript

4 May 1996: Palestinian and Israeli negotiators met in Taba for the opening session of final status negotiations on the most intractable issues of the Israeli–Palestinian conflict: refugees, Jerusalem, Israeli settlements, borders, and water resources (deferred from the interim talks). The meeting was largely symbolic, being held to show that the peace process was on track with what was agreed upon at the Oslo accord. Serious negotiations were to begin after the Israeli elections on 29 May 1996. The victory of the Israeli right-wing party Likud, and the election of Benjamin Netanyahu as prime minister, had led to a crisis in the peace process. The new Israeli Prime Minister stated that Israel wanted to renegotiate parts of the previous agreement. This hardline position, taken before the parties had started substantial negotiations, leaves little hope

for the refugees that Netanyahu will grant an end to their forced exile. As the prospects for a political solution on the refugee issue diminish, Palestinian refugees continue their struggle. Hence the football arena in Jordan remains an area of political expression and resistance.

Notes

1. The author wishes to thank Rania Maktabi, Hans Hognestad, Aage Tiltnes, Kjetil Tronvoll and Are Hovdenak for useful comments.
2. Ref: firasiii–netcom.com (27 January).
3. Editors' note: this text was written prior to the Hamas suicide bombings in Israel in late 1995 and early 1996, and the Easter bombing of Lebanon by Israel.
4. Palestinians number 800,000 consisting mainly of the Palestinian population that did not escape during the uprooting following the war between Israel and her neighbour states in 1948. It is these Israeli Palestinians that might play in 'mixed teams'.

Chapter 6

Football: Politics and Power in Cameroon

Paul Nchoji Nkwi and *Bea Vidacs*[1]

Introduction

In 1990, the Indomitable Lions, the national football team of Cameroon changed sporting history by reaching the quarter-finals of the World Cup, football's most important international event. This was the first time that an African team had reached this far in the competition, and many spectators felt that the appearance of the Cameroonian national team was the most remarkable event of that year's competition. Thus, their early elimination from the 1994 World Cup in the United States was a shock not only to Cameroonians but to their many fans all over the world.

This chapter examines the interplay of ethnicity and nationalism in Cameroonian football. After a brief overview of the development of the sport in Cameroon, we outline the roles ethnicity and nationalism play in the general workings of football in Cameroon, finally, focusing in on *Bonjour l'Amérique*, the radio programme which covered the 1994 World Cup, and from which people grappled with Cameroon's elimination from the competition. We will call attention to some of the main questions they were dealing with. In analysing the way the programme changed over the course of the World Cup we intend to show how sport is used both as an instrument of control by the government and as a means for the expression of popular disaffection.

The Development of Football in Cameroon

Cameroon was first colonized in 1884 by Germany. After the expulsion of the Germans in 1916, the territory was shared by Britain and France who administered their respective portions under the League of Nations aegis and later as United Nations mandates. Consequently, football developed according to very different patterns in the two areas, and to this day it continues to express the collective identity of the two groups.

In Cameroon, as in most former colonies, football first spread in the 1920s, as an unorganized activity (see Tsanga 1969) copying the exclusive leisure activity of the colonizers. It was only later that it became part of physical education in colonial schools, thus its practice often became a sign of prestige. For example, what evolved eventually as the Southern Cameroonian (former British Cameroon) national team, was largely made up of young graduates from St Joseph's College, Sasse. However, it was not until the 1930s and 1940s that clubs began to emerge, and regular championships and cup competitions began only after the Second World War.

The years following independence in 1960 were marred by civil unrest and the enormous destruction of human life. With the assistance of the French, Ahidjo, the first president, outmanoeuvred other nationalist forces. Civil unrest and guerilla warfare emerged as a consequence, and Ahidjo ruled the country for more than twenty-five years with an iron hand. However, for a while at least, sports and culture were apparently considered non-subversive areas. While the State had absolute control of most critical areas – social, political and economic domains – culture and sports enjoyed relative autonomy. And so, Cameroon football was left to develop along regional and ethnic lines with minimal government intervention. However, as Cameroon began to gain more visibility because of its football, the state increased its role and controlled sports in general, and football in particular, more closely.

Ethnicity, Regionalism and Nationalism in Cameroonian Football

One of the factors that makes football theoretically so interesting is that it is possible for its spectators to identify on various levels at the same time. The very structure of sport competition puts into effect a form of 'segmentary opposition' where, depending on the level of locality of the players – whether neighbourhood, town, region or nation – the inclusiveness of loyalties of the audience will vary. Local groups may be set against each other when local groups from the same region play, but will be united on the next level when they are playing against a team from a different region, country or continent. Thus, sport is both a divisive and unifying force. We are going to demonstrate this point by discussing how the forces of ethnicity, regionalism and nationalism play themselves out in football in Cameroon.

Cameroon is a multi-ethnic nation. The most significant divisions are between the Francophone east and the Anglophone west, and the Muslim north and the Christian south. The Anglophone–Francophone divide stems from the colonial legacy of the British and French administrations after 1916. However, it has to be understood that the term Anglophone has begun to function as an ethnic designation. Anglophones, who make up about 25 per cent of the population, see themselves as much maligned and betrayed by their French compatriots, inasmuch as since the time they voted to join Cameroon in a UN supervised plebiscite in 1959, their rights to autonomy and self-expression as a people with 'Anglo-Saxon' traditions have been steadily diminishing. PWD (Public Works Department) Bamenda, mentioned several times in this chapter, is the most important Anglophone team in Cameroon, and as such, it commands the loyalty of Anglophones. In addition, there are over 250 different ethnic groups in Cameroon. There are as many ethnic groups in the English-speaking areas as in any other region of the country, but in most contexts being Anglophone overrides other distinctions, and is used widely both as a term of reference and of self-appellation.

The most important ethnic groups to be mentioned in this chapter – in addition to the Anglophones, who inhabit the South-West and North-West provinces – are the Bamileke, from the Western province of the country, the Beti from the Centre province, and the Bassa and the Douala from the Littoral province. The Beti live in and around Yaoundé, the capital, and the Centre province also happens to be the 'home province' of Cameroon's president, Paul Biya. The five other provinces have not gained much prominence in national football so far, although the 1990s have seen the rise of some northern teams.

This ethnic diversity is reflected both at club level and in the national team. Many Cameroonian clubs are organized on an ethnic basis. For example, Canon of Yaoundé, which was arguably the best African team in the late 1970s, had a core of six or seven players like Abega, or Manga Onguéné, who came from the same cultural niche, the home province of the Beti. The rest of the team was made up of a few good players picked from other ethnic groups and regions.

Many first division teams have been established on an ethnic basis: Union of Douala, Racing of Bafoussam and Diamond of Yaoundé were, and still are, teams with a Bamileke flavour; Canon of Yaoundé and Tonnerre of Yaoundé are based in the Beti region and have been dominated by Beti players; Dynamo of Douala is a Bassa team. However, we witness here the complexity of the ethnic picture, because only Racing, Canon and Tonnerre are located in an area where the ethnic group they represent is dominant. The other two teams mentioned above are teams of migrants who established themselves and formed a team which originally was ethnically based. By now, for the most part, the players and coaches may come from anywhere even in ethnically based teams. The deciding factor for the ethnicity of teams is the identity of their administrative leadership and the ethnic composition of their fans (see Clignet and Stark 1974). These often tend to be completely homogeneous. For example, in the 1995 competitions, Dynamo, a Bassa team, which had been relegated to the second division for the past five years, attracted a very large crowd of Bassa spectators, many of whom had not come to the stadium since the relegation of the team to the second division. At the same time it is also true that the very large teams, such as Canon and Tonnerre, have supporters – at least in Yaoundé – among other ethnic groups as well as the one with which they are primarily associated. Nevertheless, it seems that the degree to which fans take the matter seriously is in direct proportion to their closeness to the ethnic group with which the team in question is associated.

Even though, especially in teams of the higher divisions, the ethnic origin of the coach or of the players does not matter for the most part in the 1990s, when the team loses, ethnic explanations are easily evoked, and players or coaches of a different ethnic group from the team, are charged with having sold the match. For example, when the football club PWD Bamenda played the finals of the Cameroon Cup in 1979 and lost to Dynamo, a Bassa team, rumours ran high about a Bassa player in PWD Bamenda, having sold the match. The underlying conflict of interest (ethnic solidarity versus team solidarity) is an easily comprehended conflict in Cameroon.

Regionalism, too, has played a significant role in Cameroonian football. From its beginnings in the 1930s, Cameroonian football was dominated by teams from the Centre and Littoral provinces, mostly from the towns of Yaoundé, the political capital, and Douala, the economic centre. In the first division league, the Centre Province alone usually had at least six teams. The Littoral region would also have at least four to five teams. In most cases, the contest for the title of champion and for the Cup of Cameroon was between the two major cities, Yaoundé and Douala. Lately, however, the monopoly exercised by the Centre and Littoral provinces is collapsing. In the 1990s it is no longer true that the best teams are theirs. In fact, in the 1993–94 football season, for the first time in history, the top positions in the championship were taken by teams not based in Yaoundé or Douala. The most remarkable change, however, has been the advance of teams from the Western province. In the 1994–95 season there were six teams in the first division from that province. Three of these six teams are of relatively recent creation and their rise to the first division may be seen as part of a new trend. This change also has an ethnic and regional component inasmuch as the Western Province is clearly identifiable with a single ethnic group, the Bamileke. The Bamileke are well known for their entrepreneurial spirit. Their present prominence in football may be seen as the result of a combination of factors. First, there is the question of means. The rising costs of playing football and the simultaneously deepening economic crisis in Cameroon appear to favour Bamileke teams, not so much because they are not affected by the crisis, but because in every community there remains one or two rich individuals who are willing and able to sponsor football for the greater glory of the community.

The other factor is that of political will. Bamileke themselves openly admit that their rise in football is part of an attempt to show the world what they are capable of in a political context where many Bamileke feel that they are being marginalized by the country's political powers. This movement for football prominence in the Western province has grown to such proportions that someone remarked that Racing of Bafoussam, which is one of the historically important, locally based, Bamileke teams, no longer has any supporters because all their one-time fans are supporting their own local teams. The remark nicely illustrates our initial statement about the divisive and unifying capabilities of football. At the same time, the overwhelming majority of Bamileke seem fiercely proud of the achievement of the province as such.

In Cameroon, as elsewhere in the Third World, football was expected to play a critical role in the emergence of a sense of nationhood. In fact, the fostering of football is part of a conscious government effort to strengthen national unity. Some of the efforts are quite high-handed.

In order to curb ethnic exclusiveness, prevent political conflicts and promote national unity, the Cameroon government passed a law on June 12 1967 banning associations based on ethnic criteria. The law of 1967 was designed 'to ensure that traditional forms of expression which contributed to the building up of a genuine national culture and offered incentives, would facilitate the mobilization of the masses in favour of national objectives' (quoted in Bayart 1973: 129–30).[2] Football was no exception.

In pursuit of this policy, the Ministry of Youth and Sports attempted to detribalize 'football in the name of national interest, arbitrarily reducing the number of teams' (Bayart 1973: 128). The ministerial instructions stipulated that no football team would be built on the basis of ethnic distinctiveness. Teams that were previously constituted along ethnic lines had to disband. Players were reallocated to a few teams of a multi-ethnic character. However, leaders of different football clubs rejected the move, and the public uproar was such that Mr Ahidjo, the president, returning to the country from a short stay abroad, suspended the measure and later the Minister responsible was also dismissed (Ntonfo 1994). Although it was public knowledge that Cameroonian football had an ethnic character, the State was prepared to condone this ethnicity tacitly if it would foster public order.

Nevertheless, participation in international sports has generated a greater sense of nationhood than any other Cameroonian achievement. The sentiment, however, is spontaneous rather than imposed from above. The second half of this chapter will illustrate, how as the focus of national pride, the 1994 failure of the Indomitable Lions, has, among other things, triggered responses challenging the government – often in the name of the nation – by ordinary citizens. In any case, sports nationalism in Cameroon has served to break down ethnic boundaries. When the Indomitable Lions or a local club are playing a foreign team, they are no longer a particular team or club; they are Cameroon.

At the same time, however, the forces of ethnicity and regionalism do not completely disappear on an international level. Rather, we find that the national team is only capable of uniting Cameroonians when things go right. When the team loses there is a tendency to scrutinize the ethnic origin of players and coaches, and to try to put the blame on whoever is not of the ethnic origin of the person doing the scrutinizing. Ntonfo, talking about the 1990 selection of the Indomitable Lions who participated in the World Cup in Italy, remarks that although almost 90 per cent of the players were of the Bassa ethnic group 'not for one moment did the Cameroonian people in all their ethnic diversity question the validity of this national team, which has besides written one of the most beautiful pages of their football history' (Ntonfo 1994: 90). He does not deny the importance of the ethnic factor in the national team, but rather points to the ethnic considerations which go into selecting the national team.

The State, Football and Politics in the 1990s

The beginning of multi-partyism in Cameroon occurred in 1990. Until then Cameroon had one political party, the Cameroon People's Democratic Movement (CPDM or *RDPC*), headed by the President of the country, Paul Biya. The most important threat to the ruling party came from the Social Democratic Front (SDF), led by an Anglophone, Ni John Fru Ndi. Political demonstrations in Bamenda were bloodily suppressed. The first years of the 1990s also witnessed the appearance of a plethora of opposition papers (see Krieger 1994). The national football team's victorious performance in Italy thus came for the government, at a most opportune time, helping to quieten political turmoil. The Lions' return from Italy was declared a public holiday, and the government took as much advantage of the national team's performance as it could, in both direct and indirect ways.

Thus, for example, there was, in the 1992 presidential election, for the first time in Cameroon's history, a serious candidate – in the person of Ni John Fru Ndi – other than President Paul Biya (the handpicked successor to Ahmadou Ahidjo). Biya's propaganda machine created an election poster divided into two panels: on one side the president, on the other side a lion with the words 'Courage Man – President Man' written over both images. On one of the panels it also says 'My President Paul Biya'. People often sarcastically refer to the president as Lion Man (*Homme Lion*). This clearly exemplifies the nature of political contestation taking place around football, and outside of football, in Cameroon. The government's attempt to co-opt the Lions' victory, which was also seen as the Cameroonian people's victory, was immediately turned back against the government by the people to become a term of derision against the government in general, and against Biya, in particular.

In the 1992 elections, Ni John Fru Ndi, the charismatic leader of the SDF, which was at the head of a coalition of opposition parties, seriously challenged the incumbent Paul Biya, who came into power in 1982. This was a significant first in Cameroonian history. The elections were highly contested, and although the opposition lost, it is a widely held view in Cameroon that Fru Ndi only lost the elections owing to fraud. Therefore, the event is referred to in Cameroon as the stolen victory, once again proving that the people are capable of verbally getting their own back.

The preparations for the 1994 World Cup in the United States took place in a climate of general disorder. Cameroon had barely qualified for the World Cup when two conflicting organizing bodies were called into being: the *Comité Technique d'Organisation* and the *Haut Comité de Suivi*. Their functions were unspecified, but it was commonly believed in Cameroon, that their most important function was to enable their members to line their own pockets.

In March 1994, a little more than two months before the World Cup, the FECAFOOT (*Fédération Camerounaise de Football*) held a secret meeting in Douala where the delegates deposed Pascal Owona, the government appointed president of the Federation and elected Maha Daher in his place. Naturally, the Ministry of Youth and Sports, and the government, objected to the 'coup d'état' and attempted to reinstate the 'official' president. FIFA, in keeping with its regulations, and its ideals of support for democracy, stepped in and presented Cameroon with an ultimatum: that if the 'democratically elected' president was not allowed to assume his functions, Cameroon would be banned from taking part in the

World Cup. Eventually, the government backed down, accepting the new president, in order to preserve Cameroon's right to participate. At the time, the election of Maha Daher was seen by Cameroonians as a blow against the government, and FIFA were regarded as the unfortunately necessary outsider who could foil the government's high-handedness. FIFA thus became the champion of democratic freedom, in a country where official propaganda claims to have introduced democracy though many feel that the government is only paying lip-service to it.[3]

It was in May 1994, that the Prime Minister of Cameroon, Simon Achidi Achu, launched *Opération Coup de Cœur*. This was a fundraiser to help finance the Lions' American Campaign. Counting upon the patriotism of Cameroonians, the population was asked to contribute money to the Lions. The donations for the most part were voluntary in name only. In government offices, contribution was as good as compulsory and depending on the locale, contributions nation-wide were more or less forced. People talk about this event angrily, even a year later in 1995. 'Even old mothers in villages had to give' or 'even prisoners contributed' are typical and often repeated comments, pronounced with great bitterness.

To appreciate the sacrifices people made, the economic conditions of Cameroon have to be understood. State employees, the easiest targets for forced contributions, had suffered several months of salary arrears, as well as drastic cuts (as much as 60 per cent) in their salaries. All this was coupled with the devaluation of the CFA franc in February 1994, which led to a rise in the price of most goods in the country.

It would, however, be an error to think that *Opération Coup de Cœur* was purely a matter of force. A great number of people contributed willingly, out of national pride or personal pride. In Cameroon, donations to good causes often measure the value of a man, thus contributing a large amount also reflects on the prestige of the giver. Giving freely occurred at all levels of society. Not only did collection sheets make the rounds in government offices, but village associations also conducted their own collections and contributed to *Opération Coup de Cœur*.

These are the conditions under which the 1994 World Cup took place for the people of Cameroon. The teams' performance however went from bad to worse in the competition. Their first match against Sweden resulted in a draw. The second, against

Brazil was lost 3–1. This defeat took many Cameroonians by surprise. The last match for qualification for the second round was against Russia, who had been defeated in all their previous matches. Had Cameroon been able to beat them by a large margin, they could have hoped to qualify for the second round as a 'best loser'. This was not to be. On June 29, Russia dealt a severe 6–1 defeat to Cameroon, thereby not only putting an end to Cameroon's World Cup aspirations, but also wounding Cameroonian national pride as most Cameroonians felt humiliated by this crushing defeat.

Media Coverage of the World Cup

From the beginning of the competition there was extensive media coverage. Matches were broadcast on television, and radio took on a very important role. A radio programme called *Bonjour l'Amérique*, became the most listened to programme of the period. It ran from 5:30 a.m. until 9 a.m. every morning. It was a call-in programme, and many said that this was the first time in Cameroon's history that people were allowed freely to express their views in the media.

As Cameroon is officially a bilingual country, soon after the launch of *Bonjour l'Amérique* an English language version *Hi America*, also began, which ran for two hours every afternoon. This was less listened to, owing to its timing, but in fact, there were contributions to *Bonjour l'Amérique* in English as well as in French, and the occasional French contribution also cropped up in *Hi America*.

Cameroonians responded to the programme enthusiastically. Phone calls came in from all corners of the country, although predictably, the greatest number of calls came from Yaoundé and Douala, the most urbanized areas of the country and, as we have shown above, historically the strongholds of Cameroonian football. One might suppose that phone calls meant that responses would be limited to a narrow well-to-do layer of society. However, calls came from phone booths as well as from offices, and, as someone pointed out, in households with telephones household members come from a variety of social backgrounds, any one of whom could easily have made use of the telephone to participate in the programme. In addition, there were daily sessions with the provincial stations of Cameroon, where 'the man on the street' interview spots were featured. Furthermore, people in Yaoundé could and did arrive at the Radio Broadcasting House to leave letters and even to participate personally, and mail arrived daily from the provinces.

We are in the preliminary stages of analysing the material which was broadcast, which one of the co-authors recorded and transcribed. Even as a first approximation, it is clear that the tenor of the programme changed over time. Before the Lions bowed out of the competition, the audience was called upon to make suggestions on the composition of the team, and in general the programme expressed the support of the nation for its team. After the defeat, the audience was invited to analyse the causes of the fiasco and to make suggestions on how to improve football in Cameroon.

Since national media anywhere in the world, but especially in a Third World country, also serves to control and manipulate the audience, it is important to examine the programme from the point of view of how Cameroon Radio and Television (CRTV) and by extension the government, handled the World Cup and Cameroon's defeat in it. The programme encapsulated a great many contradictions. On the one hand, it was an expression of Cameroonian nationalism; on the other, in the context of defeats and problems as they piled up, it became an indictment of the government. Finally, it served to smooth things over without bringing about any resolutions.

First of all, it is clear that *Bonjour l'Amérique* began to gain in importance as Cameroon's situation in the World Cup worsened. It was almost openly admitted that, especially after Cameroon's humiliating defeat by Russia, the programme served as a safety valve. Immediately after the match, journalists started talking about the importance of remaining calm. More importantly, by allowing the people to speak in an almost uncensored manner, to vent their anger, bitterness and disappointment, the government was hoping to forestall more drastic action, either in the form of an attack upon the residences of the players and coaches, or in the form of some unspecified revolutionary action. Judging by the texts of the contributions, a large number of Cameroonians blamed the government for the poor performance of the Lions, and their anger and humiliation may well have physically turned against the government. Thus, for example, a few days after

Cameroon's defeat by Russia, a Francophone caller said the following:

> every author of this defeat, everyone who one way or another had a hand in this, starting with the Prime Minister, Mr Kontchou [the Minister for Communication], and others should resign, because, gentlemen you are enjoying yourselves, but such a coup could smear the entire government. And it is also for this reason that we demand that the Head of State should, really, open a very important page in this story, because if not, he too will be considered an accomplice of the first order.

No drastic action took place, perhaps at least partly due to *Bonjour l'Amérique*. Callers were apparently satisfied with breaking verbal taboos. At the time people were surprised and jubilant over the amount of freedom of speech allowed on the programme, which stresses how this was a first and unique occasion. Even months after the World Cup, people on the streets of Yaoundé derived a certain satisfaction from recalling the programme, saying, usually as closure to the discussion, 'the people spoke'.

After the elimination of the Indomitable Lions and a suitable 'mourning period' CRTV attempted to change the tenor of the broadcast by inviting concrete suggestions and propositions for the future. In this, they were only partially successful because, for the most part, the callers continued in the same vein. Three major events stand out in the course of the post-elimination phase.

First, on 9 July 1994, a press conference was held by the 'Minister of Communication, Special Envoy of the Head of State', on the controversial *Coup de Cœur* funds. Augustin Kontchou is seen by the majority of Cameroonians as a liar. He earned his nickname of 'Zéro Mort' after his denial of the death of students, in the course of political demonstrations, at Yaoundé University in 1991. The population greeted his press conference with doubts, some people going so far as refusing to listen to it, saying, 'I know they are lies'. During the press conference, the Minister accounted for every penny of the funds (the veracity of which account was doubted by many), while affirming that each player had been paid all his bonuses for his participation in the competition. As no player came forward to deny this, the latter is most likely true. He also promised that *Cameroon Tribune*, the government daily paper, would publish a full list of the fund's contributors and the amounts contributed. This, however, never happened. A few lists were published in the days following and then the matter was never heard of again. In conversations this fact is often brought up to prove the bad faith of the government. As already mentioned, it is a widely held view that the collection was organized to enable various government officials to line their own pockets.[4]

The much debated subject of the non-payment of players' bonuses had a wider significance in view of the fact that Cameroonians as a whole had been faced with a situation of non-payment of salaries. Thus, when people were discussing whether the Lions were entitled to their pay, or whether they could be expected to perform for the nation without pay, they were talking on at least two levels: about the players and, more subtly, about themselves. Kontchou's affirmation that payments had been made to the players in effect closed the debate, in spite of people's scepticism on the matter.

This press conference signalled the beginning of greater government control on what could be said on *Bonjour l'Amérique*. Journalists from that day on rebutted callers' criticisms of the handling of the *Coup de Cœur* money by using the press conference as a point of reference.

One exception to this increased control was the second significant event in the radio coverage of the post-elimination phase of the World Cup. This was the interview on 16 July 1994, with Joseph-Antoine Bell, one of the ace goalkeepers of the Cameroonian team. Bell, arriving in Garoua in the north of the country, agreed to an interview. This was to be broadcast at eleven o'clock, after the scheduled programme and coincided with the departure of the Chadian president from an official visit to Cameroon. The interview started later than expected owing to Idriss Deby's departure, and ended when it was suddenly interrupted by music, apparently under the orders of the Minister for Communication (see *La Nouvelle Expression*, no. 174).

Bell is a controversial figure in Cameroon because he speaks his mind and is often critical of the way football is managed. He does not seem to take a particular side; he is critical of mistakes no matter where they come from. He also provokes intense feelings in people. He has unconditional supporters and unconditional detractors. Much of the debate on *Bonjour l'Amérique* concerned him, and during the World Cup public opinion was firmly against him, partly because his performance was not at its best, and partly because he was seen as indifferent to the fate of the team. A young

Anglophone man confided to one of the authors that he could not accept Bell's performance because after failing to save a goal he laughed, thus implying disdain for his country.

Earlier, in the course of the 1990 World Cup, Bell had been nicknamed Nelson Mandela when, supposedly by government order he was prevented from playing in the competition because he had organized the players to demand their bonuses. At that time he was seen as someone who was willing to sacrifice himself for the common good. In the 1994 World Cup he was seen as putting personal interest before national interest. In the 1992 elections Bell supported President Biya's bid for power, by announcing on national media that among the available candidates, Biya was the best. This political affiliation may well have contributed to the negative view people had of him during the World Cup.

None the less, Bell's appearance on radio following the World Cup and his iconoclastic stance once again turned public opinion in his favour. All the more so, as the cutting short of the programme, in conjunction with other events in the aftermath of the World Cup, once again put him in opposition to the government. Firstly, a few days after the programme three journalists were suspended from their positions at the radio station for having allowed the interview with Bell to pass, thereby interfering with coverage of the Chadian president's departure. Secondly, about the same time, Bell was invited for a debate organized by the opposition newspaper, *La Nouvelle Expression*, in a Douala hotel. The event never took place because police with teargas dispersed the crowd who had gathered to attend the debate. These two events restored Bell's image as an iconoclast, and his Jubilee later in the year was attended by enthusiastic crowds in Douala.

Another recurring subject on *Bonjour l'Amérique* was the head-coach, Henri Michel, who was French. He aroused the resentment of Cameroonians in many ways. His appointment came after Cameroon's qualification for the World Cup in replacement of a Cameroonian coach. Although anywhere in the world coaches are the first to be blamed when the team is not performing well, the complaints directed at him went deeper and addressed issues which had little to do with either Henri Michel or football.

Both Anglophones and Francophones resented him, but with a somewhat different focus. Anglophones complained about French dominance and the fact that it would never occur to Francophones to think of appointing a non-French coach, even though Cameroon is officially a bilingual country. For example, on 30 June 1994 an Anglophone woman caller said the following on *Hi America*:

> So as a contribution on how to solve the problem now, I think [all] we can do is try to avoid this idea of having to lean on France, France, France every day . . . Why should we always go to take coaches only from France every day? Cameroon is a bilingual country, why have we never taken a coach from say England, from even America, which is not a football country, even Germany which . . . a country we know, really

Francophone complaints put the matter somewhat differently, laying more stress on the fact that there were a great many equally qualified Cameroonian coaches, so why should a foreigner, a Frenchman at that, be chosen for the post. Others went so far as to refer to a French plot to undo Cameroon in the World Cup, by way of revenge for the fact that France herself had not managed to qualify for the event while Cameroon had. Henri Michel was also blamed by the audience of *Bonjour l'Amérique* for having mismanaged the team for personal gain (either by benefiting from lucrative contracts, or somehow gaining money from the test matches he had the team play). This is the kind of accusation which is also levelled at the political leaders of Cameroon. Here again, verbal ridicule is an effective weapon against people perceived to be in a position of power.

One of the co-authors, a white (Hungarian) woman, received a number of highly ironic remarks, in markets and other public places in Yaoundé: she was addressed as Madame Henri Michel during and for several months after the World Cup. The message was clear: Henri Michel was seen to embody all whites, and especially all French people, and the crimes he committed against Cameroon were emblematic of the crimes all French people commit against the country. In fact the only way I found of relieving these tense situations when I was identified as Madame Henri Michel, was to tell people that I was not French, at which point everyone relaxed and the tension disappeared.

The third and final incident at *Bonjour l'Amérique* witnessed the re-emergence of censorship in its most obvious form. The day after the Bell interview, on 17 July 1994, a few hours before the end of the World Cup, once again Augustin Kontchou, the Minister of

Communications appeared on *Bonjour l'Amérique*, on a special edition where all questions were supposed to be answered. In answer to some challenging questions, the Minister called upon Bell and Massoua II (the then Minister of Youth and Sports, to be dismissed a few days later), to call the studio and present their version of the facts. A journalist shouted excitedly that Massoua II was on the line, they were connecting him . . . Then came music. The programme finished there and then, with no explanation and no technical problems evoked – just music – and the listener was left wondering whether the problem was with his own radio.

Conclusion

A brief analysis of the radio coverage of the 1994 World Cup has allowed us to demonstrate the following points. Football is politics in Cameroon. By taking credit for the victory in 1990, the government was also forced to take the blame for the failure in 1994, as is witnessed by the contributions to *Bonjour l'Amérique* and *Hi America* which called for the resignation of the Prime Minister, or otherwise openly blamed the government. Verbal ridicule, for which there was ample scope on the radio, as well as on the streets, is one of the only ways that people have of turning the tables, and deriving satisfaction from avenging some of their usurped power. Shifting the blame to one person, Joseph-Antoine Bell, did not succeed, largely owing to the high-handed nature of the attempts to silence him. More successful, though most likely unintended, was the shifting of the blame to Henri Michel, the French expatriate head-coach of the national team. The latent, and not so latent, animosity of Cameroonians to their 'ancestors', the French, came out in virulent forms during the two programmes. Most successful, however, was the silence that ended the programme. The debate was never opened again, and we have shown how Bell's meeting with the press was prevented from taking place.

This silence, however, left many unresolved issues festering. More often than not when people were talking about football, they were also talking about their daily lives and their social reality. When people spoke about unpaid bonuses for players, they were also speaking about unpaid salaries; when they insisted that national coaches were as well qualified as expatriates, they were also talking about the relationship of Cameroon to France; and finally, when they implored the government to take the matter seriously they meant not only the plight of football, but the plight of the country.

Notes

1. The fieldwork for the research was supported by the Wenner Gren Foundation for Anthropological Research.
2. Bayart's text is quoting from a political response of the Presidency to a statement by members of Ngondo, the traditional assembly of the Douala, from *Bulletin quotidien d'information de l'agence camerounaise de press*, 2 August 1972.
3. There was a sequel to the FIFA story when during the summer and autumn of 1995, the Ministry of Youth and Sports suspended the Federation for alleged embezzlement of funds, putting in a Caretaker Committee in its stead and, under threats from FIFA, the Ministry had to finally back down and reinstate the old bureau of the FECAFOOT.
4. The *Coup de Cœur* accounts made a later appearance in May 1995 when radio and government newspapers suddenly announced that a final accounting had been made of the Coup de Cœur money, and 'naturally' everything was found to be in order. In the view of most people the publication of the accounts at that precise moment had more to do with trying to divert attention away from allegations of embezzlement directed at the Federation, than with a wish to inform the public.

Chapter 7

Soccer and Violence in War-Torn Africa: Soccer and Social Rehabilitation in Sierra Leone

Paul Richards

Introduction

The debate about soccer and violence is dominated by images and assumptions of young men behaving badly. Recently, Armstrong (1996) has argued that much of the literature on this topic is unduly influenced by a widespread moral panic rooted in the changing relationship between work and social order in a post-Industrial society. Put bluntly, contemporary society at large does not know how to cope with its strong young men, raised in a decades old, working-class tradition of disciplined manual labour. Young men turn to soccer hooliganism as an expressive idiom reflecting their plight, in a highly ritualized and organized activity, mainly directed at rival hooligans. It may not be much fun for those who have to police it, but it ranks low on the list of objective dangers faced by the general public. Perhaps it also has self-healing and socially constructive properties; by and large, hooligans turn into solid citizens. They may be more solid in their citizenship for having passed through a hooligan phase.

The point I want to pick up from this all-too-brief attempt at summarizing a complex argument rooted in extraordinarily rich ethnography, is that there is no fixed and determinate relationship between soccer and violence. Causation flows both ways: there may be positive as well as negative aspects to the purported relationship; there are strong social reasons why the relationship should be misrepresented, and the coupling of soccer and violence will vary as social circumstances vary. We are likely to find major variations between industrialized, non-industrialized and post-industrialized societies.

The purpose of the present chapter is to explore a radically different coupling of soccer and violence in contemporary non-industrial but highly globalized rural war-torn Africa. I shall be considering mainly the case of Sierra Leone (but with some additional reference to neighbouring Liberia). Specifically, I ask what models of rule-based social interaction are available to young people forcibly recruited to 'anarchic' war, where the promoters of conflict have violated and invalidated the social understandings upon which rural civil society was based. The great virtue of soccer as a template for social regeneration in a war-damaged social landscape may be the simple but fluid abstractness of the co-operative scenarios that the game portrays. Here – if you like – the 'hooligan violence' precedes the soccer. Soccer may be one of the antidotes to violence.

The New Social Disorder in Africa

The social order is easier to destroy than to create. Security agents in white-dominated Rhodesia and South Africa developed an applied anthropology of social destabilization during independence struggles in that region. More recently, this anthropology of social destabilization has found applications in other conflicts in sub-Saharan Africa (Wilson 1992; Furley 1995). In West Africa, insurgent movements in Liberia and Sierra Leone have built upon guerrilla methods elaborated in the long 'dirty war' in Mozambique (Ellis 1995; Richards 1996a). A range of tactics is deployed specifically to corrode the local social confidences upon which civil society in rural Africa depends for its continuance. Two among these tactics are:

1. Instrumental attempts to heighten local social tensions, for example, burning the houses of only one religious or ethnic group not because the insurgents have a religious or ethnic agenda, but because they want to divide village neighbours who formerly exhibited mutual tolerance and accommodation (Richards 1996a).
2. Forcing young people to take part in atrocities against key

figures in village society, thus blocking return to social acceptance should young conscripts later seek to escape insurgent control (Amnesty International 1993; Goodwin-Gill and Cohn 1994; Richards 1996a).

Puzzled international commentators have described this allegedly purposeless post-Cold War conflict in Africa as a 'coming anarchy' (Kaplan 1994; Luttwak 1995; Bradshaw 1996) and relate it to Malthusian pressure on natural resources. It is probably better regarded as an instrumental application of the theory of modern guerrilla warfare for purposes of renewed 'primitive accumulation' in a continent subject to 'marketization', donor-enforced 'structural adjustment' and resultant state recession (Richards 1996a).

Descent into Violence: Liberia and Sierra Leone

Liberia and Sierra Leone are two small, resource-rich countries dominated by their capital cities and patrimonial political formations. During the 1970s and 1980s young radical intellectuals from throughout the West African region, inspired by pan-Africanist ideals and Libyan revolutionary populism, began to envisage a new kind of bush war to overthrow entrenched and corrupt capital city élites and neo-patrimonial political regimes (Yeebo 1991). The theory was based on the assumption that army coups were invariably reactionary. Hopes for a progressive break with neo-patrimonial politics were pinned on the idea of popular struggle spreading from the grass roots. The struggle against Obote in Uganda, and the subsequent economic and political success of the Museveni regime were thought to be hopeful portents (Yeebo 1991).

The subsequent evolution of events in West Africa is obscure. Much radical energy seems to have been centred initially in Ghana, where the June Four Movement was used by Jerry Rawlings as a stepping stone to power. Elsewhere, Thomas Sankara, the leader of a coup against patrimonial authority in Burkina Faso, was another focus around which radical sentiment gathered. Disillusioned with Rawlings, some Ghanaian radicals then began to pay attention to plans by a Liberian economist, Charles Taylor, to lead a Museveni-style revolt against the ill-educated and barbaric military dictator of Liberia, Samuel Kanyon Doe (Yeebo 1991).

It now seems that Taylor was less a revolutionary than an agent of a certain kind of business expansion into the still heavily forested Liberian interior (Block 1992; Reno 1993; Tarr 1993). Taylor's plans were to constitute a 'Greater Liberia' – a term that revives older Liberian claims to some of the forested and mineral-rich borderlands of eastern Sierra Leone. Drawing extensively upon Renamo-style terror tactics, youth capture and an instrumental use of historical tensions between forest-farming populations and a Mandingo merchant diaspora, his movement, The National Patriotic Front of Liberia (NPFL), launched its guerrilla campaign at Christmas 1989 and was initially very successful: it soon came to control nearly all Liberia outside of the capital Monrovia (Ellis 1995).

Taylor then helped form and arm a second small dissident movement, mainly recruited from exiles and economic refugees from the one-party regimes of Presidents Siaka Stevens and Joseph Saidu Momoh in Sierra Leone. This second movement – the Revolutionary United Front (RUF) – comprised ex-student radicals, some local political dissidents from the Sierra Leone border region, and former army officers and NCOs implicated in a coup plot against Stevens during the 1970s. It launched an invasion of Sierra Leone from the eastern border with Liberia in March 1991, assisted by Liberian and Burkinabe veterans of Taylor's movement.

Initially, Taylor's NPFL and the RUF (through the influence of Taylor) seem to have enjoyed some political backing and funding for arm's purchases from Francophone interests in the region. Taylor was a protégé of Blaise Compaore, the officer who over-threw Sankara in a second coup in Burkina Faso. This coup was widely thought to have enjoyed the tacit approval, if not connivance, of the French. Sankara was apparently a committed radical, but Compaore (nominally a radical) was in fact closer to the conservative Ivoirian president, Houphouet-Boigny.

French business interests in the region are strongly entrenched in the Côte d'Ivoire. A central fact about the Ivoirian economy is the rapid agrarian economic development that has turned the country into the world's largest cocoa exporter in the past thirty to forty years. Cocoa and coffee (the main export earners, since Côte d'Ivoire is not rich in minerals) became less attractive crops in the 1980s and 1990s, as world prices continued to decline. Cocoa-butter may one day be produced from a diversity of feed-stocks through enzyme engineering. Concomitantly the tree-crop economy had become over extended. This dubious progress had been bought at the price of one of the world's highest rates of tropical deforestation. The forests had been cut, intentionally, to fund an economic take-off that increasingly was beginning to falter. Meanwhile, a more eurocentric France was beginning to cut back on its economic subsidies to its former colonial African empire.

Not surprisingly, businesses in Côte d'Ivoire eyed the 30 per cent of Liberia still in high forest (Parren and de Graaf 1995) with considerable interest. Liberia and eastern and southern Sierra Leone were also rich in minerals (iron ore and alluvial diamonds, in particular) that might help provide an additional lease of life for French investments in Abidjan. It was assumed (probably correctly) that American and British business interests in the region, which the French sometimes refer to as 'Guinee anglais', were in long-term decline. The idea of support for a 'progressive' Taylor to unseat a 'barbaric' Doe must have seemed an attractive and even praiseworthy proposition.

Compaore was Taylor's first protector (Tarr 1993; Ellis 1995). Allegedly, he helped recruit and train some hardy revolutionary types for Taylor's cause, and later for the RUF in Sierra Leone. Perhaps the best that can be said in defence of the Burkinabe president, and of Houphouet (his father-in-law), in this matter, is that they failed to prevent the training, supply and passage of these would-be revolutionaries through their countries to begin the conflict in Liberia. The revolutionaries themselves were more concerned to secure loot than to establish the political programmes they proclaimed.

It soon became clear that the Taylor programme was politically insincere (Yeebo 1991; Tarr 1993). The attempted mobilization of revolutionary and ethnic sentiments was instrumental to Taylor's longer-term presidential and business aims. Pandora's box was opened. Several distinct and competing militias were formed by rival backers. Each used the same range of socially-destabilizing techniques deployed by the Taylor group. An international peace-keeping group (ECOMOG[1]) was formed, ostensibly to bring a halt to the unrestricted carnage in Liberia. ECOMOG was dominated by the Nigerian military, who seemingly had an anti-Ivoirian business agenda of their own in Liberia (Ellis 1995). Taylor helped launch the RUF into Sierra Leone, perhaps mainly to destabilize ECOMOG. In addition, the forested and diamond-rich border region between Liberia and Sierra Leone which was under attack by the RUF, would have been a useful economic appendage to the new Abidjan-focused economic region Taylor and his backers sought to carve out from the western end of the Upper Guinean forest block.

Taylor 'appointed' Foday Sankoh, a disgruntled ex-corporal from the Sierra Leone army, who had been dismissed and jailed for his alleged involvement in a coup plot in 1971, as 'governor' of Sierra Leone (perhaps an intentional revival of an old colonial appellation). Threatened by the RUF, the government of Sierra Leone then helped supply a new militia, ULIMO[2], which was formed around an alliance of Doe loyalists in the Liberian army and Mandingo refugees from NPFL terror in Liberia. This group of irregulars assisted the Sierra Leone army in beating back the initial RUF invasion of Sierra Leone. It then continued across the Liberian border to oppose the NPFL in Liberia.

Later ULIMO split into two factions, mirroring an earlier split in the NPFL (where one faction was led by the NPFL's main guerrilla strategist, Prince Yormeh Johnson, the other by Taylor). The peace-keepers in Liberia then encouraged the formation of yet another anti-NPFL militia (the inaptly named Liberian Peace Council) from elements in the former Armed Forces of Liberia (Ellis 1995). All these competing factions employ the same set of tactics for recruitment, social destabilization and military action. They live by looting, gem-stone mining and logging. Temporary peace deals and truces soon break down, and new factions emerge with depressing regularity.

Social conditions in the remote forested areas of up-country Liberia and Sierra Leone fed the conflict. Dominated by the capital city, and in recession, neo-patrimonial states found it harder, through the 1980s, to ensure the social and political incorporation of the increasing number of youths in the population. A key demographic fact is that Liberia and Sierra Leone, in common with most African countries, have more than 50 per cent of their population under the age of eighteen. For young people, the economic decline meant that schooling systems broke down and donor-imposed stringencies limited the number of jobs available for disbursement via political patronage. In addition, for political reasons, the Sierra Leonean state allowed communications with the border region with Liberia (never good at the best of times) to degenerate almost to the point of non-existence. Large numbers of youths – many of whom were school drop-outs – were to be found in this diamond and timber-rich border zone, hustling for a living on the very margins of society (Zack-Williams 1995; Richards 1996a, b). Some young people proved willing converts to the rebel cause. Others were captured and forced to join, but soon began to identify with the RUF programme. Social exclusion and disgruntlement with the State became the main motives for rebellion, ensuring that the RUF insurgency outlived the support of Charles Taylor (see RUF/SL 1995), who had meanwhile been forced back on to the defensive in Greater Liberia by the proliferation of rival militia.

After more than five years of war, pervasive war-weariness assails both countries. High-level peace negotiations have been tried in both conflicts. A 1995 peace deal in Liberia has since broken down. There seems a better chance that a deal between a democratically elected government and the seemingly less factionally divided rebels in Sierra Leone might prove more durable. But attention has to be paid to conditions on the ground. Here matters are not so easy to assess. Much will depend on how quickly and effectively alienated rebel youths can be reabsorbed within a community and a society rendered fragile by war.

Over half the population of both countries are living as refugees or internally displaced people. Rural social structures have broken down. Social amity has been deliberately targeted by rebel tactics. But established social values have also been undermined by the experience of displacement. The socialization of an increasing youth population has been hindered by interruptions to schooling. Many young people have been swept up into the militia from their pre-teenage years and now barely know of any mode of life other than violent conflict and looting.

A somewhat hopeful sign, in Sierra Leone at least, is that several centres of provincial civic politics and culture remain more or less intact within the war zone. Citizen groups in Bo and Kenema (two of the principal and relatively secure towns in the war zone) are currently very active in reaching out to rebel groups in the countryside, seeking to bring about their social reincorporation, even ahead of any peace deal with the RUF. Some of these activists are very clear about the difficulty, perhaps impossibility, of reviving older social forms and understandings, since the war has destroyed (or at best made problematic) the delicate tacit agreements upon which peaceful coexistence in conditions of great poverty previously was made possible. New idioms of social incorporation must be invented.

Social Resources for Peace?

In peace negotiations, the Sierra Leonean government of President Ahmed Tejan-Kabba and the RUF rebels in 1995/6 agreed on a process for encampment, disarmament and rehabilitation of former combatants. At the time of writing the rebel groups are concentrated in off-road camps where they are relatively safe from army counter-attack while negotiations for a final comprehensive peace settlement are concluded. Meanwhile, the young fighters are anxious for any sign that they will be reabsorbed within the wider community.

Many RUF fighters have been five years alone in the bush. During that time, not only have they missed several years of acculturation, but they have also been deployed to attack their own communities. Almost everything that belongs specifically to the community – including kinship – has been damaged by this experience. At times, even the families of the fighters balk at the idea of reabsorbing these young captive rebels, believing that they have been for ever 'turned' against society by rebel magic.

What remaining links to wider society do these young people retain after having been deployed for up to one third of their lives in socially destabilizing acts of terror? It seems that some of the most important links are those that depend upon a 'global' or explicitly multi-cultural framework of cultural reference. We are speaking in general terms of the popular cultures of youth (see PEA 1989) – including music, sport, and multi-cultural masquerade – and elements of world religion.

Contact and confidence-building are the first issues, and 'remote' electronic media (notably radio) have a central significance (Richards 1996c). Two traders of my acquaintance, buying rice in rural areas north-west of Bo, were recently apprehended by rebels of the Sixth Battalion of the RUF. The young fighters claimed they had all been seized as pre-teenagers in 1991 in the border districts, and trained to fight by Burkinabe mercenaries. Based in bush camps in the forest ever since, they kept in touch with social currents in the rest of Sierra Leonean society only through radio and occasional trading contacts. No longer killing villagers, because of a general expectation that the war was coming to an end, they still felt free to loot the items they needed for their subsistence. Torch batteries were among the first items they took from my friends: 'for their radios', they explained.

The traders asked why they did not simply dump their weapons (they had run out of ammunition) and follow them back to town. They said they were too nervous to return to Bo without a firmly guaranteed amnesty. Meanwhile, the young rebels (many hardly more than fifteen years old) listened assiduously to the music programme broadcast by the local FM station in Bo for any signs that peace was coming, and that they might at last be welcome to return. Local disc jockeys have for some years been sending out subtle and soothing messages, without it being necessarily obvious that these were addressed to combatants. This has being taking place well ahead of any formal peace deal.

My rice-trading friends were released by their captors after three days, with specific handwritten instructions requesting a song by South African pop music star Shaka Bundu to be played for 'the boys in the northern jungle' (as they described themselves). Popular music (and a request on the local radio) is one of the first steps through which these young captives begin the task of rethinking themselves as peaceful Sierra Leoneans, and escape the reputation they have acquired in local eyes as outcasts and 'monsters' through the RUF's application of the Renamo-style techniques of violent social estrangement.

Once direct contact resumes, and rebel fighters begin to assemble in camps, prior to returning home, resources beyond a shared interest in popular music programmes will be urgently required.

Along with inter-cultural street masquerade (Richards 1996a), a shared enthusiasm for soccer is an interesting resource for peace-making, because it is one of the relatively few widely enjoyed but 'neutral' items of cultural common property – unspoilt by war – through which these alienated youngsters might begin to experiment with the direct reconstruction of their social identity. Camped, the ex-fighters will play soccer. It is important, therefore, to begin to analyse what scope soccer offers for modelling new social relationships in the kind of post-conflict settings described. The advantage of soccer is not just its general popularity, but also that as a cheap and universal team sport it has a social character without specific social reference. It is nobody's game, but everybody's. As a 'global' play of conflict and co-operation it offers a neutral space through which combatants and society at large might begin to seek some mutual accommodation in a 'shared space' before getting down to the hard tasks of re-forming specifically Sierra Leonean social identities and social understandings.

Seeing Society in Soccer

The interest of Sierra Leonean youth in soccer crosses most social divisions in the country. Rich and poor, Muslims and Christians, women as well as men, all enjoy the game. Soccer pitches are found in the remotest villages as well as in urban areas. The game can be (and is) played by barefoot enthusiasts on the roughest of pitches, with a minimum of facilities (rag balls if need be, and bamboo sticks for goals).

According to reports, Freetown has women's teams and a nascent women's league. In December 1994 I interviewed a woman who was involved in plans to launch a league for women's soccer in Bo. She was the manager of one of the four teams intending to play in this league. Having persuaded a physical-education instructor from the police force to coach the side, she was making plans to secure the small sponsorship necessary to buy a team-strip. Interviewed on the day before the RUF launched its attack on the town of Bo in December 1994, she was understandably preoccupied with the safety of her family, and in 1996 I have still to hear whether the league was subsequently launched.

Soccer is regularly used as a way of linking local populations and groups of outsiders. Once, when leading a team of students from Freetown on a fieldwork trip to a village in up-country Sierra Leone, I was invited to pick and captain a side against the village eleven (or fifteen as it happened) as a way of 'announcing our presence'. After attacks on the Sierra Rutile mine at Mobimbi, RUF rebels are said to have organized a soccer competition to help improve relations with the local population.

What useful social lessons might young Sierra Leoneans see in soccer? I offer the following ethnographic vignettes, in order to raise debate about what the game might contribute to healing some of the most glaring social wounds of war.

Referees

It is Saturday afternoon in Mandu, a large Mende village north of Bo. Mandu is the headquarters of Valunia Chiefdom. A feeder road to the railway in Bo was constructed early in the twentieth century, and Lebanese traders ventured to Mandu to buy palm produce. When the British introduced a poll tax, the first of these Lebanese traders paid tax for the entire chiefdom, to be reimbursed in palm produce at the farmer's convenience. The road remains untarred. Mandu is now a Saturday gathering-point for village-based fieldworkers for the main rural development agency in the region – the German-funded Bo-Pujehun Project. Today, the health workers from the area have challenged the agricultural extension workers to a match.

The game is billed as a novelty event – women and men – and fancy dress. Arriving at the field (belonging to a local school) we meet twenty-two very fit young men already changed into two sets of distinctive strip. There is no sign of fancy dress or of any women participants. I am asked, 'will I take charge of the game?' Fortunately I am with a colleague who is a qualified referee, and after some discussion he agrees to step in. My friend calls the sides together and points out the obvious – there are no linesmen (indeed no lines). Off-side will be hard to judge. The players will have to abide by whatever he decides.

The game begins. It is energetic and skilful, despite the dust (rendering some of the action invisible to the crowd at times) and the fact that many of the participants are playing barefoot on gravelly ground. The green side scores a goal. The referee is immediately besieged by the players of the red side, and some of the spectators, protesting off-side. The clamour will not die down. Scuffles break out among players and the referee is jostled. Serious accusations begin to flow – the referee made a mistake, he is incompetent, he is biased – maybe he even took a bribe before the match began.

Unwilling to be insulted further, my friend walks smartly off the pitch, and heads for home. As if by magic the scuffling players are brought under control by their peers, and the crowd retreats to its rightful place. My friend is entreated not to abandon the game. He gives a little speech. He came to the match merely to accompany me. He had no warning he would be asked to take charge of the game. He has no linesmen. There is no way he could make accurate off-side rulings in such circumstances. He told everyone that at the outset. Offended and insulted by their actions, he makes it clear once again that he will blow as he sees fit, like it or leave it.

There is a general murmur of assent. Yes, indeed, a game played at speed and with passion cannot be regulated without a referee. Better to abide by the referee's rulings than for the game to be abandoned. Somebody mutters the proverb 'bad osban beta pas empti os' (a bad husband is better than an empty house). Order returns and the game is played out in a friendly spirit, resulting in a 1–1 draw.

Rules

The scene now shifts to the grassy patch in front of a house in Bo town. Bo is the main urban centre of provincial Sierra Leone. Two days previously the town came under attack from a small contingent of a hundred or so rebels of the RUF. The attempted invasion was beaten off by an uprising of citizens. Clearing the town of insurgents, the civil defence later drove off the army as well, and imposed its own curfew, with vigilante patrols extracting summary revenge on looting soldiers and checking the credentials of incoming refugees to identify rebel would-be infiltrators.

Now the army has returned with reinforcements. These reinforcements include new rocket-launchers with a louder than usual explosive bang. They serve little tactical purpose since the rebels are by now well hidden in villages back from the roads, but the noise they make serves to terrify citizen and rebel alike.

It is the school holidays and the small boys from the surrounding compounds have gathered on the grass for an impromptu soccer game with a rag ball. They are all between nine and eleven years old, typical of the age-group the rebels had set out to capture as recruits in their raid on the town.

The game rages for twenty minutes or so, but is interrupted by an enormous racket from the brigade headquarters as the new rocket-launcher is test-fired. Some young women nearby cry out in terror. The soccer players decide to rest from their game for the time being, and begin instead to recapitulate the major incidents of the recently completed 1994 World Cup.

Nearly every game has been seen on video by each of the participants. They are children from low-income households, but there is a good steady electricity supply in Bo, and there are many video parlours showing a mixture of mainly Indian and Kung Fu films, and war movies of the *Rambo* genre (Richards 1994). Entrance costs only a few pence. The video parlours also show sporting and news items copied from the satellite connections owned by wealthier members of the Bo community. Most young people in

Bo are familiar with media events such as CNN coverage of the Gulf war or the video made by Prince Johnson's people of the torture and killing of Liberian dictator Samuel Doe (Davidson 1992). It was through video shows that these young soccer players had gained intimate knowledge of nearly all the main matches in the World Cup.

As we sheltered from the sun under a dusty ornamental palm, the topic turned to the use of the red card. It seemed that the young participants had almost complete recall of red-card incidents in the World Cup competition. Each was now subjected to elaborate examination. Fairness was weighed in the balance. The objectivity and eyesight of each referee passed under scrutiny. Older boys struggled to remember the origins of each of the match referees, coaching the younger boys in where the countries in question might (or might not) be found. The argument then swept up and around the question of the national bias of match officials. A global social order was constructed before my eyes – shaky in details but recognizable in its larger outline. The games and results themselves seemed but mere incidentals. And then, as if reminded by the engines of war in the background, their attention swung back to the social purposes of the referee. Without an official there cannot be a game. Beggars cannot be choosers. Referees and their red cards are a necessary evil. 'Bad osban beta pas empti os.'

Something I had recently been told came to mind. Apparently there was a brave human-rights lawyer working for one of the agencies in Monrovia whose job it was to motor out to the roadblock checkpoints and teach the Geneva Convention to militia fighters. These under-age warriors were at first baffled, but later intrigued (I had been told), to find that war had rules. It crossed my mind that the lawyer might have been more readily understood had he started with the rules of soccer.

Trust and co-operation

In the midst of the war we were interviewing young people in Bo about their likes and dislikes in video entertainment. Many placed sports videos high on their list. Soccer was mentioned often.

What was it that was so attractive about the game? One young man said that watching soccer made him understand a great deal about human nature. Was it the glory of victory or the tragedy of defeat that attracted his interest? No, he said, he paid less attention to the competitive aspects of the game than to what was happening to players on the same side. Studying the game closely made one understand team effort. Some players were too selfish. Others combined and co-operated well. In life, it was the people on your own side you had to watch and understand, more than your opponents even.

Organization

East Freetown is a major concentration of working-class and migrant communities. I had been invited to meet the youthful organizers of a team competing in a local cup competition. The members of the side were teenage migrants from the north-west of Sierra Leone, several were living in East Freetown as 'street' youngsters (see PEA 1989). The organizers were devout Muslims who had succeeded in attracting the support of a Norwegian temperance organization. The donors had no presence on the ground, and a shrewd suspicion that their investment might not be reaching the intended recipients. Some feedback was required. Having helped fix some contacts with local evaluators I went along 'for the ride'.

In fact, the club was impressively genuine in what it was setting out to achieve. Soccer was the focus for the group, and the attraction for its young members, but the organization had a general social welfare agenda in addition to Saturday sport. Many migrants fail in city life through no fault of their own. The club existed to play soccer, but it also saw itself as an instrument for the reintegration of young migrants into rural life when life on the streets became unbearable. My colleague, Serrie Kamara, tramped with representatives of the club committee deep into the bush in north-western Sierra Leone to examine a large and apparently impressive co-operative farming project for club members, funded with the assistance of the Norwegian donors.

Back in Freetown we were invited to the post-match celebrations following the club's participation in a local street-league cup final. They had lost the match. I arrived as the members of the committee had ranged themselves on the stairs of a hired canteen ready to greet the players and officials of the winning side. The winners arrived in triumphal mood. Clutching their bottles of soft drink a little too hard in order to control their disappointment, the losers bravely stood their ground to offer praise and congratulations to the opposing side.

The club was run by teenagers, but with patronage from senior figures. Good discipline – from managing a fixture list through to offering congratulations to their noisy opponents at the celebratory party – was an entirely justified source of pride for the young people involved in running the club who significantly lacked other opportunities to hone their organizational talents.

After five years in the bush as militia fighters the young conscript fighters of the RUF have few social assets above and beyond an ability to combine and co-operate on operations. For some ex-fighters, their principal skill (after several years of missed education) will be a knowledge of ambush tactics (an activity requiring considerable co-operation and reserves of self-discipline). Running soccer competitions at the camp may be one way of building quickly and constructively on that tenuous sociological capacity.

Conclusion

This chapter is speculative, and descriptively it is manifestly 'thin' rather than 'thick', but it may serve to direct attention to the role of football as a universal idiom for the generation and practice of certain kinds of social knowledge. Under-age fighters in wars such as those currently being fought in Liberia and Sierra Leone have been drastically desocialized. Resocialization of combatants who may have spent more than a third of their lives in bush warfare is no easy task. The cultural infrastructure (of shared understandings and collective representations) has been stretched dangerously thin by these experiences of anarchic struggle. Easily understood, cheap and widely popular, soccer is sufficiently free of cultural content to be an effective medium for the forging of co-operative skills from scratch.

This makes us think again about soccer violence. First there was violence, and then there was soccer. Perhaps soccer is one of the basic ways in which conditions of radical desocialization can be reversed. Perhaps only in a post-industrial society could such a simple possibility be neglected in favour of the more popular notion that rich and settled 'tribal' loyalties are a cause of soccer violence.

Postscript

Sports associations, including football clubs, are a recognized element in the 'social capital' of civil society (Putnam 1993). Recently, I had the opportunity to talk over the possible role of soccer in the social reintegration of ex-combatants with some organizers of soccer in the town of Bo. Already, it was known that 'rebel' combatants sometimes slipped into town to watch important games.

Each section (quarter) of the town of Bo has its own playing field, serving as a focus for youth and community activities. The fields at Durbar Ground and Ahmadiyya Secondary School (the latter serving as focus for two quarters – Bo Number Two and Njaiye Town) were visited, and their organizers interviewed. In most cases pitches are open areas dedicated by convention to the game, without stands or other facilities. There are no allocated clubhouses. Most weekdays there is a match in progress – boys under-15, intermediate, senior, women's team, or a practice – from about half-past four in the afternoon until dusk (about 6.30 p.m.). Players have team-strips, but not all have boots. Pitches are bare, gravelly patches, generally with netless goals, some are entirely improvised. Ball supply and maintenance is a constant worry. Cheap plastic balls wear out quickly on gravelly ground, and frequently burst in play, sometimes bringing matches to a premature end. Considerable numbers of people, predominantly youths, from each quarter turn out each day as a matter of pride to support whichever 'home' side is playing that evening. Spectators turn up even for informal training and friendly matches, but interest is greatest in the various regular inter-quarter league and cup matches.

Team organizers were articulate about soccer's social role, especially for Bo youth. Clubs apply a disciplinary code to spectators as well as players. For example, young people who escape 'household duties' to watch matches are banned for a certain number of matches. Violent and ill-disciplined players face exclusion by club officials in addition to referees' sanctions on the field of play. Players grumble about 'incompetent' or 'dishonest' referees, but concede that annual coaching events by the Sierra Leone Amateur Football Association (at Bo School) have improved the general standard of conduct at matches. The organizers at Durbar Ground were explicit that 'good' games and 'good' public order go hand in hand – that football is a medium through which social skills can be acquired. Since Durbar Ground is a Muslim praying ground it is thought especially important to stress discipline and the avoidance of drugs and alcohol among players and spectators alike. As one informant observed, the potential of soccer for facilitating post-war conciliation cannot be under-estimated as it is such a popular rallying point for youth.

Notes

1. ECOMOG stands for Economic Community of West Africa Monitoring Group.
2. United Liberian Movement for Democracy.

Chapter 8

The Use of *Juju* in Football:[1] Sport and Witchcraft in Tanzania

Anne Leseth

Why does one football team win consistently and another lose? Certainly the winning team will have players who are more talented. But why are these players more talented and where does their skill come from? These are the questions which football magic deals with in Dar-es-Salaam in Tanzania. Traditionally witchcraft is practised in *ngoma* (traditional dances) related to dancing competitions. The dancing group which attracts the biggest audience is the one which wins.[2] The victory will be credited, not on the performance in itself, but on the *dawa* (medicine) used by the medicine man. Old people told me that the use of *juju* in *ngoma* dances is necessary for the survival of Tanzanian tradition and culture. Today the practice of witchcraft also takes place in modern sports and games, and seems to be most widespread in football. In this chapter I will discuss the use of witchcraft in football, a practice which for many Europeans probably appears as highly 'exotic'. I will not enter into a discussion on witchcraft in *ngoma* dances, but rather call attention to the cultural continuity between *ngoma* and football when it comes to the practice of *juju*.[3]

Football and Witchcraft in Tanzania

Some Tanzanians trace the origin of football back to traditional sports like *Mieleka* (wrestling) and *Nagga* (a traditional game similar to rugby), while others claim it has a British origin. The Tanzanian Football Association (FAT) was formed in 1935 during the British colonial period. After independence in 1961, the leadership of sports in Tanzania was organized by the Ministry of Education and Culture. The National Sports Council (NSC) was formed in 1967 and is the only sports institution, after the Ministry, which is responsible for all sports development and supervision in the country. FAT is responsible for the organization of training and tournaments throughout Tanzania. It is the best organized Sports Association in the country and holds annual league tournaments, from district to national level.[4]

In Tanzania, as in many other countries in the world, football is an extremely popular sport which draws hundreds of thousands of people, mainly men, to games every day, players as well as supporters. Football as a key to masculine culture seems to be a virtually world-wide phenomenon. In Tanzania, the popularity of football must also be related to the strong social dominance which men possess. As a sociologist at the University of Dar-es-Salaam stated: 'Sport in Tanzania is equal to football and football is equal to men.' But in Tanzania a victory in football can be accredited not to the excellent footballing skills of a team or to technical virtuosity, but to some mystical powers. The witchdoctor is a leading character in creating *juju* power. He is consulted by a representative from one of the competing teams before a crucial match. (He cannot 'treat' two competing teams.) Witchdoctors in Dar-es-Salaam agree that training is important for football players in order for the team to have a better chance of winning. But in addition to that there must be witchcraft – 'Huweza kushinda bila ya uchawi' – you can't win without witchcraft, the witchdoctors say. One of them explained to me how this *juju* power was practised:

> An important football match was going to take place at the National Stadium in Dar-es-Salaam one Saturday afternoon. Team X had been frequently defeated by their rivals for a long period, which was very humiliating. The night before this match, some people from team X entered the stadium with a goat. Right there on the pitch the goat was buried alive. The following day, the players of team Y would be running over the goat, and thus lose their strength and endurance. The buried goat would ensure the victory for team X, unless, of course, team Y used any similar powers against them. On entering the ground, team X did not pass through the gate, but they climbed over the wall surrounding the stadium. In this way they avoided being affected by *juju* power which could have been smeared on the gate by members of the rival team. In addition to the goat, this act made the rival team Y very nervous.

'So, did they win?' I asked. 'Why shouldn't they win after doing all this *juju* business?' he replied, 'the rival team went down by three goals to nil.' The match result is in this way magical and the victory can be explained with reference to the best 'treatment'.

In pre-colonial times, most people in Tanzania believed in the efficacy of witchcraft, but they differed in methods and techniques of combating the practice (Mesaki 1992). Cases of witchcraft were treated by local authorities, elders and courts according to their degree of seriousness. The missionaries of black Africa saw witchcraft as a sign of a general backwardness (Mesaki 1992). During the colonial period (from 1896 to 1961) the Germans and the British tried to control the use of witchcraft. Witches were killed or condemned to death. By prohibiting traditional games and dances which they found barbarian and pagan, they tried to abolish the witchcraft beliefs which were practised, especially in traditional dances. The introduction of modern sports was an important tool in this process of civilizing Africa into conformity with the Western world view (see in particular, Mangan 1986). Through ball games and athletics, the colonial rulers believed Africans would become more civilized. The British administration (from 1919 to 1961) systematized the control of witchcraft by legislation. A witchcraft ordinance was first drafted in 1922. The Act prohibited the practice in all its manifestations (i.e. naming, actual practice or even pretence) and spelt out stern penalties for any breaches. The post-independence government retained the witchcraft ordinance to demonstrate official abhorrence towards the illogicality of witchcraft beliefs and practices (ibid.).

The practice of witchcraft in football can be understood as a traditional belief persisting in a modern sports context. People I met in Dar-es-Salaam disagreed on notions related to the use of witchcraft in football. To become a professional football player in Tanzania, implies being a 'drop-out' from the school system. It is difficult to combine education and sports. Most football players in the first division (league) have had a maximum of seven years of education. Therefore, some Tanzanians argue that the belief in witchcraft must be related to the players' level of education. They claim witchcraft beliefs are contributing significantly towards the fall of footballing standards in the country. A member of the National Sports Council puts it this way:

Exercises are the only way to success! The belief in witchcraft is deteriorating in sports. We are now moving forward scientifically. But instead of concentrating on planning their football by putting more emphasis on training, football coaches and players concentrate more on this *juju* business.

But there is not necessarily a correspondence between education and belief in witchcraft. The journalist Wilson Kaigarula wrote in the Tanzanian newspaper *Sunday News* (15 December 1984):

Witchcraft is a primitive phenomenon that thrives on the psychological weakness of people who have been brain-washed into believing that they can be assisted, by the so-called witchdoctors, to prevent negative events and predetermine good things. It is a great pity that the victims of the primitive propaganda include enlightened people, amongst whom are science graduates.

But despite this condescending attitude towards the practice of witchcraft, there are people who justify their belief by claiming that witchcraft is a part of the Tanzanian tradition and that it is necessary for the development and persistence of Tanzanian sports and culture. As a former football manager, Mr Abu, explained to me:

Our Government and the National Law don't believe in witchcraft, but in football the use of *uchawi* is a positive fact. It's a way to speed things up. You can't win without *uchawi*. So you see, our traditions will always be part of the new things, the modern life. If not, we will die.

The arguments above reflect two different ways of explaining witchcraft beliefs; focusing on rationality and cultural continuity respectively. But despite official abolition of witchcraft beliefs, the practice still persists, in sports as well as in everyday life. Mesaki (1992) argues that because witchcraft is hard to grasp, it is also difficult to devise effective ways of combating and checking its manifestations in the modern State. Yet why is witchcraft hard to grasp and why does it persist in football?

Witchcraft and the Element of Unpredictability

The use of witchcraft in football is not only common in Tanzania. In West Africa, beliefs in witchcraft are so strong that not many years ago some of the teams used to make sacrifices on the pitch before kick-off by slaughtering goats, sheep etc. The urban Zulu in South Africa have football teams which used to slaughter a goat before the season, 'to open the doors to luck', and the end of the season used to be marked by another slaughter (Scotch 1968). These witchcraft activities are differently named in football countries: *juju*, 'voodoo', etc. The belief in witchcraft explains the inexplicable: why one football team wins and another loses. The practice of witchcraft rationalizes the element of unpredictability in football which is not only related to the Tanzanian or African experience, but is a common experience within the world of football. I was told by a Tanzanian footballer that (during the World Cup tournament in Italy in 1990) President Menem of Argentina watched TV while sitting in the same position and on the same chair whenever Argentina played. To do otherwise could have brought misfortune upon his favoured team. People cope with the experience of unpredictability in different ways and attach different labels to it. Hognestad (1995) makes a useful distinction between a game and a ritual to explain these dynamics of football.[5] Football must be understood as both game and ritual, as a ceaseless endeavour to break the equilibrium of life. Hognestad argues that the elements of unpredictability and uncertainty are contained within the ritual framing of the football match. He quotes one Scottish football fan who says that when he hopes for his team to win it is like a prayer: 'You're there praying that this will happen and it does happen . . . they score the goal you were praying for and you get ecstatic . . . you know . . . you're saying: please give us this goal, and when it does happen it's just great' (ibid.: 48). There are an endless number of stories about how fans and even club managers all over the world believe in doing or not doing certain things in order to bring luck to, or influence the performance of, their teams. Even in 'rational', post-colonial nations, the top international players prefer playing in the same jersey throughout their careers: the Dutch player Johan Cruyff consistently wore the number 14 shirt in the 1970s. But the parallel between the use of witchcraft in football and European fans' prayers is not uncomplicated. The differences are rooted in the question of rationality.

The Evolutionary Paradigm

John Mbiti (1969) argues that most of the distorted ideas about witchcraft and magic in Africa have come through European and American popular writers, missionaries and colonial administrators. Within a scientific discourse, the use of witchcraft in football can be explained as primitive and as a kind of social pathology. This way of thinking about magic and witchcraft has been a dominant paradigm among anthropologists as well as among the colonial rulers and missionaries in Africa. The anthropologists Edward Tylor (1871) and James Frazer (1922) have had a decisive influence on the anthropological understanding of witchcraft, magic and sorcery. Their distinction between magic, science and religion led to an evolutionary paradigm in which the belief in witchcraft is to be understood as a primitive system of belief. Evans-Pritchard (1937) went a great deal further than his predecessors in trying to understand witchcraft beliefs among the Azande and how it presents itself to the Azande themselves. But in his writings there is more than one remark about the difficulty he found in shaking off the 'unreason' on which Zande life is based. As he states: 'Witches, as the Azande conceive them, clearly cannot exist' (ibid.: 18). Evans-Pritchard returns to the fact that science is ultimately the only system which can explain how things 'really are'. While Evans-Pritchard wanted to understand the logic of witchcraft, Max Gluckman (1956) was concerned with witchcraft as a language to express conflict, but nevertheless as a 'distorting obscurity' (ibid.: 108). Gluckman argued that science represents, from the African point of view, an extremely limited system for explaining total scenarios. While science explains *how* a given process occurs, witchcraft explains *why* the process occurs in the first place. Scotch (1968) draws on Gluckman's conflict theory in his discussion on witchcraft and football among the urban Zulu in South Africa. Scotch argues that the use of witchcraft in football can be understood as a response to change and a way of meeting the exigencies of new life-situations. This perspective is interesting, but too simplistic in its functional and tautological explanations. Peter Winch (1970) makes a crucial point when he criticizes Evans-

Pritchard's approach on witchcraft. Winch disagrees with the Evans-Pritchard argument that the criteria applied in scientific experimentation constitute a link between our ideas and an independent reality, while magical methods of thought do not. Winch (ibid.: 81) puts it this way: 'The trouble is that the fascination science has for us makes it easy for us to adopt its scientific form as a paradigm against which to measure the intellectual respectability of other modes of discourse.' Winch argues that it is necessary to investigate the role such concepts as witchcraft have in a society, rather than trying to falsify its existence.

Following Winch's argument, the practice of witchcraft in football must be understood in relation to a highly complex system of socio-cultural processes. Witchcraft in Tanzania is one of several answers to misfortune. Witchcraft is invoked, as a protection against disruption and an insurance for success on the one hand, and a retaliatory agency on the other. But the belief in witchcraft must also be related to a kind of Tanzanian moral philosophy which is very alive, not only in sports, but in everyday life. People have an idea of equality. It is important to be good, but at the same time you shall not be too good or be too aware of it – for a reason. If you build a house which is much bigger than your neighbour's house, you are exposing yourself to *juju* power. You cannot feel completely safe.

In competitive sports, people 'make justice' through this idea of equality by explaining a victory with reference to a magical power, *juju*. When there is a competition in *ngoma*, there is no referee there to adjudicate on who is the winner. The dancers have an intuition themselves of being the winners according to the response from the audience. But you should not claim out loud that you are a winner. If you do, you are exposing yourself to *juju*.

Nothing harmful happens 'by chance', everything is 'caused' by someone directly or through the use of mystical power. Thus, I think it is fruitful to deal with witchcraft in football, not as a tautology but as part of a cultural field of lived experience. This implies an understanding of science and witchcraft as two more similar systems of beliefs, as two kinds of representation or ideas about our being-in-the-world. As Michael Jackson (1989: 101) puts it: 'It is not enough for us to decide whether witchcraft is a social pathology . . . for our task is to throw light on the lived experience that lies behind the masks and façades of category words.'

The Use of *Juju* and the Morality of Conduct

The use of *juju* is efficacious in competitions. An interesting point is that *ngoma* and football, as two apparently distinct cultural practices, have an 'intrinsic connection' when it comes to the use of *juju*. In *ngoma*, the element of competition is in a way 'hidden' when compared to modern sports like football. As I have mentioned in the introduction, people's notion of competition in *ngoma* differs from notions of competition in modern sports. The dancers are 'competing in creativity', rather than in cleverness, to get attention from the audience. The idea of equality makes the practice of *juju* crucial in football as well as in *ngoma*. When two Tanzanian football teams are going to play a match, no one will claim that one team is better than the other. Both will rather say 'we cannot win'. In order for there to be a loser, *juju* must therefore be applied. But at the same time, the competing teams have to be on approximately the same level if *juju* is going to work. This idea of equality is related to practice, it is a morality of conduct rather than a morality of being. Mbiti (1969: 214) argues that this 'dynamic ethic' is the very essence of African morality in general. It defines a person for what he *does*, rather than for what he is.[6] I find this dynamism of great interest, because it illuminates the importance of the *practice* of *juju*, rather than *juju* as a 'thought' or a belief system.

The use of witchcraft in football is not part of an everyday discourse, but rather a shared experience and a secrecy. This allusiveness was striking when I tried to get some information about the use of witchcraft in football during my stay in Tanzania. It was always me who broached the subject with football players and coaches, in the directorship of sports and among the public: 'Have you ever heard of the use of witchcraft in football or sports in general?' Perhaps my way of asking was too direct. Very often people avoided answering the question or gave me a very ambiguous reply like:

> I have heard of *juju* in football, but never seen it, because it is not possible to see witchcraft. It is a tradition. But I don't believe in it. Football is not *uchawi* (witchcraft). Football is exercise. There are people who believe in it. It helps to get a victory. Some believe in it, others don't. It is important to win. To win is good! To deal with *uchawi* in football is a secrecy, so I haven't seen it. It is difficult to get any

information of how *uchawi* is used when you don't see it. *Uchawi* is different things I cannot know what it is.

The problems I had in grasping people's experience and knowledge about the use of witchcraft in football, almost made me give up the subject. But then I got to know Faibi. Faibi had been a football coach for many years. Now he worked within the National Sports Council. One day I met him in town, and on the way to his office we chatted about football and sport. I said I was interested in the use of witchcraft in football. Did he know anything about it? Surprisingly, Faibi answered without hesitation:

> Yes, *juju* is in action right now – people believe in it – the football players use it. Most of the football clubs have formed what they call executive committees. These are not normal committees, but committees within other committees. Their main duty is to plan all the witchcraft arrangements required to enable their teams to win. A lot of the club's money is kept aside for 'executive' activities. Players, leaders and other officials of these clubs claim that defeating a rival team in football depends on how their team has fully prepared itself in *juju* affairs. If you don't believe in this, you risk being suspected of collusion with, or being used for the interests of, the rival teams. So it is a complicated matter. When I was a coach for one of the big teams in Tanzania, people from the executive committee came to me and asked whether they could do this and that *juju* thing with the players of my team or not. I said all right, you can do what you want, except cutting and vaccinating the players. Vaccination implies cutting the skin of the body, and putting some magical powder in the wounds. The *mganga* (witchdoctor) came to the team before the match, and told the players what to do.

We had reached Faibi's office, and then he started whispering to me: 'Of course, it doesn't work, but this *juju* business has a psychological effect. Therefore I permitted it, even if I didn't believe it myself.' Faibi gave me his hand. 'Well, I think I have answered your question, madame,' he said and went into his office.

From this moment on, my curiosity in this subject rose considerably. Those who willingly started to talk about the subject were often men like Faibi, former football coaches, old people or people who dealt with *ngoma* dances. Footballers, on the contrary, always told me that they didn't know about this practice and that they didn't believe in it. During my stay I got to know two witchdoctors (*mganga/waganga*) in the suburbs of Dar-es-Salaam who taught me the practice of *juju* in more detail.

The Sacrifice

The *mganga* argues that when it comes to football, exercise gives you more experience and improves your skills, while *juju* gives your spirit power. But you can't use *juju* on a team which is not training. If a local team are going to play against a national team, the local team will be defeated. It will be no use giving them *juju*. Wherever there are people, there are dangers. Among the spectators at a football match or among the audience watching *ngoma* dances, there are potential witches. Thus the football players have to protect themselves, not only against the rival team, but also against the people watching.

The *mganga* will make *juju* which can be used against the rival team. He will also find medicine to protect the team from *juju* which can possibly be used against them. *Juju* is made by a *kafara* (plural: *mafara*), a sacrifice. The goat (noted earlier) which was buried on the National Stadium was a *kafara*. Birds are also used. A member and ardent supporter of one of Tanzania's first division teams, told me a story about how ten years ago he had travelled sixty kilometres searching for *kinega* – a certain bird – which was to be sacrificed to enable his team to defeat its traditional rival. This bird was later slaughtered, burned by fire, and its ashes smeared on to each player of the team on the day of the match. Pigeons are easier to find and are frequently used as a *kafara*. Pigeons are messengers, both in a direct and in a figurative sense. When the *mganga* smears the blood from a pigeon on the gate of the pitch, the message is clear: '*Juju* is here.' *Kafara* can also be smeared on the skin or clothes of the player, like the *kinega* above, and thus the players are protected during the match. All or some of the players of the team can also be asked to do 'certain things'. One of Tanzania's most famous football players, who has now retired, told me that not only had the players to hide certain 'things' in their socks and shorts, but sometimes club officials and fans used to sleep at the cemetery the day before a crucial match. The *mganga* explains that on the cemetery people get strength from the devils and the witches. They dance with them and they are empowered by witchcraft to resist *juju* from the rival team. In addition to the *kafara* and the 'ritual' actions, the words of the *mganga* are necessary to make the *juju* power work. Through prayers and sayings in Arabic, the words are said to work through the *kafara* and thus the *mganga* 'blessings' are extremely potent.

The *waganga* have various ways of performing their skill. Some have learned their work from their fathers or grandfathers, while others have been educated through methods of Koranic medicine (see also Larsen 1995). A specialist in traditional medicine can read the character of a person by knowing the person's astrological sign or star, as well as her/his name and the name of the parents. Dr Abu had acquired his knowledge from his father, who was an important *mganga*, while he in turn had been taught by his father and so on. Dr Sogon, who titled himself Dr Professor, was educated in practical astrology and Koranic medicine, and was in many ways a more 'modern' *mganga*. Dr Professor was known among football teams for his success in making *juju*; while Dr Abu preferred to treat people who suffered from serious diseases, rather than football teams. He even claimed that the use of *juju* in football was an evil practice. So I went to Dr Professor to participate in a ritual 'treatment' of a football team.

How to Make *Juju* for a Football Team

A local football club have sent the entire team[7] to Dr Professor's office, a small mud-hut in a suburb of Dar-es-Salaam. The office consists of one room, about twelve metres square. All the players are sitting down on the floor in a circle. I am seated on a bench against the wall. Dr Professor informs the players about my presence and they accept my being there. The team have brought with them the names of the players of the rival team and a living black hen. Dr Professor tells me that they use a black, rather than a white, hen for magical purposes. The first thing to do is to examine the power of the team by using practical astrology. This is possible by making a *kafara*. By this practical astrology, Dr Professor will find out which elements the players of the rival team are made of. The four central elements in practical astrology are fire (heat), water (liquid), wind (gas) and stone (solid). The goalkeeper of the rival team is 'fire-hot'. Then Dr Professor makes a *kafara*, an egg, and throws it on to the fire. In this way he has destroyed the goalkeeper's power. The next step is the hen. Dr Professor holds the hen around its neck while lighting some incense on the floor which is intended to 'fill' the hen with incense and mystical powers. Dr Professor starts mumbling prayers in Arabic and the players are asked to close their eyes. The Professor takes the hen in a circle around each players head, seven times for each, all the while mumbling Arabic words. These words will provide the players with the power that works through the *kafara*. When this part of the treatment is finished, everybody is asked to leave except the coach. The players are given pieces of paper with their personal astrology written on. It is very important that the players wear these scraps of paper during the match. If a player loses his he has to go off the pitch.

When all but the coach have left, the killing of the hen remains to be done. Dr Professor steps out into the backyard were he cuts the hen's head off. He gives the head to the coach and tells him to burn it and bury the ashes on the pitch.[8] The coach is also given three *mafara*: a big fruit (papaw), an egg and a handful of sand, with which the coach is told to do 'certain things'. He will boil the fruit and afterwards put some of the water on each player. Dr Professor has written in Arabic the names of each rival player on the egg. The coach is told to bury this egg on the pitch. The handful of sand he is also told to boil in water. Then he is going to smear the liquid on to each player. The goalkeeper is going to smear this liquid in his hands. The rest of the sand must be mixed with the sand in his goal. After all these instructions, the coach leaves Dr Professor's office. While shaking the *mganga*'s hand, he claims that he is now calm and fearless about the match.

The final session of treatment is done without the players or the coach. Dr Professor makes one more *kafara* to destroy the power of the eleven players of the rival team. In this case, he uses the coconut as a *kafara*. He writes on it the practical astrology of each player of the rival team, and puts the signs (fire, water, wind, stone) on each of the eleven coconuts. In this way, each coconut represents a player of the rival team. Dr Professor goes out in the backyard and, while mumbling prayers, he destroys the coconuts, one by one. Now he has rendered the power of the rival team useless and the match can start.

The Business in *Juju*

The success or failure of a football team is invariably attributed to the skills of the *mganga* as well as to the natural talent of the players. The *waganga* earn lots of money from the clubs for their treatments, *if* the team wins. In this case, the team won 6–0, and Dr Professor got his reward. The executive committees spend huge sums of the club's money in their endeavours to bring victory for their team. Hence, witchcraft in football is big business. *Waganga* have enriched themselves enormously through the 'wages' they receive from leaders of the various clubs. There have also been several incidents of fraud connected to their practice. Some practitioners are real experts in the business, like the *mganga*, but there are others who supply cheap, false articles for the sake of gain. Some football officials have taken huge sums of the club's money claiming that it is required for witchcraft purposes, while in reality the money is pocketed for private use. The leaders then arrange a trick: they hire people to do 'certain things', certain movements which make the players believe they use *juju*. I was told a story about a young boy who was given some money to walk into the headquarters of the rival team. He just entered the club, greeted those who were inside and walked out again, saying nothing. This incident was enough to frighten the officials and players into believing that this strange being was either a spirit or a ghost who had been called up by the other team. And when the players came on to the pitch, they were so seized with fear that they couldn't help conceding two quick goals.

There are those who believe in witchcraft in football, explaining it as a Tanzanian tradition, and there are those who use it for commercial purposes. But the business in *juju* and the belief in *juju* must be seen as two aspects of the same phenomenon, rather than as contradictory practices. Dealing with football as a business venture can be a way of coping with the experience of unpredictability related to the game. Players and spectators all over the world believe in doing 'certain things' in order to help win a match. Many of us play the pools and check our coupon every week. We spend huge sums of money trying to predict the results. Both fans and players prepare for a match and try to influence the strength of those on the pitch. The world-famous Argentinian player Maradona, has at least a hundred pairs of boots to choose from every time he is going to play a match. But it is not only because it is practical to have many shoes when you are a football player. Each pair also has its history, and is in a way magical.[9] These practices and beliefs differ in content from the practice of *juju*, but can be understood as 'magical elements' within the ritual framing of the match.

Concluding Remarks

The morality of conduct which can be related to the practice of *juju*, makes it necessary to understand *juju* in football as a complex system of social, economic and psychological phenomena related to concepts of ethics and justice. The idea of equality is a cultural experience which makes sense of the continuity between *ngoma* and football. This experience is continuously being re-created within cultural practices. But how is the result of a football match, which usually expresses an inequality, to be explained? The victorious team does not win only because of their skills, but because it uses the best *dawa* (medicine) and because it has the best *mganga*. When Dr Professor makes a treatment for a team that wins 6–0, his treatment can explain much of their success. In this way, the players are somehow 'released' from the responsibility of winning. In Western countries, there are many stories of football stars who can't handle success. People in Dar-es-Salaam told me that it is your responsibility not to behave as if you are better than others. But it is not your responsibility if you and your team win a football match. It is *juju*.

Glossary*

Dawa: A medicine, medication, anything supplied by a doctor, including a 'charm' or a talisman, used by native medicine-men. All words in African languages which are translated by 'medicine' also have the meaning of 'magic anecdote'. Most 'medicines' are intended for good purposes, but some serve evil intentions.

Juju: The word *juju* has two different explanations emerging from its linguistic origins. It can be from French creole, joujou – 'plaything' or 'toy'. It probably refers to worry-beads or ornaments worn by people as amulets for protection. Some Muslims say that the word comes from the Koran – *yajuju* and *majuju* (plural). They believe that the different explanations converge in the meaning of 'evil spirit'. In Tanzania *juju* is used as a nickname for *uchawi* (witchcraft).

* References: Knappert (1990) and Johnson (1939)

Kafara: An offering, a charm. The coach for the football team is given one or several *kafaras* from the witchdoctor. A *kafara* might be an egg, the head of a chicken, a goat or even a human being.

Mchawi (plural: *Wachawi):* A witch, either a woman or a man, who practises black magic *(uchawi).*

Mganga (plural: *waganga):* A medicine-man and a wizard. His practice is mainly under the permission and control of the government. He is a specialist of various kinds of traditional and Koranic medicine.

Ngoma: A drum. *Ngoma* is extended to include any kind of dance or music in general. When people talk about *ngoma,* it is thus often with reference to the whole dancing context: the drummers, the dancers, the singing and any other instruments used.

Notes

1. *Juju* is a Kiswahili nickname for the Kiswahili word *uchawi* (witchcraft). In football-related contexts *juju* is the most common expression. African people rarely draw the rather academic distinction between witchcraft, sorcery and evil magic. The term 'witchcraft' is therefore used here in a popular way to designate the harmful employment of mystical power in all its different manifestations.
2. The principle of winning in *ngoma* is not equivalent to that in modern sports. In *ngoma,* you can technically perform a dance badly, but nevertheless you and your group can attract a big audience by singing an entertaining song while dancing.
3. This chapter is based on fieldwork carried out in Dar-es-Salaam, Tanzania, between 1992 and 1993, which also led to my thesis in social anthropology (Leseth 1995). I introduce a broader interpretive framework for examining bodily practices in general, and football and witchcraft are not discussed explicitly in my thesis. I am grateful for helpful suggestions and comments on this chapter made by Hans Kristian Hognestad and Eduardo Archetti.

4. At the district level in Dar-es-Salaam, football matches are a daily activity, both during and after tournaments. In Kinondoni district in Dar-es-Salaam, where I stayed, there was a football match every day from Monday to Sunday between 6 p.m. and 8 p.m.

5. Lévi-Strauss (1966: 32) distinguishes a game from a ritual in the following way: 'The main difference between a game and a ritual is precisely the creation, in the former, of a state of disunion between winners and losers. On the contrary, the function of a ritual is to create an organic relation between groups that initially are separated.'

6. In Western culture, Descartes' epigram: 'I think, therefore I am' is dominant and in great contrast to an African consciousness about the self as defined by Mbiti (ibid.): 'I am because we are, and since we are, therefore I am.'

7. It is not necessary for the entire football team to see the witchdoctor before a match. Sometimes the team sends a person from the executive committee or only the goalkeeper or the coach of the team.

8. The ashes have a certain symbolic value not only in *juju*. In England, it was very common for football fans, to make wills stating that upon their deaths, their ashes should be scattered across the pitch. To some extent, there is the underlying belief that this will bring victory to the team. Others believe they will be able to continue watching their teams after their death.

9. Eduardo Archetti introduced me to this illuminating example.

Chapter 9

Legislators and Interpreters: The Law and 'Football Hooligans'

Gary Armstrong and *Malcolm Young*

> So what is the function of criminal justice? It has a dramatist's function. It exists to say: we disapprove. It has rhetorical power. Prison cannot be practical, so the criminal justice system is mainly symbolic. In the old days, the men in wigs marched through the town to the assizes. And that, basically, is what the apparatus of the law does now.
>
> (Programme Notes from a play 'Murmuring Judges' by David Hare)

Introduction

This chapter considers the way the concept of 'football hooliganism' has been loosely structured and demonized by those defining a phenomenon that has often been glibly and too easily categorized as deviant and disgraceful. Our analysis uses an anthropological perspective. In the absence of a better term, we will use 'Partisan Fanship'[1] to denote what is more loosely defined as hooligan activity. We argue that partisan fanship is part of a complex social process which is constructed and played out almost as carnival (Turner 1974). It is largely misunderstood, misinterpreted and misrepresented, and this has led inexorably to vilification and a profound over-reaction. The complexity of the cultural context, we suggest, is more usefully considered by exploring the Geertzian 'webs of significance' (1975) which surround not only events at the ground on match day, but necessarily encompass the responses of the media, the activities of the police, and those who implement the legal process. The history of dealing with those involved, we contend, is better understood if their activities are seen to be part of what Turner

(1974, 1982) described as a 'processual social drama', in which all of the actors influence the events – and each other – as part of an interactive cultural dynamic.

The Power of the Law

A general principle of British law declares that, in most instances, opinions are not evidence. However, as Nietzsche reasoned, 'knowledge is power', and so almost inevitably those holding the reins in the domain of law enforcement have the power to impose their own opinionated version of events on to those whose voice in the discourse is muted or silent. In the public realm, where events surrounding the activities of partisan fanship are played out, there is rarely any shortage of witnesses to an incident. Yet the opinions or versions of reality that are subsequently generated often seem akin to those crime-statistics which we all sense are flawed, but which consistently retain the ability to create moral panics (see Young 1991). These official presentations or 'institutional truths' (Young 1993) provide a working capital for those in the domains of power, but they rarely reflect an absolute reality. Rather they gain their strength from their symbolic import, so that like the annual crime-statistics, there is simply no other version of events available to the public domain. Thus, the opinion that partisan fanship is to be equated with unacceptable hooligan activity continues to stand almost as a symbolic reflection of a belief in the 'left hand of darkness', which is then contained in the media soundbite, perhaps to be re-created by a politician seeking to enhance his or her credibility.

Football Revelry – A History of Control

The idea of football hooliganism might suggest that it is a new phenomenon, yet it has its roots in the age-old masculine pursuit of revelry. The game, it seems, has always troubled the authorities, perhaps because it reflects the spirit and wayward energy of the mob – *mobilis vulgus* or 'fickle crowd' of the early eighteenth century. Legislation has long been used to control football-related disorders. As far back as 1314, football was banned in London in an attempt to preserve public tranquillity, for it was feared the tumult and disorder surrounding these games might encourage sedition and treason. However, because there has never been a definition of 'hooliganism' nor any specific criminal offence of 'football hooliganism', it is necessary to consider the entire concept, and not merely take the authoritarian perception as truth. A crucial and often neglected factor in the situation under discussion is one which encompasses an infinitely fine set of gradations of an activity – is the response of an audience which fails to comprehend the nuances of what is occurring, and so codifies the entire gamut of behaviour as deviant. An energetic factor which evolves from complex notions of masculinity, a strong identification of club and town and some degree of personal flexibility further reinforces the stereotype. In their pursuit of the docile body that all institutions of power crave (Foucault 1977, 1980), the authorities seek appropriate responses and almost always ensure these are judgmental in form. This means that the public commentator, the media, the police, the politician, the social statistician and other conformist members of society help control the processes that stigmatize by establishing boundary-maintaining devices which ultimately render the fan simplistically defined as hooligan, and subsequently fined, imprisoned and degraded.

Since the 1960s the defined label 'hooligan fan' has increasingly been invoked as a problem for us all, so that moral entrepreneurs, ranging from journalists to academics and from policemen to football administrators, have enjoined law-makers to impose extra punishments and create new moralities in an effort to combat what they claim is escalating violence at matches. A convenient receptacle for a variety of prejudices, the 'hooligan' label has been applied to behaviour ranging from banter and shouting or the swearing that has for generations been the norm at the game, to the throwing of a toilet roll during a match. The need to link football fandom to disorder has seen the 'hooligan' label applied to incidents of assault that occur hours after the game and at locations miles from the ground. We would argue that the ideology of a 'problem of violent hooliganism' needs to be constantly set against the reality, for in England and Wales half a million people attend the 46 football league and cup matches every week of a thirty-five week season. Scotland has twenty games and 200,000 spectators weekly. In point of fact the relative rarity of violent ground-based disorder and the lack of social chaos in the streets surrounding the ground needs to be emphasized. Even the activities of those partisan fans who seek fights with opposing fans result in rare instances of injuries more significant than minor bruising. And although the Heysel stadium disaster had tragic consequences, the reality is that serious injury is not deliberately sought, and the death of a partisan fan occurring solely because of conflict is an extremely rare statistical event. For such fans know the rules of the game and know that any brawl is governed by a code much more subtle than a legal one, and that all this occurs in a domain where revenge is not pursued by seeking the protection of the law.

Even as this essay was drafted early in 1996 elderly men who had supported a team for decades were banned from grounds because of their swearing, and another excluded for throwing a digestive biscuit on to the pitch. This redefinition of what constitutes 'hooliganism' has become a dynamic process, a changing cultural form that influences not only the participants but also the classifying bureaucracies. The tendency throughout has been to demonize, so that apparent sinister behavioural mutations of cabalism and organized atrocities are increasingly presented; even though the evidence from prolonged participant observation (Armstrong 1996) suggests that the carnival of conflict is now acted out in venues largely removed from football. These carnivals of conflict, as detailed ethnography shows (ibid.), most often revolve around complex social rituals involving consenting male adults, and have clear parallels or commonality with the masculine games of bravado and status which anthropology has reported in societies across the globe. In these British jousts, the idea of 'their boys' coming up against 'our boys' is as close as the contestants get to defining their behavioural forms, for they simply live out the nuances and fine gradations of contest, conflict, male daring, honour and shame, pursuing these in a world which provides the essence of identity for young men across what is often a fifteen to twenty year period of attachment to meritocratic and ego-centred quasi-groups, which nevertheless defy anyone's attempts to assume leadership status (Armstrong 1996).

Standing outside these domains, and almost inevitably mis-understanding the form of partisan fanship, an undeniable 'institutional' truth argues there has been a moot change from the 'normal' hooliganism allegedly witnessed only two or three decades ago, to a degenerate vision in the 1990s of the 'patho-logical' hooligan. This has necessarily required the imposition of a regime of punitive sanctions accompanied by a rhetoric which always presents itself as serving the interests of deterrence. Through the enactment of a burgeoning set of legal controls, the guardians of moral and social welfare can thus claim to be defending a collective sentiment. But, of course, we might well ask who really needs protecting, and look with cold objectivity at just what it is that partisan fanship actually requires of its members.

The 'Hooligan' in Action

A decade of anthropological observation[2] suggests all participants take a complex set of ritualized procedures into the public domain, and that these operate simultaneously on several levels, with a multiplicity of meanings, even for those who are engaged in the performance. For the participants, the activities of partisan fanship are essentially pursued as a mannered, stylized and coherent drama, containing elements of script, production, direction and stage-craft. For the young players in these social dramas, the ultimate significance that their webs of meaning create lies in an ability to test events before an audience of colleagues and adversaries who provide the applause, the approbation and the status that come with an adrenalin rush of fear and excitement. A statement that 'fifty of their boys' are in some adjacent pub will mean little to the uncommitted fan. However, participants and informed observers will understand the statement in the light of procedures in the forms of dress, style of language and other social processes which ensure the drama follows certain approved and time-honoured lines. The fans strut, pose, tease, cajole and generally try to make 'their boys' lose face in finely nuanced games of dashing and daring. This requires the actors to show aspects of a specific masculine style, that they all understand to be about gaining or losing status. In a clear majority of cases these dramas are played out for the participants, and are not gratuitously undertaken to provoke outsiders or those who do not understand the genre. In many ways the activities clearly mirror those of the game itself, with its crucial dimensions of masculinity, sense of self and place, physical contest, costume, and an indefinite end result that might lie somewhere between glory and disaster. Properly played out, the match as social drama has the ritual element of theatre that Turner (op.cit. 1982) described, but its ending – unlike that of the theatrical play – is always unknown. For the committed fan, the game can thus generate a fission as the team melds together and creates moves that any choreographer might die for. It can also engender fierce despair when it all goes wrong. In their ancillary activities, a fan will be awarded high status for invading 'their space', for coming unscathed through this act of 'face' and for 'showing bottle'. Again the language says it all, and the nuance in 'giving it the big 'un', or 'walking through' (their fans in a pub) is part of a drama that simply cannot include those who look in from the outside. In all of this, however, the drama contains production assistants who are constrained by their own vision of events; so the uncommitted crowd, the police and club officials, all tend to bring a moral outrage even to those relatively mundane activities that the fans in the drama see only as part of the turbulent processes that mark the event as lying between the poles of transfixing agony and transforming ecstasy.

But even this is too simplistic, for the effect of cultural diversity is such that even partisan fanship is constrained by a vision that allows the participants to understand the clearly pre-determined boundaries, and be outraged themselves by certain activities inside, or external to, the group. For they too have their structures of normality and pathology. Thus all of the mostly masculine parties to the event – the players, the alleged hooligans, the police, the sports journalists, the officials and stewards, the politicians – can denigrate and attach 'shame' and degradation to a set of binary others. Indeed the ethnography clearly reveals how the fans have a fierce understanding of those who transgress and who are said to be acting beyond what is within the bounds of partisan fanship. In all of this, it is the interpretation of events which is crucial, for the various performers tend to speak somewhat different languages. Most encounters encompassed under an externally imposed banner of 'hooliganism' are a form of masculine cultural collateral, to be bartered in a competitive and ranked system that trades in futures even as it operates as a cascading anti-structural drama which contains the elements of what Turner (1964, 1969) described as 'communitas' and 'liminality' (for the liminoid).[3] In this act of moving to the margins, Turner argues, 'an emphasis on spontaneity, immediacy and "existence" throws into relief one of the senses in which communitas contrasts with structure [and] is of the now; [while] structure is rooted in the past and extends into the future through language, law and custom' (1974: 99–100). His vision of 'liminality', developed from Van Gennep's work on *rites de passage* (1960), describes the carnivalesque aspect of operating in the betwixt and between situation of marginality, a place where a time for reflection on the constraints of the structural process occurs. Whether the opportunity is taken up however, is another matter, but even the least reflective of 'the boys' is aware that genuine violence is *not* the motivating force behind his gatherings. Indeed, though the performers periodically enjoy the performance aspects of threat and disorder, this leads to violence and serious injury only on rare occasions.[4] This is because the carnival is actually founded on constantly circling and tension-filled modes of thought and action which are based in masculine and regionally specific ideologies of 'honour' and 'shame', 'reputation' and 'hardness', 'ritual presentation' and extremely 'coherent and mannered responses' (Armstrong 1994).

The Vision from the Barrier

Those performers in the drama who act as commentators or umpires tend to contextualize these ideologies in terms of unambiguous condemnation, and the police response generally has two dimensions. The first dimension lies in the official account set in the form of the press release, or the evidence placed before the court or at some tribunal. This almost always presents the police as righteous and humane advocates of 'the people' who work to enforce a publicly acclaimed morality that is well defined and legally exacting. The second, or unofficial reality, has included the following ambiguous control measures and the use of extra-legal irritants, including occasions of extended detention of alleged hooligans who fail to be charged; 'instant justice' in the form of assaults; ejections from the match made on spurious grounds; forced removal from public transport; the turning back of hired coaches and other vehicles; refusal of entry to grounds for no easily identifiable reason; and the blanket photographing and video recording of fan identity for police databanks. That many of these unofficial measures are witnessed by the public at large yet fail to attract condemnation says much about the way the 'hooligan' identity has been preached against. Few can even begin to contemplate the support of an alleged hooligan in the face of a detractor's vision of his condemnable actions, for the law requires and shapes the evidential and semantic boundaries; while the public vision is directed by the police and focused through the

media, who are served up the court case, the soundbite and the
public-relations presentation.

According to police evidence presented to the 1990 Home
Affairs Committee (HAC), hooligan gatherings had been increasingly composed along quasi-military lines from the mid-1980s,
with highly structured roles founded in what can only be interpreted as original sin motivated by 'outright wickedness' (pg: 10).
Allegedly committing a variety of crimes to finance football-related
atrocities, some six thousand known and *suspected* (our italics)
hooligans were biographically profiled on a centralized database,
and categorized for their often unproven involvement in a set of
classified crime-events, entitled 'Drugs', 'Fraud', 'Auto-Crime' and
'Others'. This again illustrates hooliganism as a growth industry,
which is not necessarily reflected in the numbers of participants,
nor in the frequency of their appearance on the streets. Rather the
expansiveness attributed to hooliganism lies in the way institutions
think, for as Foucault (1970) argues, institutions overcome
individual thought and strait-jacket minds and bodies. Thus an
ever-expanding set of antagonists becomes imperative, for, as
Douglas (1987: 92) persuasively argues:

> Institutions systematically direct individual memory and channel
> perceptions into forms compatible with the relations they authorize.
> They fix processes that are essentially dynamic, they hide their
> influence, and rouse our emotions to a standardized pitch . . . Add to
> all this that they endow themselves with rightness and send their
> mutual corroboration cascading through all levels of our information
> system. No wonder they easily recruit us into joining their narcissistic
> self-contemplation. Any problems we try to think about are auto-
> matically transformed into their own organizational problems. The
> solutions they proffer only come from the limited range of their
> experience. If the institution is one that depends on participation, it
> will reply to our frantic question: 'More participation!' If it is one
> that depends on authority, it will only reply 'More authority!'.
> Institutions have the pathetic megalomania of the computer whose
> whole vision of the world is its own program.

The Legal Framework

As with the demonization of the 'drug fiend' and subsequent
explosion in drugs legislation in the 1960s (see Young 1994),
so the legislators have used an increasing number of Acts of

Parliament to justify claims that a spirit of mayhem rather than carnival is at large in the hooligan domain. Various civil and criminal laws have been utilized, ranging from the ambiguities in some perceived breach of the peace that has been contained over the centuries by the 1361 Justice of the Peace Act, to the specificities of the 1991 Football (Offences) Act. The 1861 Offences Against the Persons Act – passed in what Pearson (1983) describes as the great year of legislation (for it included a first complete Larceny Act and the Malicious Damage Act) – has provided for a variety of assault and wounding charges; while the 1936 Public Order Act, and its expanded re-creation in the new 1986 Public Order Act – declared by the then Home Secretary as 'a law against hooligans' – provides for charges of Violent Disorder and Threatening Behaviour. As with those nineteenth-century street-visible offences of drunkenness, these are subjective matters which exist within the minds of those in the institutions of control, and which allow the police the discretion to offer opinions about, or define just who it is who suffers the variable effects of such inexact concepts as 'harassment, alarm or distress'.

Since the 1980s, fans have faced more serious charges of Affray, Unlawful Assembly, Riot, and Conspiracy to Cause Affray. However, definitional and evidential problems have seen the forces of authority faced with many embarrassing court-room dismissals and claims for compensation. Other laws were aimed specifically at the fan, for example, the Sporting Events (Control of Alcohol) Act of 1985. This Act was based on the premiss that to drink is to be a hooligan, and set out to control alcohol use in vehicles travelling to games, and to put a stop to the time-honoured activity of having a drink before the match by denying those who had done so from gaining access to the ground. Other laws setting out to create a Foucaultian docile body have aimed to exclude hooligans. For example, the Football Spectators Act of 1989 sought to introduce ID cards, and to confiscate the ID cards of any miscreants. This proved unworkable, but restriction orders for those convicted of 'football-related offences' abroad were introduced. These bilateral agreements saw prevention measures ranging from an outright ban from football grounds, to the conditions that fans report to police stations on match days. One inquiry, responding to the establishment belief in control and the denial of liminal activity, suggested electronic tagging as a potential measure (see The Taylor Report: 1989); while the Football

(Offences) Bill created three match-day crimes of 'throwing a missile', 'trespassing on the field of play' and 'chanting racist or offensive words'. The missile, of course, need not be some Exocet, for a biscuit can suffice; while the control of chanting seems set to challenge an ancient match-day norm of denying a referee's parentage.

These extra measures were introduced despite the Association of Chief Police Officers stating (in the HAC document) that they considered the existing legislation to be totally adequate for dealing with hooliganism. Meanwhile, with regard to the legislation, the policing of football has been increasingly pro-active, with control measures becoming a product of local emphasis and pre-match intelligence briefings. In this situation, arrests are often enacted with a gusto which seems not to be practised on others who commit similar acts elsewhere in society. Again there are few to question the validity of any extra-legal aspects of police action, for the 'institutional truths' encompassed in the negative vision of hooligan ideology have no source of alternative legitimization; and post-1990, a fierce commercial imperative has actively sanitized the football ground, to encourage the attendance of women, children and spectators who are, in general, viewed as the 'respectable' and a civilising influence on young men. A new morality has thus been imposed so that any appearance or reflection of the spirit of carnival, with its swirling social dissonances, can lead inexorably from surveillance to arrest, even for the simple misuse of words and gestures. That this is not the case in other areas might be worthy of note here: the carnivalesque nature of the TV series 'Gladiators', for example, demands that the audience be partisan, even down to orchestrated yelling and chanting for the heroes and against the villains, in what is evidently a very controlled display of solidarity. In other situations the acceptance of expressions of dissent and xenophobia are present for all to witness, allowing us to reflect on why any success at Wimbledon 1996 by an opponent of England's new young tennis hope, Tim Henman, saw crowds howling in a furious rage that would have had them ejected from football grounds and arrested. And no doubt, television commentary from a different location would not have been as benign or approving of the fans' partisan and disorderly activities as was the case at Wimbledon. Again the Euro 96 football competition saw home-grown television commentators committing intellectual double somersaults in their attempts to give licensed support to some of the intense partisan fandom that could be seen on the terraces, and which in other circumstances they would no doubt have been happy to deny and deplore.

One might argue, as Marcuse (1970) has, that Britain suffers from 'surplus repression' in that it is governed by a range of regulations and controls far beyond those necessary for an orderly or safe existence. Yet for many, such repressive forms and strictures help generate the forms of release they seek, especially in those leisure pursuits where excitement, creativity and risk are part of the equation. The opportunity to exercise some form of choice in these carnivalesque activities, however, is always limited by socio-economic circumstance and tradition, yet some young men still choose this drama to provide an excursion to the anti-structural edge, and they understand clearly that this edge has a visible return route which allows them to pull back from taking the plunge into the total social chaos that must lie beyond the pale of the liminal phase. In this milieu, emotions of terror and moments of the sublime coalesce, enabling an individual to experience the exhilaration of standing at the limits of a social process, which, concomitantly, can even engender innovation. During these times, individuals in such collective gatherings experience the specificity and separateness of those peculiar 'occasions' (Faris 1968) in which they are liberated from everyday convention and cliché; and when, for a while, they can operate between the polarities of pure and positive joy and the negations inherent in the potentially violent spectacle.[5] This ultimate violent extreme is, of course, unacceptable to the judiciary and the police (and to many academics), who are forever trying to correct it by the use of the law. Other agencies pursue the discipline of docility and pacificity, resorting to a Victorian belief in curative athleticism, or youth clubs and adventure trips; while politicians argue for educational measures to inculcate their own vision of moral citizenship into the young, working-class male. The real problem, however, is that even though such policy-making proposals might well assuage some political pundits, the carnivalesque play activities they seek to cure cannot be channelled into such benign pastimes, and across thirty years a range of punitive and educational measures have clearly failed to prevent the next generation from joining the hooligan cohorts. For, as the American cultural critic Christopher Lasch (1978: 100) has written:

> Games simultaneously satisfy the need for free fantasy and the search for gratuitous difficulty, they combine childlike exuberance with deliberately created complications . . . Yet the 'futility' of play, and nothing else, explains its appeal – its artificiality, the arbitrary obstacles it sets up for no other purpose than to challenge the players to surmount them, the absence of any utilitarian or uplifting object. Games quickly lose their charm when forced into the service of education, character development, or social improvement.

The Legal Process

Although keen to avoid being charged with serious offences, those individuals we know were involved in partisan fanship were never really antagonistic towards their police controllers, for they understood that the police perform a necessary part in the social drama. Rather the fans sought to side-step confrontation, always keenly aware it was unwise to offer the police violence; and in most encounters, the fans would accommodate the vagaries of police demands, and felt – without receiving any support for their beliefs – they in turn should be allowed a degree of performance before the inevitable intervention in their inter-club theatrical rituals of resistance occurred. As constantly denigrated actors in what was always viewed as a hooligan discourse, the fans were forever able to try to cheat the social restraints, to raid the impositions placed upon them and to construct reactions to their positions of enforced marginality (see De Certeau 1984). In all this, however, they only ever gained power enough to create some minor discomfiture (Hebdidge 1988: 18), and little else.

In the court, the demands for the 'institutional truths' to be sustained were seen as obvious by the fans, and even though many were found guilty of some offence that failed to reflect what had actually gone on, few considered what they had done to be shameful or wrong. Moreover, regardless of the problems the law had in distinguishing framing temporally and factually accurate charges from what were often switching and swirling ritualistic confrontations, it often made good economic sense for fans to plead guilty to a minor charge, a fine could be less than accumulated travel costs and the lost wages that an adjourned case could generate. A fair and just hearing with an eventual acquittal was not something that participants in partisan fanship ever believed to be part of the equation. Guilt itself was rarely on the agenda, even for those facing serious charges plea-bargaining was understood to be a logical and crucial addendum to the fact that the court appearance was only one further aspect of the appearance and performance that the drama encapsulates. As it happens, the events are played out in terms that the institution demands, while the underlying constructs of liminality, *communitas* and carnival lie outside the realms of what the actors in either the judiciary or magistracy – or even the accused themselves – can comprehend or accept as material evidence.

And despite the perceived pathological malevolence of those dubbed with the 'hooligan' epithet, the intensity of prolonged participant observation suggests that few players in the social drama were arrested for or charged with specific assaults. Mostly they were charged with the ambiguous activities encompassed in some charge of public disorder (see Cook 1978; Trivizas 1981; White 1984) – the ambivalence of which even seemed to provoke Justice Popplewell to conclude his mid-1980s enquiry with the suggestion that a specific law of 'disorderly conduct' would be entirely suitable for fans. Again others have sought to control the artefacts of football support, with shadow Sports Minister, Dennis Howell, suggesting a law against the 'desecration of the national flag' as a means of preventing English fans from draping it over foreign fields (the *Evening Standard*, 20 January 1988).

What is being prosecuted then is not the random, indiscriminate assault or some premeditated, far-right instigated, political act of violence, but a combination of the semiotics of contests embodied in notions of 'hardness', 'masculinity' and 'reputation'. These ancient constructs are now set in opposition to the newly sanctified commercial match-day ideals, with their attempts at the 'embourgeoisement' of the game. In these circumstances, indignation about the fans is often as much aesthetic as it is political, for as icons of a loosely but usefully defined working-class illiterate they can be identified as relics of barbarism. In addition, their perceived anarchy and rejection of the values of restraint coincides with a growing insecurity arising from mass unemployment, short termism, loss of faith in church and state and the other institutions of control. Unable or unwilling to challenge the symbols these fans present, or even to see them as perhaps holding the key to questions that they should be asking about the 'truths' surrounding these uncertainties, those with political and institutional power are able to proselytize and argue for new laws, new powers, more control, new technologies of surveillance and intelligence-gathering, etc. For only this, it seems, can save us from each other.

More Docile Still – the Expansion of Surveillance

Adopting Bauman (1991) we can suggest that even as the police interpret events to suit their vision of the social drama, so, in particular, they are driven to an increasing use of technology and the surveillance camera, to an extent that is only just beginning to be understood by some of those concerned for civil liberties. Now the ubiquitous camera-surveillance teams rely on the fans not only to provide the material to generate arrests, but also to sustain the subsequent police proclamations of success in these metaphoric 'wars' against a 'hooligan' fraternity. Assisted by a recognition in English Law that video-recorded football-related disorder can now ascertain the Mens Rea of the defendants to a jury (Regina versus Clare 1995), this recent legal precedent sets the scene for a world where the police will no doubt increasingly edit the highlights to present a two-dimensional view of what is inevitably a multi-dimensional drama. And to combat the Thatcherite vision of 'enemies within', tactics comparable to those normally associated with despised totalitarian regimes are now being used. Specialist riot squads, overt and covert mass surveillance, random photography and body searches of ill-defined suspects are all part of a world that easily employs restrictions on movement, and where undercover officers listen for conspiratorial conversations that are used in show-trials which are re-presented to the public by a largely uncritical media (Armstrong and Hobbs 1994).

This identification of the demonization of the partisan fan seems to have occurred almost in parallel with Thatcherism, with its denial of the concept of society and disdain for any form of display of collective working-class culture. Since the 1980s, successive administrations have pursued the idea of an individualized, privatized, bourgeois mentality, and seem to find any collective gut display of cultural solidarity to be both incomprehensible and threatening. It seems not at all coincidental that the police have pursued all-seater stadiums and encouraged family-unit participation, so that the traditional macho football supporter is confined to individual seating that destroys the old terrace locations. Of course this mirrors the political denial of any collective activity which has the potential to represent an alternative vision of how things might be. As we have intimated above, partisan fans are disdainful of the legal process, never seeking the protection of the law in their jousts, which are governed by more subtle codes than those the law can enforce. However, law is a universalistic and imperialistic code which does not allow for partisan opposition to its demands. This is significant in relation to arrests for 'partisan' activity, for the 'operational imperative' (Waddington 1994) is not just about using the new and extended powers granted to the law enforcers, but is concerned to use these powers to engender the restoration of a vision of order to the drama. As a matter of fact, Public Order charges are usually invoked rather than those of assault and battery, for there are few complainants or willing witnesses to partisan fanship skirmishing. Semantically then, the problem for the controllers is always in the spectacle, for the show is carried out in public space, and is now increasingly available for all to see as a result of the expansion in micro TV recording systems which can follow events with ease. What we have is a historical and hegemonic struggle about what sort of social dramas are to be allowed to occur in public spaces; and whose code of conduct will prevail. As New Age Travellers, Ravers, Pagans and other collective, predominantly non-commercial assemblies, which remain unpenetrated by the regulatory and bureaucratic controls of the State, have found, such social action is anathema to those holding the reins of authority. And like the participants in these demonized groups, those involved in the inherent social drama that accompanies partisan fanship are simply not willing to have their games bowdlerized and licensed for acceptable commercial consumption.

The criminal justice system today has a dramatist's function then. In the court-room the 'men in wigs' still pass judgment on, or argue over, evidential opinion, while those who are truly 'walking through' the streets (to paraphrase and meld the fan's language with Hare's comment in the programme notes to his play) are the actors who at one extreme are engaged in a complex play, while the production assistants are using an expanding armoury, and in the words of Kohn (1994), 'talk like Tesco but dress like NATO'. Using rhetoric and political power, these warriors of officialdom set out to convince a wider public by pro-active measures, and frequently and publicly claim to know the script even before it has been written or performed.

This, we suggest, has become a truly Foucaultian world, where an overriding philosophy is attempting to legislate a phenomenon out of existence, and to surveille and control classified hooligan bodies to the point of extinction.

Notes

1. The players in this male domain of partisan fanship simply speak of themselves a being 'one of the boys' and adopt a range of specific symbolic indicators – dress, drinking ability, style and other denominators of a somewhat obsessive fandom – to say who they are. They clearly have a vision of what hooligan behaviour is about, but generally only refer obliquely to the activity, speaking usually of it as being 'out there' and those who are 'into it'.
2. The authors are social anthropologists. Gary Armstrong is a fan, and has spent a decade and more carrying out detailed ethnographic enquiry among those involved in partisan fanship. Malcolm Young is not even an uncommitted fan, but spent the last decade of a thirty-three year police career carrying out participant observation on the way that institution thinks.
3. Turner argued for the use of the concept of 'liminality' to be restricted to those ritual periods in small-scale societies which *all* must pass through, and to use the term 'liminoid' for anti-structural periods, such as those personified in the counter-culture of the 1960s (1978: 287). The question of whether to use 'liminoid' for those periods when only *some* of the members of society experience a rite of separation is not pursued here.
4. The tendency is always to recall the excess of a disaster on the scale of Heysel Stadium and to ignore the reality that week in and week out, across cities and small towns of the land, 'the boys' are strolling and posing, and deriding their opponents, and scoring points by 'walking through' them, or 'giving it the

big 'un', and later recalling these 'triumphs' over their pints at a thousand and one venues; and with none of it making the news bulletin.

5. The match itself is often a brutal contest, with metaphors of warfare (see Lakoff and Johnson 1980) sustaining the TV commentary; so that we hear of 'attackers shooting' at goal, and 'defenders parrying their thrusts'; of goals 'killing off' the opposition, or 'leaving them for dead'; of 'defenders fighting for possession' or 'massing in an effort to keep the attackers out'; of 'victors taking the spoils', and 'clashes between old rivals' that might encompass a 'relegation battle' described as an attempt to fend off the 'fatal drop' to ignominy and loss of face. In the light of this, it is perhaps surprising that 'partisan fanship' sees so little violence in its inter-club rivalries.

Chapter 10

The Jambo Experience: An Anthropological Study of Hearts Fans

Hans Kristian Hognestad

Preface

This chapter discusses the 'Jambos', a nomadic tribe which has the Lothian districts of eastern Scotland and predominantly the district of Gorgie in the city of Edinburgh as its main territorial base. However, as the words of one of their folk-songs reminds listeners, they have even been to Perth and Paisley. As part of a thesis, submitted at the University of Oslo in April 1995, this Norwegian anthropologist carried out eight months fieldwork among the Jambo-people in 1992/93 (Hognestad 1995). The reader might sense some parallels here to the master-narratives of classical modernist anthropological field studies: a young white man decides to go somewhere and do a study on some alien 'tribe' and discover its exotic culture and customs.

As the secrets of the Jambos were gradually revealed, their life-stories and practices appeared as extreme or simply alien to this ethnographer: first of all, Jambos' main concerns were related to the support of Heart of Midlothian FC or Hearts which is a more commonly applied term in the Scottish football vernacular. Due to their numerous near-misses in league and cup competitions they have been labelled 'The Nearly Men of Scotland'. Hence, fandom à la Hearts is a far more traumatic and bitter affair than in many other versions of obsessive support. Secondly, this was Scotland, and since a participant-observation method was applied, the ethnographer's liver was tested in new and demanding ways. This should be understood as part of a more complex pattern of having 'gone native'.

Introduction

In a time when people's lives are becoming more and more privatized, economically and socially, football as a public phenomenon stands out as one of the few remaining generators of huge collective rituals in many parts of the world. Although the experience of being a football supporter can be a very private thing (Willis 1990; Hognestad 1995), this experience is generally tied to a sense of communion made real through the continuous act of following one team. In an age when the hegemonic focus is on individual careers and concerns, football has become unique as a catalyst for questions of social identity, self-esteem, morality and solidarity. For many fans support is a question of maintaining these values in a diversity of ways. Football has got a universal mythology about winners and losers, glory and defeat. Yet, the emotional identification with a club is a feeling which often exceeds a mere quest for success. On the night before the 1996 Scottish Cup final between Hearts and Glasgow Rangers, a Jambo told me that: 'If Hearts win tomorrow, Edinburgh will explode, and, you know, we'll just celebrate for weeks. But obviously supporting a team like Hearts, you realize that the club-feeling does not depend on success. That is a feeling which goes much deeper.'[1]

This strong sense of a 'club-feeling' is continuously carved out in relation to a series of relevant Others. Football necessitates a meeting between different teams from different places and with differently composed identities. Throughout the history of football, fans and players have expressed these antagonistic aspects of the game. The fact that football seems to have always had a certain violent potential must be understood within this perspective.[2] In the world of contemporary Scottish football violence is not a major trait of a match-day routine in the way it was, particularly during the 1970s and 1980s (see Giulianotti 1993b). Yet, ardent support in Scotland resembles Geertz's notion of 'deep play' (Geertz 1972). Symbolic pride is tied to support and football is therefore frequently made into 'a matter of honour'. Even though violence is the ultimate way of vindicating honour (Pitt-Rivers 1966; Armstrong 1994), the quest for honour must first and foremost be related to identity. The vitality embedded in the identification with a team has been carved out and continuously maintained through various constructions of enemies and rivals. Staged in ways resembling Turner's account of a social drama (Turner 1974;

Armstrong 1994), the 'us versus them' polarizations are generally most vividly dramatized within the domestic football-universe in games between local or regional rivals. For the Jambos, these polarizations were prevalent in games against their city-based arch rivals Hibernian FC (known commonly as Hibs), or against the dominant Glasgow teams, Celtic and Rangers.

Symbolic capital in the shape of stereotypical images, caricatures and sarcasm are often applied in these processes of opposition in ways which resemble Bakhtin's account of 'the carnival laughter' which is . . . 'mocking and deriding, and at the same time gay and triumphant' (Bakhtin 1968: 11–12). A peculiar aspect of Scottish football is the way religious identity has come to play a significant role, mainly owing to the hegemonic position of Celtic and Rangers who have gained their huge support through appealing to sectarian loyalties (Murray 1984; Walker 1990; Boyle 1994). Even though Hibs were founded by Irish–Catholic immigrants (Mackie 1959), this connection to their sectarian origins has faded significantly in the Protestant dominated Edinburgh of the twentieth century. However, both Hibs fans, commonly known as Hibbies, and the Jambos are known for utilizing sectarian songs and symbols as a means of constructing imagined differences.[3] The established associative link between Hearts and Protestantism must first and foremost be considered as an element in the formation of a local rivalry. Mackie (1959: 30) writes: 'Hearts needed a local teaser, a stable-mate which would stir the club to great deeds. Was it by chance that the two names happened to alliterate-Hearts and Hibs?'

However, as a ritual, football should not be considered as a one-dimensional representation of something else, positioned in realities beyond its own relevant contexts. Football provides a connection to an authentic social reality in its own right. Rather than regarding actions and events taking place in football-related contexts as mere mirrors of wider socio-cultural processes, they must be valued as: 'part of a general process of the way society models some of its central existential, moral and political issues' (Archetti and Romero 1994: 47).

This chapter focuses less on the expressionist aspects of fandom and more on the subjective experiences, including how supporters conceptualize and reflect their own participation; the meaning of football and, in a particular sense, the meaning of Hearts.

A Different Reality

Football has developed into a cultural form which has the capacity
to unveil and generate what the theologist Paul Tillich (1957) calls
'a passionate concern'. A Jambo reflected upon the football ground
as a concrete representation of one of his greatest loves in life in
the following way:

> It's funny, Tynecastle isn't a particularly nice ground, but I've been
> there since I was a wee laddie. I've seen the glorious Hearts team of
> the 1950s play there. I remember the roars from way back. I've seen
> 'The Terrible Trio'.[4] When I drive up Gorgie Road for work every
> morning I automatically turn my head to catch a glimpse of this
> wonderful place.
>
> (Dave, aged 48)[5]

As such, football generates concerns founded on bonds of loyalty
and often tied to a sense of belonging and a feeling of continuity.
In the words of Scottish social psychologist Gerry Finn (1994a: 101):
'Football-fans not only identify very closely with the club they
support, the club symbolically becomes part of their own identity'.
Hence, football in its widest sense may happen anywhere.
However, the ritual aspects of football are more exclusively tied
to actual games. Through the privileged male participation in
football it is possible to sense a resonance to Victor Turner's
accounts of ritual and liminal phenomena as marked by com-
radeship between equal individuals (Turner 1969: 96). As a ritual
football generates elements resembling his accounts of 'anti-
structure', even though Turner applies this concept in relation to
rites of passage in particular traditional small-scale societies (ibid.).
The specific version of football ritual considered here, taking place
in a complex society, is in many ways self-contained with its own
moralities, commitments and loyalties. These have not been
developed hermetically, yet they are just occasionally aimed
politically towards the wider society in a direct way. Rather than
viewing football fandom as constitutive of sub-cultural formations,
the football-space considered here is seen more as constitutive of
a different reality. As such, 'anti-structure' may serve as a concept
for marking this step into a time–space guided by *different* codes
of conduct.

Entering the ritualized frame around a football match is for a

fan often experienced as passing a threshold where the sense of
the immediacy and authenticity of active support tends to
transcend all other concerns. The wider social event includes the
sharing of drinks before and after games, travelling together to
games, etc., and it is repeated with a certain frequency during the
football season. Within a British context since the 1890s, Saturday
afternoon has been firmly established as 'the football day' for the
fans. Even though a certain displacement has taken place with
the recent increase in live Satellite TV coverage, which means that
games today are played most days of the week, this notion still
holds true. Saturday is *sacred*, as the following comment by a
Hearts fan illustrates:

> The thing is that because we've been doing this for so long and
> anybody who knows you well enough to know who you are, they
> wouldn't even suggest [*laughs*], 'Oh, there's something happening
> next week I want you to come to.' And you ask: 'what day is it?' . . .
> 'Saturday afternoon, 3 o'clock' . . . well, yeah, I mean they wouldn't
> even consider it. The one thing that is always a hassle is weddings.
> Because usually, when somebody's getting married it is usually a
> Saturday and the actual wedding will be in the afternoon and in the
> evening you'll have a wedding reception . . . again, if people know
> you, they'll invite you to the reception at night, they won't invite you
> during the day [*laughs*] because they know you'll be at the game but
> if it was somebody outside your close circle of friends, they'd probably
> have difficulties in understanding that. If they would say, 'There's a
> wedding on and you ought to be there,' and you turn around saying
> 'Well, there's a football match on, I'll have to be there' . . . eh, if they
> don't have a grasp of the situation, with the way you support your
> team and that, they would say: 'Well, there's something wrong with
> you!' [*laughs*] Major problem!
>
> (Rab, aged 33)

As a ritual, football thus entails something more than just a form
of entertainment. Even models which portray football as a leisure
activity, as opposed to work and the things people do to provide
an income for themselves and their families, run the risk of missing
the point. It is not experienced as a pastime for the ardent
supporters:

> For someone who is not wrapped up in football, they probably find
> it quite humorous and comical how people can get so wrapped up in
> it. I think it's part of their social background, part of their social fabric,

if you like . . . obviously getting an education, having a job and considerations like that are important for other aspects of your life, you know having a job pays your bills, which football doesn't . . . Football is something else, but it's not a pastime. For myself, I haven't been willing to take a job that involves working on a Saturday.

(Stephen, aged 24)

The passion for football and the close emotional bonds that the fan ties in imaginative ways to one specific team, means that fans regard themselves as active participants in the drama of football. This experience prevails among the supporters and should be intimately tied to the various meanings of established imperatives such as 'get behind your team!' and general notions of unnerving support. Neil had been supporting Hearts for forty years and viewed the sense of loyalty that football generates, along with its intrinsic existential qualities as the basis for his own involvement:

I've got a lot of things . . . but football is different . . . you can go to a concert and find that it's not very good and you decide not to go back, and you don't . . . now, I often get utterly disillusioned at Hearts matches, saying to myself: I'll never go back, but I always do . . . because it's something that . . . I think if you're a fan of the sport and you have a favourite team, you can't get away from it. It's part of you.

(Neil, aged 54)

The identification with the club is frequently grounded on matters of an existential nature and is for many fans experienced as a 'string' that goes through their lives from childhood to old age. The late journalist and Hearts fan John Fairgrieve writes in his book about Hearts in the aftermath of the 1985–86 season that:

You see it's all very well to talk about football being only a game. In the most literal of terms, it is probably just that. Only a game? In the hearts and souls and minds of thousands of millions it is one hell of a lot more than a game. For God's sake, rugby is a game, cricket is a game . . . Football is so much more than a game. Football is a way of life, a cherished thread of existence, for so many. When the thread breaks, even if its renewal is inevitable, people do cry.

(Fairgrieve 1986: 141)

These statements were written shortly after Hearts were beaten 2–0 by Dundee in the last match of the 1985–86 season, which meant that they lost the championship title by the narrowest of margins. Yet, Fairgrieve's words have a clear resonance in contemporary accounts from Jambos in general. For a lot of fans the football space is experienced as an arena protected from other concerns in life, a space for liberty and imagination, but also a real space for ecstatic joy and utter despair, 'virtues' which have established football as a unique cultural form. After the local derby match between Hibs and Hearts in August 1992, I met Scott in a pub. He proudly stated that . . . 'when someone asks me what I do for a living, I tell them I'm a Hearts supporter.'

In view of this, the identification with football and a specific team provides the prime time–space, while other spheres of life and activities take on a secondary importance with regard to authenticity. In this respect, the sense of continuity which the football community gives, seems to be a very important asset:

The football gives you some sort of constant in life. You know in these days you're under so much pressure at work, families, whatever . . . I think everybody feels this pressure to perform in one way or another and it's very important to have things that you know you can rely on . . . and you know it's going to come round every week. For me personally it's great to know that you can go to the football and get away from all the pressures that you have in your life . . . and you can go there and you know you'll get no hassle from anyone . . . eh you're doing what you wanna do and you're with the guys that you like and, eh, it's just great.

(John, aged 32)

This last passage in which football is valued as a 'release from reality', might suggest that football thus becomes a kind of escape from 'real life'. That is, if football is regarded in terms of a 'false consciousness'. Simultaneously, this 'release' may be interpreted as a space for continuity, thus providing a strong sense of identification with a community which seems to change slowly. As the sociologist Anthony Giddens argues, the significance of 'anchorage' in the context of post-modern societies, plays an increasingly critical part in many people's lives. Maybe Giddens did not have football in mind when he stressed the importance of different cultural settings to 'allow a faith in the coherence of

everyday life ... achieved through providing symbolic interpretations of existential questions' (Giddens 1992: 38).

Nevertheless, it seems that football for the ardent fan provides
an arena for the experience of coherence and continuity. As an
activity, football is certainly closer to this description than Giddens'
notions of 'free-time' as a way to 'kill time' in between the aspects
of life which are regarded as the more consequential: work, family
and education (ibid.: 113).

Play it Deep

Most fans started going to games as children together with their
fathers or another male member of the family. A writer in the
Hearts fanzine *Dead Ball* describes the peculiarity of football as a
space where generations meet:

> So a football team (and a football league) provides a solid foundation
> where generations can meet. You may hate your father's taste in
> music, clothes, politics, but you share something important in your
> heart. The only people who miss out on this experience are those
> unfortunate enough never to have known their fathers – yes referees.

> (*Dead Ball*, no.10)[6]

Whereas this last reference to referees fits well into the usual
humour about the 'game's neutral authority', the first passage
points to the fact that football happens within its own time–space
as a continuous cultural form. In view of this, both a contrast and
a relation to other spheres of life is provided. Something of a
'second home' is created, and yet the club does not solely represent
a link of identification for the individual fan. As an activity we
might label non-utilitarian, football provides an existential space
for play and, as such, a release from life as it is experienced in the
context of survival, duties, necessities and obligations. In this way,
the football space acquires the qualities of a playground in the
sense that it is liberated from the hierarchies and 'responsible
actions' normally associated with other areas of life, such as work
and family. As such, football opens up opportunities for the
supporters to imagine and experience qualities of life through play,
where the aims are not directly linked to goals outside the confines
of its own time and space. As Huizinga points out, order is
established in a temporary, limited sense within the playground

(Huizinga [1949] 1980: 10), since the playing always proceeds according to a certain set of rules. In football this is quite obvious in the practice of singing and attempts to *outsing* the opposing fans, which often have a carnivalesque content (Hognestad 1995). Both play and carnival are, in the modern world, commonly associated with the infantile. Carnivals are arranged in kindergartens and children are the only legitimate actors in playgrounds. Football establishes a line of continuity which usually goes back to the days of childhood and this carries a great significance for a lot of supporters. The strength in the experience of a club identity and the concerns related to the performances of the team must be understood in this perspective:

> I'm a married man, well settled. The most second important thing in my life next to my family is the Heart of Midlothian. I can't stop following, it's like a drug. Apart from the work and the football I play golf, eh, and I love gardening . . . but when I'm out in the garden I'm always thinking of Hearts and when I'm at the golf course I'm thinking of Hearts . . . next game coming up; how badly we've done, how well we've done . . . it's always in the head, you know.
>
> (John, aged 38)

The game produces big clubs, run as huge commercial enterprises, with glamorous histories. Football is fairly unique in the way that even clubs with minor success can retain a strong social integrity and continue to attract a large support. This must be related to the fact that football clubs become a significant part of people's social identity (see Finn 1994a). The team thus comes to represent a complexity of sentiments, memories and other experiences forming elements of the biographies of individual fans.

In Scotland, the two Glasgow teams Celtic and Rangers, have dominated the entire history of Scottish football. A few days after I arrived in Edinburgh for the first time, I watched Hearts lose 2–1 to Celtic in the quarter-final of the League Cup. To contextualize what it can be like for a Hearts fan to go through thick and thin with the team and how closely Hearts fans may identify themselves with the club, the following description of this game is particularly enlightening.

> Most Hearts fans have seen quarter-finals and semi-finals where we have been put up with Celtic or Rangers . . . we don't seem to have the final bottle to go with them and funnily enough that game was a

perfect example where we should have destroyed Celtic and allowed
a silly goal to take the whole thing away from us . . . and we started
to see things; fouls for Celtic . . . the game's being unfair to you. You
start to criticise players, the manager, the referee . . . and you talk
about the Celtic players and at the end of the game you feel that you
should have won . . . but we didn't and the answer is to go back there,
since you're a Hearts supporter . . . I sometimes think that the players
don't realise how low the fans are . . . you come away and you're
absolutely gutted . . . you know. You go to the game thinking: I might
be in the semi-final tomorrow, happy and joyous, I might be happy
to see us winning the cup . . . the next day it has vanished and it's
like someone has ran a knife up at you: It's away, that thing isn't
there for you anymore and you gotta say to yourself: well, what's
the next thing coming up . . . and the next thing you come along with
is on the Saturday against Motherwell and . . . OK it was another
game, but you win!

(Alex, aged 42)

In this story the optimistic logic of the fan appears; even in the
aftermath of defeats experienced as devastating there is another
game coming up which will, after all, kick off with a clean sheet
for your own team. It is further noteworthy how the Jambo quoted
above says '*I* might be in the semi-final tomorrow' and '*I* might be
happy to see *us* winning the cup.' This indicates an idea of how
closely fans may identify with their club and corresponds to Finn's
findings exemplified through fans' inclination to talk about the
club in terms of 'we' as much as 'they' (Finn 1994a: 101).

To follow Hearts every week is not an 'easy option' and every
Jambo seemed to have similar things to say about the difference
between themselves and someone supporting more glamorous and
successful teams. Hearts fans tended to regard the lack of success
as signs of their feeling of a superior loyalty towards the club,
and of solidarity and solid commitment:

I reckon Hearts have the most loyal support in the land, having a
core of 7,000 fans who will watch them at Tynecastle no matter how
the performances of the team are like on the pitch. Take Rangers, for
instance. Now they have an average of 40,000 spectators at every
home-game. In the early to mid-1980s, when they were playing shite,
they had crowds of 3,000 to 4,000. That shows what kind of part-time
supporters they really have.

(Stuart, aged 22)

Since Glasgow football has been so dominant within Scottish football, the feeling of animosity towards either Celtic or Rangers, or both, regularly found its expression in the course of pre- or post-match chats among Jambos. In their minds, Hearts' lack of success evidenced a kind of patience and endurance which Rangers and Celtic fans would surely not know anything about. Their support for Hearts was for reasons regularly presented as honourable in themselves. There are, however, more iconic manifestations of club identity depicted through past and present legendary players and whole teams.

The Hero is a Jambo

Hearts had their great era in the 1950s, when the legendary former Scotland international, Tommy Walker, was the manager. They were particularly famous for having scored 132 goals in thirty-four matches during the 1957–58 season, when Hearts won the league championship, taking a record of 62 out of 68 possible points. For a team like Hearts this was not normal, and represented even then a break with an established mythology of 'near-misses'. John Fairgrieve who followed them at this time describes how Hearts in those days of perfection stopped being Hearts:

> Heredity matters. So does environment, naturally. Then there is a long apprenticeship, during which one goes through the fire. Hearts always have great expectations, which, with crushing inevitability, fall in ruins, usually just before or just after the New Year. Occasionally, very occasionally, a cup or a title does come to Tynecastle, and belief is temporarily suspended. When they were scoring all those goals in the late 1950s, we celebrated well enough, but, somehow, deep down, there was this strange disappointment. It was as if we feared Hearts might become mere pot-hunters, like the people at Ibrox or Parkhead.[7] Soon enough, however, everything returned to normal, and we were able to relax.
>
> (Fairgrieve 1992 [1976])

Whereas fans of successful sides like Rangers or Manchester United may go through the odd fear of failure, this particular account suggests that Hearts fans live through the odd fear of success! While the Hearts team of the 1950s were mythically associated with an elegant and forward-minded style of football, including great individual profiles, they are normally associated with a physical style which the initiated observer of the game could easily have identified as 'British'. Even though outstanding individual skills are appreciated, the most important aspect here is related to whether a player is ready 'to play for his jersey'. This phrase refers to a certain attitude based on commitment and 'guts', combined with a soldier's attitude, and preferences often identified along with working-class values (see Bourdieu 1984; Bromberger 1993a). Among Hearts fans I found nothing suggesting any antipathy against technical finesse. On the contrary, the problem for Hearts and other Scottish teams was, among Jambos, often pointed out in terms of a lack of 'artistic touch'. However, as long as a player was valued as someone who would 'play his heart out for Hearts' he was generally accepted among the fans.

In 1992 Scott Crabbe was playing for Hearts. He was one of those players who had supported the club as a child before becoming a player. Whilst never an outstanding player, he did score some vital goals from his position in midfield and was generally regarded as someone who would never give up. Via this combination he qualified to the status of 'a proper Jambo'. The Hearts manager at that time, Joe Jordan, wanted to sell Crabbe, claiming that he did not fit into the team's style of play. Crabbe publicly announced he did not want to leave the only club he had ever cared for, but was eventually sold to Dundee United. After his last appearance at Tynecastle, he took off his team-shirt, kissed its club crest and threw it into the fans as a farewell gesture. When Dundee United came to Tynecastle a few weeks later with Scott Crabbe in the line-up, he got a very warm welcome from the Hearts fans, and I even overheard Jambos cheering Crabbe on during the match. The usual booing which players who have left a club at an earlier stage in their careers are subjugated to in performances against their old team, never happened here. Scott Crabbe wanted to stay, but being a professional footballer he had to leave in order to get a game of football. Later that year he was also spotted as a spectator on the Tynecastle terraces, as Dundee United's game that day had been postponed.[8] The important consideration here is that Hearts fans were speaking of Crabbe as 'one of us', an antidote to professional footballers who, since the early 1970s, have been judged as greedy and primarily involved because of the money. Crabbe was regarded as a fan as much as a professional footballer, thus adding to the belief that he was part of the Jambo community, as this obituary-like tribute to him, written by a fanzine writer, proclaims:

> The guy loved Hearts as much as the supporters loved him. He was a die-hard Jambo through and through and showed it in the way he would run over to the crowd (after another Crabbe wonder-goal) and kiss the club crest on his shirt, because he knew what Hearts meant to the supporters.
>
> (*Gorgie View*, issue 5)

Players, although they are professional footballers, are considered by most fans as their representatives on the pitch. Inevitably, the professional staff at the club come and go, whereas the commitment of the fan is usually tied to a lifelong contract with the club as an 'imagined community', and not with the individual players. John (aged 38) put it this way:

> I feel that the Hearts players should be playing for me. Especially with following the Hearts for so many years, no matter who's in the team, eh, let me tell you, Hans, it's not the players I support. It's the club. And I feel that they, when they're off-tuned, should be playing for me, not just me . . . there are other guys like me who have followed them for years and years . . . The club belongs to the fans, not the players. The players come and go, the club never changes. It's always the Heart of Midlothian; from the first division days, relegation etc., etc., they play for us, not their wages. And yeah, I'm disappointed with players over the years . . . I feel they should play for us, you know, eh, like Scott Crabbe. I wish we had eleven Scott Crabbes in the team.[9]

As a consequence of a commitment usually regarded as lifelong, some fans install themselves as the truly authoritative voices of the club. Before and during my fieldwork a few conflicts between the fans and the management at the club demonstrated this. These disputes were especially related to the manœuvres of the club chairman and commercial owner at the time, Wallace Mercer. His attempt to takeover city rivals Hibs and join them with Hearts, combined with a suggested relocation of Hearts' 100-year-old base in Gorgie to a greenbelt site outside Edinburgh, mobilized the ethical dimensions of support. The various Hearts fanzines (see the chapter in this collection by Giulianotti) were, in particular, conveyors of this critical approach towards the club leadership. But a general antipathy spread rapidly among the Hearts fans, expressed through chants and demonstrations.[10]

What was witnessed in Edinburgh in connection with these issues is congruent with an anthropologist's report of the activities of the fans of the Argentinian team San Lorenzo de Almagro. After their team had gone through a bad spell, including relegation from the top division, the fans manifested their loyalty, love and sense of solidarity by hailing the club and the strip through various chants. Simultaneously, however, they denigrated the attitude of those they regarded as shifting, unloyal and greedy: namely managers and players. The fans imagined the club as part of their own identity and regarded themselves as the club's legitimate protagonists (Archetti 1992: 230–1).

It is within this perspective that questions of self-esteem and pride among football fans must be understood. As mentioned above there are several ways of maintaining honour or restoring lost honour in football. Violent incidents between rival fans have decreased significantly in Scottish football over the last decade. The following story is from a particularly disastrous day for the Jambos which did, among other responses, cause spontaneous, violent rage. Before the last game of the 1985–86 season it was felt that only a mathematical miracle could deny Hearts the champion-ship title. Yet, after Celtic beat St Mirren 5–0 and Hearts lost 2–0 at Dundee, 'the impossible' did happen. Many Hearts fans were in tears inside and outside the ground, but some resorted to more expressive means:

> It was the worst night in my life. They had gone thirty-one games undefeated and then lost it all like that. I basically just spent the first hour after the game fighting with Dundee fans. Then we went back to Edinburgh and started looking for Celtic supporters and every Celtic supporter we saw, including one in a restaurant, got absolutely fucking piled. Then we went out and got pished and just sang ourselves hoarse . . . I went to work on the Monday morning and nobody said anything to me. Even the Hibs supporters I worked beside didn't say anything because the first person that said anything was gonna get a broken jaw. I think even the Hibs supporters were sort of . . . not so much sorry, but maybe genuinely felt that because we had gone so long without losing and actually coming away with the whole season winning nothing, which is basically the story of our lives . . .
>
> (Lindsay, aged 32)

A week after the game against Dundee, Hearts also lost the cup final against Aberdeen. The feeling that 'luck always escapes' is applied by Bromberger (1993a: 128) in the case of fans of the Italian side Torino, who support a team which have not been nearly as successful as their Turin rivals Juventus. It is a feeling of injustice, instigated by a belief in fate, that causes pessimism and cynicism. As the above quote indicates there is also a parallel being drawn between the fate of the team and their own life-experiences when the narrator concludes the story about the team's misfortunes adding: 'which is basically the story of our lives.' Raw pain is a significant part of the total football experience for these supporters.

Relativizing the Other

Despite the fact that football, in a lot of respects, thrives on rivalries (Fairgrieve 1986), I also witnessed how the 'us and them' polarizations dissolved altogether into new and more inclusive patterns in certain situations. This was particularly the case during the three trips abroad I participated in, to Prague, Liege and Madrid, respectively. Away from the domestic universe, the fans were generally wanting to party and in a carnivalesque state of mind (see Giulianotti 1993b), and the actual performances of the team mattered less in these contexts (Hognestad 1995). As a trend this should partly be related to a deliberate negation of the well-established notorious reputation of English football supporters. As Jambos were generally in the mood for carnival rather than riot during these trips, stereotypical images of Scottishness were often applied as pragmatic means of marking out their difference from the English. Hearts fan Eddie Edinburgh (aged 31) told a story where the dynamic synthesis of alcohol and Scottishness was given a particular value. Together with about twenty-five other Jambos he travelled to Germany in July 1993 to follow Hearts in a pre-season friendly tournament with German and Dutch teams:

> During this tournament there was some trouble between Dutch and German fans. We were drinking away in this pub and a bunch of German supporters came in and asked us to join them in fighting the Dutch fans. We just said: 'no, we're only here for the beer.' About ten minutes later, the Dutch fans came in, asking for extra power in fighting the German fans! So, again we said: 'no – no, we're only here to drink.'

A lot of fans stressed the importance of flying the Scottish flag in certain situations to signal that they were in it for the party and the drink rather than the violence. The sensation of drinking and partying with hundreds of fellow Jambos in foreign localities was combined with an inclination to include outsiders: locals and preferably fans of the opposing side. During the games abroad, the usual denigration of the opposition, with chants and verbal abuse, tended to give way to sentimental singing sessions and a less exclusive celebration of the Jambo community.[11]

It is interesting to note that 'the other' in these foreign football-related contexts is not culturally outside Scotland. Within the Jambo logic 'the other' is a Hibbie (Hibs fan), a Tim (Celtic fan) or a Hun (Rangers fan). The other is at home, and in the present context these are enemies to play with in malicious ways. On our way back on the bus from Spain, where Hearts had lost 3–0 to Atletico Madrid, someone managed to tune in to BBC Radio 5 and a live commentary of Rangers' European match against Levski Sophia in Bulgaria. The greatest cheer of the trip occurred somewhere in the south of France, when the Bulgarian side scored as the game went into injury-time, and knocked Rangers out of the competition. In a malicious fashion Jambos on the bus revelled in jubilant chants of 'no Huns in Europe'.

By way of conclusion, the football-mad Norwegian writer Dag Solstad said in an interview with a Norwegian newspaper quite accurately that 'football is football', implying that football has itself as both means and end (*Dagbladet*, 3 September 1995). Hence, as a sport and as a cultural form, a distinct set of rules and a distinct logic have been developed, which are related to other socio-cultural forms and processes in complex ways. For these reasons it is important to grasp the ways football opens up possibilities for experiencing and creatively expressing a variety of existential concerns and other desires. As a ritual, it might be false to compare football with rituals of a more religious or philosophical nature (Archetti 1992). Yet, in this case, Jambos told of how they regarded their status as Hearts fans as the most important consideration in situations of self-presentation, even outside the obvious football contexts. Belonging to the Jambo community thus forms an integral part of their total social identity, providing people with an essential existential basis. The value of this identity was significantly regarded through qualities related to continuity and a sense of a lifelong commitment. Their identification with the mythology surrounding Hearts as a football team must thus be understood in view of a more general experience among football supporters as themselves as the legitimate protagonists of the team they support.

Notes

1. As the initiated reader will remember, the Danish winger Brian Laudrup went riot in the Hearts defence that day, giving the Glaswegian side a 5–1 victory.
2. The earliest accounts of physical battles between Hearts fans and fans of their local rivals, Hibernian FC, date back to the 1870s, shortly after the founding of the two clubs. See Mackie (1959).
3. A chapter of my unpublished thesis deals with chants and the understanding of chants among Hearts fans in more detail (Hognestad 1995).
4. A nickname for the three Hearts strikers at this time: Jimmy Waurdaugh, Willie Bauld and Alfie Conn.
5. John Bale (1991) uses the term 'topophilia' to denote supporters' identification with the ground of their team, as a place charged with memories and emotions.
6. During my fieldwork Hearts had the biggest number of fanzines in circulation in Scotland. Apart from the one mentioned here these were: *Always the Bridesmaid, No Idle Talk, Gorgie View, Trophy Please?* and *Still Mustn't Grumble.* Of these, only the two mentioned first are still being produced at the start of the 1996–97 season.
7. The home-grounds of the Glaswegian clubs Rangers FC and Celtic FC, respectively.
8. In a similar way, during a cup-tie at Rugby Park against Kilmarnock in February 1996, the Hearts captain Gary Locke, who was suspended for this game, appeared amongst the Hearts crowd.
9. It is no doubt easier for a 'local lad' to qualify himself to the status of a Jambo in the minds of the fans, than it is for others. However, during a couple of games in February 1996, I witnessed

how Hearts' new French goalkeeper, Gilles Rousset, and the Italian midfielder, Pasquale Bruno, had generated a new and more 'cosmopolitan' kind of cult worship.

10. The ground issue evolved as a consequence of governmental recommendations, drafted in the so-called Taylor report in the wake of the Hillsborough disaster in 1989, regarding modern-ization of football grounds in Britain. The various incidents and debates which developed in connection with Mercer's management at this time, is treated in detail in one chapter of my thesis (Hognestad 1995).

11. I deal with these processes in more detail in a chapter of my thesis (Hognestad 1995).

Chapter 11

Enlightening the North: Aberdeen Fanzines and Local Football Identity

Richard Giulianotti

In terms of stimulation, attending a Scottish football match is often a more literary than visual experience. As events on the pitch stoke the perennial national inquiry into 'what is wrong with our game', the spectator may be attracted to other matters in hand: specifically, the humour, invective and insight of the 'football fanzine' already bought outside the ground. As 'magazines dealing with a single aspect of popular culture',[1] football fanzines are now an established product of modern football culture in the UK.[2] Yet, the definitive characteristics of fanzines underline their marginality. Traditionally, fanzines are produced by club supporters for fellow fans, on a (nominally) profitless basis; and are completely autonomous from football authorities, club officials or mainstream media – hence the 'edge' they bring to coverage of major issues within football.

Although an apparently new and highly modern phenomenon, football fanzines find their parentage in 1970s pop culture alienation.[3] From 1972 to 1976, the proto-fanzine *Foul!* performed as football's juvenile sibling to *Private Eye*'s political satire, combining Pythonesque humour and wilful nostalgia to mock modern football's avaricious players and authorities (Redhead 1991: 41–5; Haynes 1995: 35–8).[4] While 'Football's Alternative Paper!' was being libelled out of existence, a new and energetic youth cultural style was taking off in British pubs and rock clubs. The musical situationism of punk rock in the late 1970s precipitated a matching rash of nihilistic ancillary literature such as the 'fanzine' *Sniffin Glue*.[5] The Merseyside fanzine *The End*, printed in the early

1980s, reflected this football and musical lineage, but failed to inspire any significant imitations prior to its demise. Accordingly, although football fanzines share a situationist format and content, their emergence and continuing ubiquity are sufficiently new for them to represent an 'epistemic break' from these predecessors. Since the late 1980s, fanzines must be seen as enlivening the mainstream of British football culture. They berate the ultimately comfortable relationships between football 'producers' and mass media, and the colourless and restricted information that flows between the two. Instead, fanzines exploit the situational publishing possibilities afforded by photocopiers and, more recently in the 1990s, computerization and desktop publishing. As I write, fanzines generally tend to sell for £1, which is often less than the price of a club programme.

This chapter examines the fanzine culture surrounding one leading Scottish football side, Aberdeen FC. Currently, there are two Aberdeen fanzines, *The Red Final* (TRF) and *The Paper Tiger* (*TPT* Figure 11.1). Each emerged from the demise of the original Aberdeen fanzine, *The Northern Light* (TNL), which had earlier spawned a short-lived civic fanzine, *The Granite Kipper* (TGK). Most editors and writers for these fanzines of the 1990s are drawn from *TNL*'s ranks, which at its peak was described by the Glasgow daily, *The Herald* (30 March 1992) as 'Scotland's funniest and most professional fanzine'. Although regarded by local press and the club as an excessively critical, indeed negative and often abusive, organ, *TNL*'s circulation peaked at some 4,500 sales between 1990 and 1991: a time of unfulfilled promise for supporters, when Aberdeen threatened (but failed) to capture the Scottish league title, on the last day of the season, from Rangers.[6] Before moving on to assess their content and culture, however, it is necessary to locate these fanzines within the intersecting milieux of the British football fanzine movement, and the local civic contexts of Aberdeen and Scottish football.

Football Fanzines: Cultural and Localist Politics

Prior research on British football fanzines falls into two general camps, grouped into 'football sociology' and 'cultural studies'. Football sociologists are attracted by fanzines' symbolic departure

Figure 11.1. The Paper Tiger

from what is regarded as the game's internecine period, the late 1970s to the mid to late 1980s. For these writers, the main sources of conflict had included inflated player wages, directorial largesse, the intensification of football hooliganism, and ultimately the highly politicized intervention of the Thatcherite State, through the 'war on football hooliganism'.[7] The close of this chapter of political strife within football is taken to be marked by the ground disasters at Heysel (Brussels) in 1985 or Hillsborough (Sheffield) in 1989, resulting in thirty-nine and ninety-six deaths respectively (Haynes 1995; Redhead 1991a and b; Taylor 1991; see also Turner 1990).[8] British fanzines therefore constitute a symbolic and an often explicit rejection of the prior typification of football fans as hooligans. By contrast, while the proliferation of European fanzines has been far more patchy, so too the distinction of club fanzines and 'militant' supporters is notably less apparent.[9]

Alternatively, historical and cultural studies writers have tended to argue that football fanzines have been pivotal to a more momentous, reflective empowerment of British football spectators. Working across a broader canvas, these commentators emphasize the fanzines' departure from traditionally affirmative and officially incorporated supporter organizations, towards producing popular and accessible media that formulate autonomous and critical narratives on the game and its authorities (Duke 1991; Jary, Horne and Bucke 1991; Taylor 1992). In blending their established financial and affective 'support' with a newly productive and participatory role in football culture, fanzine writers and their 'community' of readers entail 'the transgression of distinction between consumer and producer' (Lash 1994: 161). The community of fans produces a 'cultural contestation' of power within and without the game (Jary et al. 1991). Fanzine writers belong to a wider social entity whom I have elsewhere categorized as 'post-fans'.[10] Ironically, unlike these cultural studies writers, they tend not to exaggerate their influence within the game, but are instead reflectively informed of their relatively powerless relationship to football players, clubs and authorities, yet are still laden with an explicit humour, irony and invective about their own identities and the sport in which they persistently invest time, money and self (see Giulianotti 1993). Neither set of writers at *TPT* or *TRF* is attracted to the elaborate, 'cultural contestation' argument regarding motivation and participation. Alternatively, as a form of *local* media (albeit with a nation-wide template), they argue all fanzines emerge in response to particular club issues which are inadequately discussed by mainstream media or fail to be addressed by the board and management.

The creative politics of football fanzines have been in the informational vanguard of a 'new social movement' within football, which includes a new œuvre of satirical plays, books and television shows, broadcasting phone-ins, fan demonstrations against directorial impositions, and fan communication links via internet web-pages. Fanzines therefore fall into the category of 'reflexive symbolic industries' (Lash and Urry 1993: 163). The very *informality* and *anonymity* of fanzines help to maximize their critical and humorous effect, through a 'riot of signs' comprising cartoons, outraged articles, scurrilous pastiches and 'thundering editorials' which often collapse into self-deprecation. Fanzines therefore fulfil a dual purpose, relating to their *symbolic* and *allegoric* functions (Lash and Urry 1993: 58). As information symbols, they seek to report 'authentic knowledge' within football that escapes or is suppressed by the mass media, whether through editorial bias or libel concerns. Local or 'football world' gossip emerges about the deviance of players, the corruption of officials, the bias of football authorities and media, or the 'reality' of fan hatred of individuals and teams. Editors and readers can step further back still, and enter the allegoric – where the 'authenticity' of information is of less value than the sheer enjoyment of fanzines uttering the previously unutterable. This provokes humour through vitriol and caricature, through 'the obvious constructedness of the whole experience', and the subsequent reflection on how these portrayals will affect or offend the individuals targeted.

The allegorical is at its most articulate when fanzine writers reflect ruefully on their own relative powerlessness within Scottish football culture. Five years into the Scottish fanzine movement, *The Absolute Game* took stock of its impact through a caricature of the mono-cultural passivity of Scottish supporters and the continuing incongruity of fanzine salesmen (Figure 11.2). In its form, this playful self-indictment enlivens Eco's (1986: 162) self-heightening 'sports chatter', 'a discourse on a discourse about watching others' sport as discourse.' But its content is of greater magnitude: while it is common to find mainstream journalists and broadcasters addressing issues with a heavy self-importance, the fanzines refuse to imitate this egotism, and take their own discourses alienatingly and onanistically seriously.

Figure 11.2. The Absolute Game

Fanzine Origins: Constructing a Football Fan Identity

While not at all divorced from the fanzine culture sweeping the UK at the time, the beginnings of *The Northern Light* in 1987 must be seen within the historical context of Aberdeen FC's successes in the early 1980s. In six years, the club won the European Super Cup, the European Cup-Winners' Cup, three Scottish league titles, four Scottish Cups and one Scottish League Cup – an unprecedented haul of trophies. In response, in 1986, Rangers commenced a high-spending strategy to dominate Scottish football, by buying in leading English and Scottish players. Aberdeen manager Alex Ferguson then departed for Manchester United to be replaced by the uninspiring Ian Porterfield, and Aberdeen entered a period of general stagnation.

Some of *TNL*'s founders wrote into the local press to air their grievances, but these went unpublished or were ridiculed by journalists for their disloyalty. Others penned critical supporters' newsletters, only to be threatened by other fan-officials with loss of position or any related perks from their voluntary posts. In late 1987, one future *TNL* founder discovered the national fanzine *When Saturday Comes*,[11] reckoned it a worthy successor to *Foul!*, and contacted a group of fellow fans with a view to producing an Aberdeen version. The first issue eventually ran to over 1,000 photocopies, sold in classic style outside Aberdeen's stadium (Pittodrie) before fixtures or through sympathetic local retailers. Further issues emerged every couple of months for the next five years, before the journal was wound up and its custodians gradually dispersed into the two informal groupings that produce *TRF* and *TPT*.

Although functioning as football fanzines, *TNL* and its offspring invariably reflect the separatist local culture of their readers. To the continual surprise of most visitors, Aberdeen and the surrounding north-east region differ markedly to the central belt of Scotland. As Rory Williams (1990: 1) notes:

> There is a consciousness of difference. It is largely from the farming and fishing communities around it that the city's population has, right up to the present day, been built up; and one sign of this can be heard in the dialect, which has sounds, words, and expressions unknown elsewhere in Scotland, let alone in Britain as a whole.

The American travel writer Paul Theroux (1983: 246) was appalled by Aberdeen's misanthropy: 'over-cautious, unwelcoming and smug' is how he judged the city, its boomtown citizens having 'found protection and solace by retreating into the most unbearable Scottish stereotypes' of which 'tartan tight-fistedness' was the most repellant. In reply to this 'vitriolic verbiage' the aged journalist and author of Aberdeen FC's history, Jack Webster (1988: 146–8) exclaimed the city to be a 'northern citadel' where 'culture is there in abundance' and whose 'race' of citizens are 'honest, hard-working and independent folk', 'their dry, piercing humour, [being] expressed with an economy of words.' These competing interpretations may be said to be opposite sides of the same cultural coin, its local subjects falling into a value-laden syntax linking the thrifty/mean, quiet/inhospitable or independent/ xenophobic. Yet it is a binary of extremes that is well known to its exponents. Giddens (1994: 94) notes that those cultures, such as Scotland, where the 'compulsive nature of modernity' (Calvinism) has been most strongly inculcated, also accommodate a counter-culture of joking and humour *against* obsessive self-control and neurotic discipline. Such forms of levity (or inversion) 'act out a caricature of the Protestant ethic – but clearly indicate that alternative attitudes are alive and well' (see Davies 1992).

The affected taciturnity of Aberdonians seems to transpose itself into Pittodrie Stadium,[12] leading to supporters being categorized as 'quiet, fickle sweetie-rustlers' by the rest of Scottish football. It's a calumny that is both critically exploited and fiercely rejected by fanzine writers as they fix a refreshingly ambivalent perspective on their fellows and themselves. Cartoons particularly have been employed to mock the few douce 'ruggies' who attend fixtures, with warming knee-blankets, plenty of mint sweets and flasks of tea. In a single issue of *TNL* (issue 11), one writer's preference for away matches is inspired by the fact that 'our own lot at Pittodrie can be exceptionally quiet at times,' while in a separate article, Glasgow writers are disparaged for suggesting that in Aberdeen 'football is only a game': 'if [the critic] would care to join us on the terracing sometime, he would soon find out otherwise.' It would be easy to accuse the fanzine writer of hypocrisy, but the two interpretations which can be drawn relate to the lack of social (or, in this case, behavioural) homogeneity within football crowds, and the satirical capacity of fanzines (even at the expense of fellow supporters) where humour rather than piety reigns supreme.

While the localist dimension underwrites the fanzines' specious content, their personnel and missions remain attuned to those which can be found elsewhere in the UK. Although earlier studies have paid little or no attention to the class composition of fanzine writers and readers,[13] research in Aberdeen and elsewhere confirms the association of these 'post-fans' with the 'new petit bourgeoisie'. This class is endowed with greater cultural than economic capital, is employed in the new service-sector, educated with new technology, socialized into enjoying consumption of popular culture, but averse to regarding itself as conventionally 'middle class' (see Bourdieu 1984). Certainly, Aberdeen fanzine writers are part of this new social strata, as they are mostly employed in white-collar work, skilled in artistry or information technology, and still on the younger side of middle age. Similarly, the fanzines are committed to 'giving the supporters a forum' for expressing their views, and for identifying any controversial issues and injustices as they arise. A common, perhaps typical, concern is that in the undemonstrative north-east too few fans write in, and that the editors may be misconstrued as some kind of self-perpetuating élite.[14] Comparatively speaking, the crux of this problem may lie in the cultural history of the club and its environs. In central Scotland the religious sectarianism associated with the 'Irish Question' promotes an increasingly ritualized identity for its football supporters.[15] Conversely, a relative agnosticism permeates the north-east which usually induces Aberdeen fans to reject explicitly the role of Irish history in the culture of Scottish football. As a *TNL* (issue 11) writer stated: 'Perhaps most important of all, we don't feel the need of religious bigotry or a misplaced idea of Irish history to fuel our passions. If the events on the park or our own good humour doesn't do it, we don't have and don't want what fires up the so called Old Firm.'[16]

An additional mission of Aberdeen fanzines, therefore, has been to underwrite this sense of differential identity and to help create some form of popular alternative that is shared by the supporters.

The most visible, symbolic consequence of this construction of identity reflects the north-east populace's marginality, self-deprecation, and their capacity to distort stereotypes about their 'otherness' to their own advantage (see McDonald 1993: 228–35). Here, I am talking of the fanzines' fetishization of a totemic figure, the sheep ('Flossy'). In predictably uninventive fashion, the more 'urbane', central-belt Scottish supporters have long typified

Figure 11.3. Bride of the Week

Aberdeen fans as being bestially orientated towards these placid but tempting creatures (Figure 11.3). The airing of such wearied verses as 'Sheepshagging bastards, You're only' (*ad infinitum*) from groups of opposing fans has, in the past decade, inspired Aberdeen fans to greet this hackneyed epithet with cheering and a mocking echo: 'Sheepshagging bastards, We're only' (*ad infinitum, con brio*). The inception of *TNL* served to convert this routine riposte into a new supporter habit. Early editions were published as 'incorporating the *Sheepshagger's Gazette*', while cartoons and newspaper clippings of stories about sheep provided a routine space-filler. Having ensured this sheep-worrying persona was 'institutionalized with pride', the more involved supporters have extended the vogue by donning ovine flags, T-shirts (weather permitting) and hat badges.

While on a parochial level this specious identity is of significance as a fanzine creation on a more anthropological level its carnival quality is striking. Evidently, it enlivens those 'rules' of carnival necessitating the collapse or inversion of social boundaries

ARTIST'S IMPRESSION OF NEW BEACH END STAND

EXECUTIVE BOXES

— CAMERON —

Figure 11.4. New Beach End

and hierarchies, in this case to mock the feeble dishonouring of the worshipping group as attempted by its Glaswegian 'others' (Ivanov 1984).[17] Elsewhere, football's carnival of rivalry involves the obscene, verbal and gestural emasculation of opponents (Marsh 1978: 25–7; Archetti 1992; Armstrong 1996). Here, the self-parodic sexual excesses of carnival are grotesque to the point of absurdity. Nevertheless, the club has responded to this participatory fandom by modernizing its public relations. Following the refurbishment and opening of one large section inside the ground,[18] a popular local DJ was drafted in to entertain the crowd; and, most intriguingly, a new club mascot was introduced: a pantomime 'Angus the Bull'. According to Lévi-Strauss (1970) (out of Eco), this emblem of the world-renowned, Aberdeen Angus beef might be regarded as an attempt to undermine the public excess of the sheepish carnival, to render respectable the animalistic mascot adopted by the club's supporters. As a symbol of the locality's affinity to the club, however, the creature has yet to soften the denizens' palate (Figure 11.5).

Figure 11.5. First Rate Second Course

The production of humour and the use of symbology represent two key resources in mapping a specific Aberdeen identity, which is largely informed by the practice of defining this construct against those of the 'others'. In this endeavour, the supporters and the club may find that they have common ground that is only contested within an anthropological imaginary. Alternatively, as a receptacle for the views of supporters, football fanzines are far less allegorical in articulating animosity towards the club's authorities when the definitive interests of supporters are jeopardized owing to the perceived lack of effective leadership.

Fanzine Agitation: Pressed into Club Conflicts

According to *TNL*'s former editor, the Aberdeen fanzines most significant, material contribution has been its 'instrumental' role in the sacking of two Aberdeen managers, Ian Porterfield (in the spring of 1988) and his successor Alex Smith (in the winter of 1992). Porterfield's private life had been a matter of extensive local gossip and his tactical negativity had alienated the supporters, whereas Smith's lingering demise brought supporters into clear conflict with the board and media. In a four-year reign, Smith won two domestic cups in 1990, but his fate was foreshadowed by the loss of the league decider with Rangers a year later.[19] The following season the club embarked upon its worst sequence of results for three decades. Mounting criticisms by supporters were frustrated by boardroom perfidy and unanimous support for the manager

Figure 11.6. Man with Football

from local and national press; fan demonstrations against Smith were even dismissed as the work of local hooligans (the Aberdeen casuals) by the media.[20] *TNL* ran a virulent campaign, and Smith was eventually sacked in February 1992, to be replaced by former club captain and local hero, Willie Miller. The role of the supporters and fanzine in precipitating these changes allowed *TNL* to play again with the irony behind their contradictory stereotype, one of supporters notorious for both placidity and nefarious vitriol. The Head of Sport at Glasgow-based Scottish Television was lambasted for failing to explain 'how fans who are the quietest and most docile in the country are also sufficiently loud and abrasive to "hound out" two managers?' (*TNL*, issue 21 1st February 1992).

The Aberdeen fanzines' form of opposition to the media is routine and dichotomous. Every issue carries several skits on media comments about Aberdeen or Scottish football generally. National media are berated for their biased treatment of Scottish football (a common grievance for Aberdeen fans), with particular regard to their support for the Old Firm. As one contributor introduced his attack: 'No one reading *TNL* should need to be told the treatment of Aberdeen in the Glasgow dominated press is atrocious' (*TNL*, issue 11). Two leading Scottish tabloids were rechristened in the fanzines as the *Sunday Mason* and the *Daily Ranger*, to reflect their apparent bias towards Glasgow Rangers.[21]

At the other extreme, the fanzines' attacks on the local media for servility towards Aberdeen FC, reflect the established views of supporters. As a one club city with the local press monopolized by Aberdeen Journals,[22] there has long been a perception among supporters that reports about players and the team's match performances are sanitized beyond recognition. Local journalists demonstrating any extended criticisms of the club are liable to become *persona non grata* at Pittodrie. Prior to one manager's sacking, *TNL* dismissed these 'duffers and charlatans whose drivelling sycophancy made a huge contribution to the slump'.

Early hostility towards the local media intensified following the mass sacking of striking journalists by Aberdeen Journals and their replacement by a young pool of inexperienced 'scab' labour, entailing a year long industrial dispute. The declining literary standards of the local media provoked further fanzine ribaldry, increasingly focused upon one hapless new local football reporter at the *Evening Express* and *Green Final*. While graffiti outside the ground disparaged this journalist's inept support for club directors, a fattening diet of ridicule was fed by his reporting inconsistencies, unfulfilled 'exclusives', surreal match reports, and susceptibility to pie-eating.[23] The reporter's bile surfaced with an inaccurate report on the closure of *TNL*, only to have this turned around by *TRF* amidst rumours of the *Green Final*'s imminent closure.[24] His final attempt to retrieve a professional reputation centred on a direct challenge to *TRF*'s editors to name themselves, rather than 'hide behind childish titles because they don't have the courage to put their names where their mouths are' (the *Evening Express*, 20 September 1995). The reply not unreasonably argued that, 'The people who matter most, the people on the streets who buy from us around Pittodrie know who we are' (*TRF*, issue 15). Unlike paid journalists, fanzine writers have literally to stand by their articles, as they sell issues face-to-face with fellow supporters.

Nevertheless, the local media's assessment of fanzines as 'not for supporters' has some credibility within the club and its older supporter associations. Following strong dissuasion from stadium stewards employed by the club, the fanzines are sold only surreptitiously within the ground. One former leader of the official

Aberdeen supporters' club was more aggressive in his hostility to the fanzines, twice threatening one vendor outside the ground. Another was informed by the club that continuing to sell the fanzine would lead to his sacking as an official programme vendor. Accordingly, the Aberdeen fanzines (particularly *TPT*) intermittently carry articles recalling supporters' negative experiences at the hands of the club autocracy.[25]

Although amused by the more irreverent aspects, club officials had come to regard *TNL* as increasingly personalized and unfair during the fanzine's later life. The most vitriolic caricatures tended to be reserved for the club's octogenarian chairman, typecast in cartoon strips according to local mythologizing of him, as frugal and cheerless in Dickensian proportions. Other club characters have been castigated, in word or image, for their blatant professional weaknesses – defenders for their lack of technique or intellect; midfield players for shiftlessness and timidity; strikers for wastefulness in front of goal.[26] Although somewhat heretical when emanating from the 'supporters', these attacks highlight the primary public appeal of *TNL*, specifically its commitment to a hitherto unknown, systematic inversion of local football's symbolic order. The humour draws upon the particularist and esoteric: established information that constitutes a local, 'restricted code' of popular suppositions, rumours and stereotypes regarding the otherwise powerful individuals who run the club.[27]

At a broader level, these criticisms of the club reflect the fanzines' consistency in scattering their critiques, caricatures and cynicism throughout Scottish football. If the powerful must be the most routine objects of attack, then the Aberdeen fanzines can only but focus upon the culture and mythology surrounding Scottish football's Old Firm, and the noted characteristics projected upon them by Aberdeen supporters: sectarian bigotry, favouritism by the national media, and a 'culture of poverty' as their social reality.[28] In one sense, the Aberdeen team's competitiveness and the supporters' abrasiveness towards the Old Firm, has assisted in the partial supplanting of one sectarian festival by a more secular (but no less intense) contest. While the Old Firm Derbys have become increasingly ritualized in their footballing and religious animosities, the Aberdeen–Rangers fixture is taken by some Rangers players themselves to be the most fervid and volatile Scottish fixture in which they now participate.

The Aberdeen fanzines materialize in print these anti-Glaswegian sentiments. Rangers and (to a lesser extent) Celtic supporters are summarily situated in vile primitiveness, their houses and streets strewn with human and industrial waste, their bodies gnarled into obese or wrecked shapes by personal abuse (Figures 11.7 and 11.8). *TPT*'s editors counter any charge of back-door racism; these targets are not discriminated against on the basis of colour or creed, merely their personal decision to follow sides renowned for their own forms of bigotry. One edition of *TNL* rejected the city's manufactured renaissance[29] with a 'Glasgow's Miles More Violent' feature (*TNL*, issue 12). And while the high-profile Graeme Souness was Rangers manager between 1986 and 1991, the anti-Rangers sentiment was at its most blatant and, possibly, its most libellous. One editor of *TNL* attempted to test the civic legality of 'comments' in various issues by hiring legal advice, which was less than enlightening. While the journal's 'common abuse' was deemed 'legal', the more personal remarks inhabited a greyer area, in which mentioned individuals might still test their merit in the civil courts with a libel action if the financial resources were available.

Figure 11.7. The Hun

And you thought things were bad for us?
You might have been a Tim!

Figure 11.8. You might have been a Tim

The Social Movement of Fanzines: Issuing a Positive Cultural Politics

Though the mockery of Scottish football's personalities and supporters are regular items for all fanzines, it would be simply wrong to suggest they are dominated by 'negativity'. All fanzines are definitive exercises in cultural politics. While *TNL* was 'provoked' by Aberdeen's footballing decline, other fanzines have emerged in response to club issues such as ground redevelopment or crowd racism. Some carry articles and features which involve the introduction of conventionally 'political issues' to the popular cultural sphere that is football.[30] The Aberdeen fanzines have all granted space to publicizing both the *Commission for Racial Equality*'s drive against racism within the sport, and the objectives of the contemporary 'new social movement': Football Fans Against the Criminal Justice Act (FFACJA).[31] However, fanzines *themselves* represent a 'new social movement' within football, and it is in this area that some divergences emerge in their various approaches towards this social status. They may be consistent in dealing positively with these liberal causes which inhabit football's cultural politics. In dealing with their own future directions, greater ambiguity reigns.

Melucci's (1980, 1985) seminal work on 'new social movements' suggests one explanation. After establishing a grass-roots identity on the basis of a specific issue, such movements are confronted with a fundamental but unavoidable dilemma in their evolution: either they become partially incorporated by the very institutions from which they had essentially differed; or they retreat into a principled fundamentalism to retain their *raison d'être*. While the former strategy represents a more rationalized and profession-alized pursuit of distribution targets and political influence, the latter strategy safeguards the outcast's critical distance and recreational atmosphere. British fanzines founded upon coverage of 'national issues' or one of the leading clubs have tended towards this professionalization, resulting in the full-time employment of staff and regular coverage in the national media.[32]

As heuristics, these ideal types generally explain the kinds of issues pertinent to *TNL*'s demise, and the subsequent formats of *TRF* and *TPT*, in their founding philosophies, and their differing approaches towards the club and its board. The former editor of the original believes these offspring are representative of the 'two extremes of *TNL*'. To some extent, issue fatigue precipitated the end of *TNL*. According to one founder, after six years it had gone 'into a groove and then a rut'. The fanzine had realized its potential, particularly by contributing to the sacking of Alex Smith. The editors 'stepped aside' to await the new generation of fanzine writers – who never materialized.[33] However, though the general policy had always been to publish what was sent in by contributors, inevitably there were disagreements over final inclusions, which were later reflected in the diverging approaches of the new fanzines, *TRF* and *TPT*. *TRF*'s editor has tended towards a 'more sedate, more predictable' journal. In terms of content and style, *TRF* is classically within the cultural politics field of football alone, aiming its comments and criticisms at the ruling figures and bodies *within* the game; for as Wren-Lewis and Clarke (1983: 131) appreciate, 'The footballing world, indeed, has its own politics.' Conversely, and with its title drawing upon Mao, *TPT* identifies with a wider conception of cultural politics; regularly quoting literary, historical and revolutionary figures to convey its antagonism towards *all* forms of hierarchy and authority.[34]

The differences between the two fanzines are illustrated more vividly in their respective discussions of Aberdeen FC's share-issue and their personal relationships with the club. In 1994, following the Chairman's death and the exhaustion of capital reserves through stadium reconstruction, the club's board decided that it should go ahead with a share-issue, the stated purpose being to buy players to compete against Glasgow Rangers. *TRF* responded positively to the eventual announcement of the share-issue, its correspondent rejecting the arguments of 'cynics' to note that 'the whole plan must be welcomed' and that, in principle, 'we are entirely in favour of shares being sold to the fans.' The article stated that 'a lot of people' opposed putting money into the club, but declared themselves 'willing to put what we can into the club, without expecting a financial return, for emotional reasons and because we have the gall to be ambitious for the club that we love.' Subsequently, the editors wrote to the club requesting a meeting, which was agreed to, but in the new chairman's absence. According to the editors, the meeting 'went well', particularly in terms of improving 'communication channels' between dedicated (rather than corporate) fans and the club's 'inner circle'. The editors concluded 'we all feel that at last the club is genuinely interested in what the fans think', though the meeting itself did not mean the fanzine had 'sold out' – a defence lent credence by the later observation of one editor (Mr Shameful Cynic) that the Aberdeen directors were buying about £1 million additional shares merely to quell any potential for shareholder rebellions (*TRF*, issue 13). A continuing liaison between the fanzine and directors was secured, and the most obvious impact of the meetings was the transformation in 'customer relations' at the Pittodrie ticket-office. *TRF* later invested directly in the club by sponsoring the players' boot-room at Pittodrie.

In stark contrast, *TPT* eschews all contact with the club and any contribution to the share-issue. The editors reason that such contact strictly undermines the objectivity that they bring to commentaries on the club. Breaching the boundary between what occurs on the park and how it is viewed off it would necessarily undermine freedom of expression. Indeed, the fanzine's very marginality is taken to provide a superior site from which to grasp events within the world of Aberdeen football (see Smith 1995: 149). This philosophy has been fully exercised in the contributors' perorations over the club's financial strategies and share-issue. In an early issue, one editor had observed, 'The move away from Joe Supporter to Fat Cat Corporate Visitor is now all but complete at our ground' (*TPT*, issue 2). He continued to explain how rising entrance prices at Pittodrie had greatly outstripped inflation over the period between 1970 and 1993.[35] The share-issue was greeted by a rival fanzine issue, emblazoned with its corporate legend 'Last of the Independents – No Sell Out'. In contrast to local media coverage, *TPT* mocked any purported 'democratization' of the club with its supporters, speculated on how the capital accumulated would be wasted on more mediocre players, and, most incisively, highlighted the fact that existing shareholders were handed nine new shares for each one held previously (*TPT*, issue 9). At its close, the issue netted £2.4 million from investing supporters, some £1.1 million shy of its £3.5 million target. Around two-thirds of that figure was spent in buying two midfield players, though *TPT* predicted that this sum would be more than recouped by the club selling its leading out-of-contract players within the next year.

TRF's public profile is likely to remain significantly stronger than its more truculent sibling. Its circulation is enhanced by a greater number of contributors and vendors, and it welcomes local and national media exposure.[36] The production of a book, with a print-run of 5,000 copies, commemorating the 'near relegation' season of 1994–95, attests to the relative institutionalization of *TRF* within the local football culture. Further exposure is guaranteed by the establishment of an Internet web-page for *TRF*.[37] In contrast, *TPT*'s classical position of greater fanzine militancy may have been decontextualized by the club's relative renaissance in the 1995–96 season. Its impact will certainly heighten, if the number of outlets increases, and the contributions chime with radical changes within the club or (more likely) the team endures another season without trophies.[38]

The Local, the National and the Shepherding of Identity

The emergence of the Aberdeen fanzines must be seen in conjunction with both local and national developments within football and civic cultures. Nationally, the fanzines have certainly been enabled by the rise of new, supporter-orientated social movements within UK football; the greater emergence of a new, educated service class having a deep affinity to popular cultural forms; and the proliferation of new media and publishing technologies, and the subsequent 'do-it-yourself' ethos that these may realize.

While these general national developments may shape the fanzines' framework, the particular, local setting largely determines the content. For example, the fanzines combine the more traditional sense of cultural differences from the rest of Scotland with the North-East's self-deprecating, often self-defeating humour: what Malinowski describes as the local 'phatic communion' of gossip, banter and joking, but transferred from street or pub to page or screen.[39] Yet they also represent a modernization of the fan culture, through the creation of post-1986 critical narratives on the club's relative decline, and the editors' parental role in the birth of a populist new symbol, specifically the sheep, and fan persona which accompanied it. The carnivalesque production of this identity is not really about 'the extent to which people feel pressure to conform to the stereotype' as 'imposed' by the other's epithets (Herzfeld 1992: 72). Rather, this persona 'fills a seemingly empty taxonomic space, and its popularity makes it possible for indifference to flourish' (ibid.: 96). In other words, it promotes a self-identity that is agreeably self-effacing and is oblivious to the sectarian fixations that pervade the 'cosmopolitan' central belt of Scotland.

Notes

1. As succinctly defined by Jary and Jary (1991: 221).
2. It may be pointed out for the benefit of North American readers that, though constituting part of the United Kingdom, Scotland has its own national football association, football team, and

national league infrastructure, each of which are entirely distinct from those in England, Wales and Northern Ireland.

3. It is possible to trace the unregulated publishing culture of football fanzines back to the pamphleteers and the working-class 'unstampeds' of the early nineteenth century (Chalaby 1995).

4. However, the Aberdeen fanzine *The Red Final* (issue 18) did call for fan information on an earlier proto-fanzine, *Football Liar*, which was distributed around Scottish grounds in the 1950s.

5. The editor of this fanzine, Danny Baker, went on to become a popular fringe broadcaster and celebrity, hosting football radio phone-ins and producing commercial videos about the game's major players' blunders. In this sense, Baker remained within an irreverent fanzine culture, but shifted his attention from music to football.

6. Sales of *TRF* and *TPT* no longer reach these heights. In the 1995/6 season *TRF* sold approximately 2,500 while *TPT* sells roughly 1,000 copies for each issue. The respective editors tend to argue that the main influence on sales is not fan interest, but the degree of marketing saturation that the fanzines can attain. The latter is dependent upon the number of vendors and retail outlets and the size of attendance at football matches where the fanzines are most commonly bought.

7. Political initiatives at this time included switching the venue of football fixtures, due to concern over crowd disorder; and preparing legislation (later aborted) that would permit only official 'club members' from attending football matches (see Giulianotti 1994).

8. The 1985 disaster was caused by fan violence, while the 1989 one was caused by a combination of dilapidated ground conditions, overcrowding, and police and steward negligence.

9. Marchi, Roversi and Bruno (1994) report that French, German, Spanish and Portugese fanzines are closely tied to the various ends and 'sides' in which the hooligan fans or *ultras* (militant, participant fans) congregate. Often these fanzines and fan sub-cultures will share the same name. Furthermore, one of the leading German fanzines, *Fantreff*, was explicitly hooligan-orientated and included a litany of letters, photographs and reports concerning hooligan activities. In contrast, the massive Italian *ultra* movement has yet to generate an analogous fanzine culture.

10. The term 'post-fan' represents a footballing application of Urry's (1990) 'post-tourist'. The 'post-tourist' is characterized by possession of personal experience and reflexive knowledge, about being a player in a multiplicity of games rather than the recipient of 'authentic' experience (Urry 1990: 100). Similarly, 'post-fans' are well aware that their involvement in football is commercially exploited by the clubs and authorities; that the players whom they 'support' have numerous personal and professional deficiencies; that the game's authorities fall somewhere between corrupt and incompetent; that media reports (especially tabloid stories) on football are largely inflated or invented; and that their personal voices matter little within the game, no matter the platitudes directed at them by those with genuine power (see Giulianotti 1993, 1996).

11. *When Saturday Comes* was first produced in March 1986, with a print run of 200 copies; it has since grown into the leading national fanzine, now calls itself a 'football magazine', and sells approximately 40,000 copies each month (Haynes 1995: 70).

12. The traditionally deep ambivalence of Aberdeen fans towards their club was perhaps foreseen by its founders in locating at Pittodrie. According to Leatherdale (1986: 1), the word *Pittodrie* is Celtic for 'place of manure'.

13. Consider, for example, the work of Curren and Redmond (1991), and Haynes (1995).

14. The general placidity of the Aberdeen support is also reflected in the fanzine editors' empathetic complaint that too few write in with contributions.

15. The cornerstone of Scottish football sectarianism is the rivalry between Rangers (Protestant–Unionist) and Celtic (Irish–Catholic) supporters. The Edinburgh clubs of Hearts and Hibs also have a historically religious divide, and it is common to find the fans of many other clubs lifting sectarian songs from Rangers in particular to formulate their own senses of supporter identity.

16. The Old Firm are the leading Glasgow clubs of Rangers and Celtic.

17. For case studies of the carnivalesque's role in determining relations between football fans, media and authorities, see Giulianotti (1991, 1995).

18. This section of the ground was popularly known as the Beach
    End, but has been rechristened the 'Richard Donald Stand',
    after the late Chairman. Figure 11.4 reflects *TNL*'s sceptical
    anticipation of the new stand's quality and congruence.

19. Needing only a draw to become champions in the final fixture
    against Rangers at Ibrox, Smith changed a settled attacking
    side into a defensive one to lose 2–0.

20. The anti-Smith campaign took many forms, such as post-match
    demonstrations (attended by fans of all ages), placard mes-
    sages inside the ground, fly-posters around the city, and
    contrived local press debates (which unanimously concluded
    by supporting the status quo). The curious but unattributed
    agreement within the national media that Aberdeen casuals
    were behind the campaign, attracted fanzine suspicion that
    someone close to the club had fed the media this line with the
    intention of discrediting and dividing the agitators. Its
    complete inaccuracy is best reflected by the fact that at one
    post-match demonstration, approximately fifty Hibs hooligans
    (supporting Hibernian FC from Edinburgh) walked through
    the protestors and caught up, and fought with, the main body
    of Aberdeen hooligans, two miles away.

21. See Finn (1991) for a discussion of the historical connection
    between Protestant freemasonry, the Orange Order and
    Glasgow Rangers. With regard to the fans' animosity to
    national media, at the Scottish League Cup Final in 1995,
    several thousand Aberdeen fans chanted 'Are You Watching
    Glasgow Press?' as they won 2–0 against Dundee at Glasgow's
    Hampden Park (commonly known as 'The National Stadium').

22. Aberdeen Journals produce three major newspapers. Its two
    dailies are the morning *Press & Journal* and the tabloid *Evening
    Express*; its weekly sports paper, the *Green Final*, is published
    for sale on a Saturday evening.

23. Part of the traditional football-spectating experience in
    Scotland involves the culinary plebianism of scoffing meat pies
    and swilling Bovril.

24. The journalist had reported that 'the foul-mouthed fanzine'
    'which appeared to have no other purpose than to attack the
    club' was winding up owing to 'dwindling interest'. The
    fanzine, reporting that the *Green Final* would cease publication
    in 1995 if Aberdeen were relegated, responded by stating that
    this 'foul-mouthed paper' with its 'burbingly incompetent

contributors in recent times', and 'which appeared to have no other purpose than attack the English language, will disappear due to dwindling interest' (*TRF*, issue 12).

25. Major Marcus B. Reno of *TPT* recalls one incident in August 1967 when an Aberdeen fan invaded the pitch and assaulted the referee, after the official had awarded a weak penalty to Celtic and then ordered a retake following a miss. After the miscreant had been heavily fined by the local courts, the writer's supporters' club organized a 'whipround' to help meet the levy – only for a member of the supporters' club committee to threaten donors with immediate expulsion if the cash was delivered.

26. A more playful representation of player weakness is illustrated in Figure 11.6. This highlights the fall-out involving one Aberdeen player and Aberdeen supporters during a match, leading to the player sending the occasional, direct message to the supporters.

27. Here, I am of course drawing upon Bernstein's (1975) distinction of 'elaborated' and 'restricted' codes of communication. While the 'elaborated' code draws upon objective, impartial and national modes of communication and is associated with a generalized, bourgeois audience, the 'restricted code' has a more subjective/localized, involved and intimate framework and is associated with a specific, working-class audience. The former might be tied to the mass media, while the latter is applicable to the particularisms and 'in-jokes' of local club fanzines. Hence, it would be easy enough for an 'outsider' to understand the arguments raised about football by Scottish or even the local mainstream media, but one would require a more acute knowledge of the particular club's culture of support to understand its fanzines.

28. Although usually a fact subject to exaggeration, Aberdeen and the surrounding Grampian region are popularly regarded as the wealthiest part of Scotland, with levels of urban deprivation lower than in other Scottish cities. Aberdeen fans are the only ones in Scotland's Premier Division habitually to mock Old Firm fans with the song 'In Your Glasgow Slums'. Sung to the tune of 'In My Liverpool Home', the song has the repeated verse 'In your Glasgow slums/In your Glasgow slums/You rake in the buckets for something to eat/You find a dead rat and you think it's a treat/In your Glasgow slums.'

29. Glasgow undertook several enormous marketing exercises to change its national identity, firstly with the 'Glasgow's Miles Better' campaign, and then through the 1990 'European City of Culture' accolade. Since then, Glasgow had been largely synonymous with a mythological history of urban deprivation, religious intolerance, razor and underworld gangs, and alcohol and hard drug abuse.

30. For example, *TNL* and its offspring have criticized Aberdeen fans involved in racist abuse (beginning with the chant-headline, 'Racists, Racists, Get tae Fuck'). More recently, both *TPT* and *TRF* have devoted a page to advertising a leaflet produced by Football Fans Against the Criminal Justice Act. This 'new social movement' asserts that the freedom of football fans to demonstrate or protest peacefully in and around grounds has been curtailed by the Act's provisions.

31. This organization declares that it 'believes the [1994] CJA will have a profound and adverse effect on the civil rights of *all* football fans,' specifically in criminalizing 'peaceful protests' at football grounds, selling on tickets at no extra cost, and various forms of 'traditional' fan behaviour (shouting and gesturing, even standing up at matches).

32. For example, the English national fanzine *When Saturday Comes* now refers to itself as a 'magazine', is sold through a national distributor and its editorial team are regularly interviewed by UK and overseas media. Haynes (1993) defends this transition, arguing that such publications now equilibrate 'a generation gap between those who write fanzines and those at the top of the football journalist profession' (ibid.: 52). However, several fanzine writers have moved into mainstream journalism in the past decade, and the spate of post 1990 football magazines (such as *4-4-2* or *90 Minutes*) reflects the greater prevalence of young male football writers. In Scotland, Glasgow's Old Firm of Rangers and Celtic have the largest selling fanzines, allowing some to employ a full-time editor and to be marketed through the club.

33. The relaunch of the Aberdeen fanzines did have separate geneses. *TPT*'s group of friends had expected a younger team of supporters to create a new club fanzine, but this failed to materialize. Conversely, *TRF* was launched as outstanding monies were used to publish the free 'issue 0'.

34. The fanzine's title comes from the Maoist dictum, 'The

reactionaries are like paper tigers; fierce to look at but they melt in the rain.'

35. The disconcerting figures showed that while prices for entry to the ground had risen 2,000 per cent (from 30p to £9), inflation had seen other prices rise at a far lower rate, for example: road tax (340 per cent) and a colour television (150 per cent).

36. At the end of 1994, prior to Willie Miller's sacking, one of *TRF*'s main writers was invited on to Radio Scotland's pre-match debate on the parlous state of the club.

37. The current *TRF* web-page can be found on: http://www.rsc.co.uk/redfinal.

38. Any future decline in the club's fanzine culture will be caused less by events within football, than by technological developments within the informal media. The expansion of the Internet and the World Wide Web is serving to enhance the opportunity for media 'receivers' to become media 'senders', in the earlier mode of football fanzine writers. These new 'narratives in cyberspace' offer more potential than print or previous electronic media – as Poster (1995: 36) notes, 'it is cheap, flexible, readily available, quick.' It may be that fanzine culture will survive this new media age only by a clear embracing of football's traditional, social form, reflected in the interpersonal transaction of selling fanzines in and around football stadiums.

39. See Pálsson's (1993: 125) usage of this concept, ironically to explain the autotelic discursive exercises of Icelandic fishermen.

Chapter 12

The Bad Blue Boys and the 'Magical Recovery' of John Clarke

John Hughson

Introduction

As a leading figure at the University of Birmingham's Centre for Contemporary Cultural Studies in the 1970s, John Clarke became an early contributor to academic discourse on soccer and social identity. He did this by connecting his broader interest in skinhead sub-culture with the study of soccer hooliganism which had been taken up by other theorists such as Ian Taylor (1971). There is a tendency in subsequent reviews of the literature to bracket Taylor and Clarke together as Marxist class theorists who explain hooliganism arising as the modernized game becomes detached from its traditional working-class supporters (Dunning et al. 1988). This is certainly Taylor's brief and, to an extent, Clarke shares it. However, Clarke goes further to suggest that what soccer hooliganism more significantly indicates is a breakdown in working-class cohesion. Principally, sections of the lower working class become detached from a class which has shifted in outlook and aspiration to adapt to the social and economic circumstances of post-war Britain (Hughson 1996). His work on skinheads highlights how these changes have affected particular sub-cultural groupings of working-class youth. Clarke (1976a: 99) speaks of skinheads experiencing a 'sense of being excluded'. Not surprisingly, this exclusion occurs in formal institutions, such as the workplace and school, where authority relations are encountered. However, in the interviews referred to by Clarke (1976a: 10) skinheads expressed an equally hostile resentment toward those from their own social background who were compliant with the oppressive 'system'. Clarke is thus insistent that the notion of community remains central to a study of the skinheads. It is at once a study about the loss of community and an attempt to regain what is believed to have been lost.

When Clarke speaks of the community's 'magical recovery' he does so with irony because his view of magic is that of the sceptic. He would see the magician as a conjurer, someone who produces effects through sleight-of-hand. Although dabbling in magic the skinhead is not a magician. While the magician's aim is to delude an audience the skinhead's magic is likely to serve as a form of self-delusion. For Clarke (1976a: 99) the skinhead attempts to 're-create' a 'traditional working-class community' which is in 'real decline'. A particular application of Anderson's (1983) notion of 'imagined community' becomes appropriate here. The skinhead imagines himself as a community member to be the true heir of a traditional way of life forsaken by other working-class youth in contemporary Britain. The skinhead conjures up a community based on perceptions of the neighbourhood in the days of his parent's youth. The visual representation of the working-class hard man in braces and boots with cropped hair illustrates the imagining. However, for Clarke, this stylistic display is not enough to revive the community in any 'real sense'. A 'real' notion of community is based on the principle of solidarity, and Clarke (1976a: 100) argues that working-class solidarity was lost in the social readjustment brought on by post-war capitalism in Britain. Thus, skinheads might talk about solidarity with explicit reference to past 'generations' (ibid.: 101), but their attempt to recapture it remains fanciful. For Clarke, the 're-creation' of community does not go beyond the projected appearance of the skinhead.

Clarke's paper is fascinating and persuasive, criticism regarding his lack of ethnographic fieldwork notwithstanding (Giulianotti 1996). His thesis on the 'magical recovery' is a useful way of explaining both the sense of loss felt by the skinheads and the disregard afforded to them by the 'community' that they claim to represent. Soccer is most important here. The highly aggressive social practices in which skinheads would engage on the soccer terrace while in support of the local team served to further divide them, not only from the 'dummoes' and 'do-gooders' of working-class youth of whom they were disdainful, but from their parental generation (to which they claim to be heirs). Unfortunately, for the skinhead, the parent culture does not welcome their particular celebration of working-class life. Although males of the parent culture may have once engaged in parochial soccer support, they did not match the violent excesses of skinhead soccer support (Clarke 1973). The older soccer fan thus tends to be as critical of the hooligan as other sections of society.

A sense of tragedy can almost be read into Clarke's paper as he concludes that social forces have worked to widen the gap between the youth sub-culture of the skinheads and the parent culture from which (even if not stated) they seek approval. However, in coming to this conclusion Clarke tends to exaggerate the skinhead as a remnant of the past without fully exploring what being a skinhead means to the person living in the sub-culture. His concentration on the 're-creation' of community leaves the question of social identity underexamined. While the skinheads might be engaged in a process of re-creation in the way described by Clarke, they are at once creating a unique social identity relevant to their time.

From the East End to the Eastern Hill

In what follows I use Clarke's notion of the 'magical recovery of community' to consider the social identity and social practice of a group of self-identifying soccer hooligans who reside in the western suburbs of Australia's largest city, Sydney.[1] This group of young men known as the Bad Blue Boys (BBB) support the Sydney United team which plays in Australia's National Soccer League (NSL). The young men of the BBB who are of Croatian parentage use soccer support as a means of expressing a social identity shaped by an extremely strong attachment to their ethnic community. Although living in a different time and in a different place, the resonances with the skinheads, as discussed by Clarke, are unmistakable. Members of the BBB declare themselves the proud bearers of a tradition of Croatian masculinity which they believe to be imperilled by the willingness of other Croatian youth to surrender a distinct ethnic identity in preference for a more urbane or 'cultured' persona. Their concern that this is detrimental to the Croatian community and their attendant claim to represent a link with the past can certainly be interpreted in terms of a 'magical recovery'. The peasant tradition of the Croatians who have come to Australia in the various waves of migration since the Second World War (Budak 1988) will steadily erode as the Australian born

generations are socialized into a very cosmopolitan and tech-
nologically advanced society. The 'old Cro. Builder'[2] of whom BBB
members speak so admiringly will no doubt disappear over the
years, and although existing in 1996, is more likely to encourage
his children to tertiary education rather than employment on a
building site.

   However, to avoid the criticisms made of Clarke, their inability
to recover an illusory community should not be overemphasized.
The 'magical recovery' does reflect a sense of loss or fear of loss.
However, this is also indicative of a social practice of resistance.
As young men from an ethnic community which has been
historically marginalized in Australian society (Skrbis 1993), the
BBB have engaged a collective strategy as a response to the
exclusion they face in a number of social arenas. Unlike other
Croatian youths who attempt to negotiate a smooth passage
through school and into tertiary education or the work-place, the
BBB enact a self-fulfilling prophecy of which they are keenly aware.
Thus, the rugged masculinity of the BBB can be seen as an attempt
to parody what they perceive as the 'stereotypical' view of Croatian
men; it may equally be seen as a declaration of affinity with their
fathers and uncles. The 'magical recovery' is ultimately ambiguous,
being at once about the attempt to reclaim 'community' and to
establish a new identity. In this latter regard, the soccer stadium
becomes the arena in which the identity is paraded. To understand
how this might work some discussion of the linkage between
soccer and ethnic communities in Australia is needed.

Soccer, Folk-Dancing and Politics

The development of soccer in Australia is tied very closely to the
history of immigration.[3] In the post-war years soccer has become
a dominant forum for the cultural expression of non-English
speaking communities resident in urban areas. Writing in the late
1970s, social researcher Rachel Unikoski (1978: 305) went as far as
to say that 'outside the sphere of economic development . . .
[soccer] is probably the largest single contribution by migrants to
Australian life'. Despite this there has been long argument within
soccer circles over whether the sport needs to shed its association
with ethnic communities if it is to match spectator levels found in
other major forms of soccer such as rugby league and Australian

rules soccer. In the early 1990s these claims were strengthened with the release of the Bradley Report,[4] which found that continuing ethnic affiliations were detrimental to soccer's expansion (Hughson 1992). Subsequently, directives were issued by the soccer authorities at both the national and state levels for competing clubs to dispense with 'ethnic' team names. So, for example, the teams Sydney Croatia and Melbourne Croatia have been renamed Sydney United and the Melbourne Knights respectively. Despite these enforced name changes, support for teams is still largely based in ethnicity. Three ethnic communities are predominantly associated with support of teams in the NSL. These are the Italian, Greek and Croatian communities in Sydney and Melbourne, and the Italian and Greek communities in Adelaide.[5] How long these affiliations will remain given the imperative of soccer officialdom to 'modernise' the game is a matter of speculation. However, it can be ascertained from what has occurred thus far, that soccer will continue to be used as a forum of ethnic celebration irrespective of 'official' attempts to sever such attachments. The retention of ethnic allegiance to soccer is likely to be most apparent in those communities which have historically maintained a strong attachment to specific soccer clubs. In this regard the Croatian community warrants notable mention. This is done with reference to the example of Sydney United.

Despite the name change from Sydney Croatia, firstly to Sydney CSC and then to Sydney United, there would be little argument from those on opposite sides of the 'ethnicity' debate against the claim that support for the team is almost exclusively from the Croatian community of Sydney.[6] This affiliation between the team and the club is strikingly obvious given that Sydney United play their home matches at the Croatian Sports Centre which adjoins a major Croatian recreational facility, the King Tomislav Club. The ground is located in the western Sydney suburb of Edensor Park, an area of large Croatian population. Match-day observations at the Croatian Sports Centre would be similar to those of Jones and Moore (1994) in relation to the North Perth Croatia Soccer Club in the Western Australian state soccer league. Jones and Moore (1994: 24) claim that, 'It is the soccer fixture that has become a major rationale for coming together as a group and publicly expressing [a] shared ethnicity.'

Over the years a home match at the Croatian Sports Centre has been something of a national fête day with Croatian newspapers and music cassettes being sold along the walkway to the entrance of the ground and the occasional display of folk-dancing and singing prior to kick-off (Hughson 1992: 12–13). After the match, supporters of various ages and both genders will celebrate a win or nurse a loss in the 'King Tom' club. It might be said that the soccer stadium and adjoining clubhouse represents a haven where Croatians can enjoy an uninhibited communal experience as Croatians – 'a home away from home' as one BBB member put it.[7]

The bond between soccer and ethnicity is not as noticeable within all ethnic communities. For example, at nearby Marconi, a club of Italian background, the linkage to ethnicity is much weaker than with Sydney United. Perhaps owing to the patronage of the local press, support for the Marconi team has become more district based. Also, the Marconi Social and Recreation Club, unlike the King Tomislav Club, holds a prominent position in western Sydney night-life and is not the domain of a particular ethnic community. There are deep-seated differences between the positioning of the Italian and Croatian communities in Australia which explain the differences in the function of the soccer club. Unlike most other post-war migrant communities the Croatians have tended to exist as an *émigré* community constantly concerned with the quest of their former homeland for independence from the perceived oppressor Serbia. The obsession with this cause has permeated all aspects of social life, and, it could be argued, has resulted in the marginalization which many Croatians believe confronts their community in Australian society (Paric 1996: 123, 138). Confronted by a mainstream culture which tends to frown upon overt displays of nationalism related to overseas political conflicts, the Croatian community are understandably wary of making public expressions of nationalist sentiments. Indeed, it is not surprising that altern- ative arenas for the communal expression of nationalism have been sought. The soccer club and park have provided both vehicle and forum for such celebrations. Although it can be argued that media reportage of 'riots' at Australian soccer matches has been exaggerated (Hughson 1992: 14–15), the carrying of political grievances into the soccer stadium has, undoubtedly, at times served as a source of crowd 'disorder'. While teams drawing support from rival ethnic groups from the former Yugoslavia are rarely brought together at the higher levels of professional soccer, this has not always been the case. A history of the crowd conflict between supporters from such groups has been sketched by Philip

Mosely (1994). A consideration of this work provides a useful historical backdrop against which the emergence of the BBB can be viewed.

The BBB and the 'Heroic Tradition'

Mosely traces the 'crowd misbehaviour' of Yugoslav soccer fans in premier competition back to their teams' emergence in New South Wales in the 1950s. By the mid 1960s three teams representing different factions had emerged – Sydney Croatia (Croatian), Avala (Serbian) and Yugal (Yugoslav unificationist). According to Mosely (1994: 34–6), each of these clubs can be said to have used soccer as a means of political expression. Mosely is particularly accusing of Sydney Croatia in this regard, claiming that at most of the matches between these teams 'some sort of crowd disorder arose'. Indeed, sixteen episodes of 'crowd misbehaviour' were reported in newspapers between 1968 and 1978. Mosely has followed up some of these accounts by interviewing opposing supporters who claim to have been present at the matches. The tale is one of physical violence featuring not only the trading of punches and kicks but, on occasion, there is resort to weaponry in the form of fence-posts, chains and knives. That physical attack did not always occur is not, for Mosely (ibid.: 38), indicative of an absence of violence. He argues that more significant damage can be caused by symbolic attack through the provocative use of 'flags, chants and insulting songs'.[8]

As indicated earlier, BBB members consider themselves the carriers of a tradition of parochial and violent soccer support. They must be distinguished, however, from the supporters involved in the 'clashes' of the past catalogued by Mosely. Although previous supporters of Sydney United might have been involved in 'crowd disturbances' they were not identifiable as a 'hooligan' group, as this term has come to be understood. By contrast, the BBB are a self-proclaimed 'hooligan' supporter group, formed prior to the commencement of the 1993 NSL season primarily to follow Sydney United and, in a secondary capacity, the Melbourne Croatian team, the Melbourne Knights. The BBB draw their inspiration from the Bad Blue Boys Dinamo, the 'hooligan' supporter group of Dinamo Zagreb (now Croatia Zagreb) a top team in the Croatian soccer league. The BBB Dinamo reportedly formed in 1986 and has several thousand members. The BBB Dinamo, like its Australian aspirants, is an organization for self-confessed soccer hooligans who cite as their major inspiration, the Italian *Serie A* supporters for their pyrotechnic displays and English hooligan groups for their perceived organizational abilities. Since the formation of the BBB Sydney, a liaison has been established between the local leadership and the president of the BBB Dinamo who is credited with providing invaluable organizational advice.

Compared to overseas hooligan groups, the BBB Sydney remains small in number and modest in their hooligan pretensions. After an initial recruitment drive a card-carrying membership numbering approximately forty was enlisted. A full two NSL seasons later, only a handful of further signings have been made. However, this does not indicate declining support for the BBB, but more, that official members become unimportant once the group establishes an identity and reputation. For some matches, members would bring along friends who might the next week bring other friends. For matches against great rivals, particularly at away grounds against opposing Sydney teams, some supporters unknown to the regular BBB would join their ranks. The BBB might remain small in card-carrying membership numbers but this does not reflect the level of 'hooligan' support it is able to muster at matches. Indeed, the BBB boasts of being the leading hooligan supporters' group to be associated with a national league team. While this claim remains conjectural it can be reasonably said that the BBB are amongst the first wave of 'hooligan' supporters' groups to appear on Australian terraces over the last few seasons. It would also be reasonable to say that the BBB has achieved more notoriety in hooligan terms than other such groups. The BBB are the only hooligan group to have been named in media criticism of crowd behaviour at national league matches. In the specialist press a debate flared in the *Australian and British Soccer Weekly* letters section following the appearance of the BBB on NSL terraces at the commencement of the 1993–94 season. One correspondent claimed that the BBB 'typify the average European soccer thug', and, in agreement with other letter writers, called upon the Australian Soccer Federation (ASF) to take action to outlaw the group. Of particular concern to a number of correspondents was the displaying of Nazi-type salutes and the racially vilifying chants and songs voiced by the BBB. These observations are not to be disputed. The songs and chants heard coming from the eastern hill of the Croatian Sports Centre on home match days are resplendent with racist goadings and are, in some cases, finished with a Nazi salute. But however the fascism of European and British soccer hooligans might be interpreted, such displays by the BBB need to be considered in a different light. Indeed, the 'magical recovery of community' is at work in such symbolic gestures.

While not a political organization in a formal sense and having no links with political organizations, BBB members profess to fascist political leanings. This would appear to have more to do with an understanding of Croatian political history than it does with a genuine commitment to that brand of politics. Members interviewed indicate that their historical knowledge has come from 'word of mouth' rather than through reading or institutional tuition. It is a history passed down from parent to child, telling of Croatians as a people of struggle and revering wartime leader and Nazi collaborator, Ante Pavelic. A number of members referred to Pavelic as a 'freedom fighter' and references to his Ustashi movement have been incorporated into soccer chants. In this regard it can be argued that the BBB work with what Fentress and Wickham (1992) describe as a 'social memory'. Fentress and Wickham (1992) contend that through the processes of group interaction individual memories can come to constitute a 'social memory'. The 'social memory' is built through a channel of intra-group communication in which the trading of narratives promotes an awareness of 'shared memories'. From this sharing of memories a group identity can be constructed and maintained over time, an agreed view of history can be reached, and this view can serve as a map to guide future social practice.

Although the narratives of the sub-cultural group might have a purely folkloric appearance to the outside observer, to the group member they are likely to assume the status of historical 'fact'. However, these narratives have an importance which goes well beyond interpretations of history. As Fentress and Wickham (1992: 88) suggest, the 'power' of the narrative is in the ability to 'legitimise the present'. Narratives provide a device through which social groups can make convenient interpretations of the present.[9] The BBB's interpretation of Croatian history must be so understood. For them, the Croatians are an oppressed people who have been engaged in a struggle 'over centuries' for national independence. It is in this light that the hero worship of Pavelic and the attendant lip-service to fascism must be interpreted. The remark, 'Pavelic might have been a fascist but he was also the liberator of the Croatian people', made by one BBB member, is typical. The 'presence' of Pavelic is impossible to escape when moving within the Croatian community of Sydney's western suburbs. A portrait of his striking visage adorns the walls of social clubs and is also given a place of prominence in the living areas of some homes. A transfer of this same portrait has found its way onto the T-shirts of some BBB members which will be worn in soccer support.

Soccer stars are also adored for their heroic qualities. BBB members have spoken of Croatian national players Zvonimir Boban and Alen Boksic as heroes. This is particularly so of Boban. While being greatly admired for his playing ability he is perhaps most admired for his part in an incident which occurred during a match in 1990 when captaining Dinamo Zagreb against the Yugoslav team Redstar Belgrade. A fight between the supporters of these teams spilled on to the pitch eventually involving several players in the confrontation. A photograph of Boban, directing a martial arts type kick toward the head of a policeman, which received international media release (*The Australian*, 15 May 1990), is often referred to in discussion by BBB members. The desired link in this interpretation is quite explicit – Boban is pictured as a Croatian soldier fighting the Serbian enemy in the form of a policeman. Here the BBB member can see the possibility of heroism being within his own reach in the arena of soccer support. Although they do not regularly confront Serbian youth during soccer support, chants and songs decrying Serbians are featured in the BBB terrace repertoire. The use of the soccer stadium as a stage for a display of belligerent nationalism determines the form of hooligan 'style' adopted by the BBB. This is addressed further on. Presently, comment is necessary on neighbourhood relations between Croatian and Serbian youth in south-western Sydney.

Defending the Neighbourhood

Although a team supported by the Serbian community does not compete in the NSL, the potential for rivalry between supporters of Croatian and Serbian background has existed over recent years at the top level of the New South Wales state league which has

included teams bearing those particular ethnic affiliations. While
the Croatian team is located in the national capital of Canberra,
some three-hundred kilometres from Sydney, the team backed by
the Serbian community, the White Eagles, are located in the Sydney
suburb of Bonnyrigg which adjoins Edensor Park. The distance
between the Croatian Sports Centre and the Serbian Sports Centre
could not be more than two kilometres. While the BBB could find
it difficult to travel regularly to Canberra, there would be no such
difficulty travelling to the games played at Bonnyrigg. It might be
questioned, then, given the strength of feelings against Serbians,
why the BBB have not pursued confrontation with Serbian youths
in this soccer context. Support for the Canberra Crows at the
Serbian Sports Centre would provide the BBB with the ideal
opportunity to confront a Serbian youth supporters' group which
follows the White Eagles.[10] However, while close proximity might
be seen as an encouragement to physical confrontation, in another
sense it might be seen as a deterrent. This has been explained by
one of the BBB members in terms of a tacit understanding that
'enemy territory is off limits'. He added, 'We don't go to their
ground, they don't come to ours, that's the way it is.' In explaining
why this was so the member elaborated, 'It helps to keep the peace,
if we went there there'd be a fuckin' riot every time.' The member
added further that this type of outcome did not greatly worry him
but that it would 'upset the oldies'.

Functionalist sociological explanations abound here. For
example, Suttles' (1972: 176) use of the term 'distancing' to describe
a natural process adopted by 'mutually exclusive territorial
groupings' to keep social order, could help to explain the 'respect'
afforded enemy turf by the BBB. However, constraints applied by
the parent culture, rather than a concern for the social order of the
neighbourhood, seemingly serve as the chief means of circum-
scribing social practice. The discussion below is revealing in this
regard. Furthermore, the awareness of an oppositional domain is
balanced by a keen sense of 'territoriality'. This was reflected in
discussions by BBB members of the responsibilities which accrue
to the factional suburban groupings within their sub-culture. While
there is considerable jibing between members along factional lines
this is usually just another source of amusement within the group.
However, a criticism made by one member gave insight into how
factional responsibility related to the defence of the neighbourhood
is a serious business. The member, from the suburban faction of

the BBB known as the 'Merrylands Boys' was criticizing the 'Fairfield Boys' for their failure to execute the removal of a Serbian flag, which was being flown in the front yard of a home within the territorial boundaries of that group. A question as to whether he seriously believed it to be the responsibility of the 'Fairfield Boys' to deal with such a display was greeted with the stern reply, 'Fuckin' oath, if that happened in Merrylands we'd get it down straight away . . . we'd burn the cunt down.' Similarities with the skinheads, as discussed by Clarke, are again apparent. Clarke (1976a: 101) refers to the organization of skinhead 'mobs' on a territorial basis in the East End of London in the early 1970s. These 'mobs' would assume responsibility for the defence of a designated 'patch' within the neighbourhood.

Clarke (1976a: 102) suggests that this defence of neighbourhood is undertaken through 'intensive violence'. He further suggests that this level of violence occurs outside of the 'informal mechanisms of social control' of the 'community', implying that skinhead youths remain relatively free from parental authority. Elsewhere, Clarke (1978: 51) has argued that one of the main explanations for the emergence of soccer hooliganism which contrasts with the parochial, even violent, soccer support of the past is a severance in soccer-supporting relations between young people and their parents. Clarke believes soccer hooliganism to be indicative of a 'dislocation' within working-class communities between adults and youths. Here the difference with the BBB sub-culture would appear significant. Parental constraint on the social practice of the BBB in various contexts including soccer support is most evident. This is indicative of a close attachment to the parent culture in contrast to Clarke's observation of a 'dislocation' of community. The constraint of parental influence is well illustrated by a comment made by a leading member of the BBB with regard to spectating positions within the Croatian Sports Centre. The member was expressing a dissatisfaction with the eastern hill end which the BBB religiously occupy at every home match. He claimed that this grassy area does not facilitate the type of 'hooligan' activities attractive to the BBB. Lamenting this he commented, 'I wish we had a terraced area like at Marconi Stadium.' When asked why, if this was so, the BBB did not occupy the concreted western scoreboard end of the Croatian Sports Centre, the member replied 'because the mums would kill us'!

Soccer and the Family

This response gives insight into a 'negotiated order' (Strauss et al. 1964) within the 'Croatian community' lived out in the soccer stadium on a Sunday evening. It seems that there is a tolerance of the BBB's 'hooliganism' as long as it is practised within the confines of their designated section of the stadium. Were the BBB to disturb the comparative tranquillity of the 'scoreboard end' they would earn the wrath of their parents and their parental generation. For their part, the BBB respect the 'right' of community elders and families to occupy the more comfortable end of the ground. Indeed, the respective occupancy of portions of the stadium by different groupings of the Croatian community is observed as a 'tradition'. This compliance with tradition is seemingly appreciated by the parental generation, reflected particularly by their warm greetings extended to the BBB by both males and females as they pass the eastern hill of the Croatian Sports Centre on the way to their own seating. A more committed form of support has, at times, been afforded by men of the parental generation when they have intervened to defend the BBB against police and private security-guards during times of tension at away matches. Men of this cohort will also, on occasion, join BBB members during post-match celebrations in the singing of Croatian folk and political songs.

This example represents a key difference from the 'familial' relationship discussed by Clarke while, at the same time, supporting his theorization on the link between such relations and soccer hooliganism. Where Clarke uses a breakdown in familial relations to explain soccer hooliganism, the study of the BBB reveals the retention of strong family bonds as a constraint on 'hooligan' activity. For BBB members soccer support is a family affair, with, in some cases, all members of a family being in attendance for home games. While the BBB might occupy a separate section of the stadium from their family members, the continuing presence of the family in the home domain of soccer support limits the BBB's achievement of a 'peak' hooligan experience to away matches (see Finn 1994a). The activity of the BBB at away matches has caused alarm, though, if not for the Croatian community in general, then to the committee of Sydney United.

However, despite being called upon by the Australian Soccer Federation to provide explanations for some of the hooligan activities of the BBB at away matches, the committee of Sydney United has lent praise to the BBB as a supporter group relevant to the contemporary game of soccer. A tribute in this regard was featured in a home match programme (13 February 1994): 'BBB supporters are those that can be counted upon to provide vocal and moral strength to the troops of Sydney United. Gone are the dark seasons of yesteryear when the supporters of Sydney United were cast as the evil of soccer hooligans.' The irony of this statement is overwhelming given the emergence of the BBB as a self-identifying hooligan group. This point was not lost on a number of letter contributors to the *Australian and British Soccer Weekly*. One writer was appalled by the readiness of the Sydney United committee to support a group which, *inter alia*, intimidates rival supporters, gives Nazi-type salutes, and wears T-shirts which clearly announce the group as soccer hooligans. The Sydney United committee have chosen to ignore this dimension to the BBB's soccer support while promoting the group for its effort and enthusiasm: 'to see the colourful and artistic banners on the famous Croatian Sports Centre Hill with the supporters bouncing whilst singing in unison is a sight which all soccer followers should be proud of.' An explanation of this defence, which is favoured by the BBB, accords with another point raised by Clarke (1978: 60). This is to recognize the 'ambiguous' position of the soccer club, which, while unwelcoming of 'hooligan' support is encouraging of what contemporary writers would call the 'carnivalesque' (Giulianotti 1991). This is so because of the conflicting demands of contemporary spectator sport which Clarke has anticipated. While wanting an orderly form of spectatorship, sporting administrators also seek colourful displays of banners and flags which are attractive to television audiences. In the case of Australian soccer, the dilemma of these competing demands is compounded by the perilously low attendance rates at NSL matches.[11] Understandably, soccer officials would be reluctant to turn away any paying customers. Accordingly, BBB members greet the Sydney United committee's predicament with characteristic arrogance. As one member put it, 'They need us more than we need them.'

The position of the Sydney United committee is further exacerbated by the relationship between the BBB and the parent generation of the Croatian community outlined earlier. For if the committee were to refuse entry to the BBB for home matches it would likely raise the ire of the 'community' as long as it remains embracing of the group in spite of the occasional embarrassments which might be suffered. Indeed, anecdotal evidence arising during ethnographic fieldwork would give some support to the claim by BBB members that they are more highly regarded within the Croatian community as representatives than the Sydney United committee. The current Sydney United committee represents something of a changing of the guard. Previous committees were comprised of older Croatian migrants who were very much of and for the 'community'. Interviews with the highest level of soccer officialdom have confirmed that previous committees were obstructive of initiatives to enforce the removal of 'ethnic' team names. One former Sydney Croatia president was quoted in the *Australian* press as advising Croatian fans to 'keep the flags waving' in defiance of the directives of the Australian Soccer Federation. With the election of the current committee which is younger, better educated and more professionally mobile than its predecessors, the fight to retain an ethnic affiliation would appear to have been surrendered. Depending on how the committee's responsibility to the Croatian community is regarded, the BBB's claim that 'they have sold us out' will be assessed.

The name change to Sydney United was received by the BBB with particular indignation. Although the change was accepted by a majority vote at a general meeting of the club membership, a number of BBB members have accused the committee of acting undemocratically. The committee is accused of using its business and management acumen to confuse a largely uneducated constituency into accepting a decision of which it might otherwise disapprove. There is much argument within the Croatian community about the impact of the name change on attendance rates at home matches. On one side there is considerable agreement with the view of a number of BBB members that many people have been driven away from soccer by the relinquishing of the traditional team name. A comment by a BBB member reflects the attitude of supporters so affected. When asked by another BBB member why he had stopped coming to the soccer this young man commented, 'I come to watch Sydney Croatia not some other team.' With regard to the committee's role in the name change he remarked, 'Yeah, they took a vote, but that doesn't mean we got what we wanted. In the old days they would have told the ASF to get stuffed.'

The current committee of Sydney United would be unapologetic about not exercising such a prerogative. Interviews with committee members indicate that they see the committee's primary goal as establishing Sydney United as a team within the NSL. To do this they regard compliance with the Australian Soccer Federation's directives on projecting a 'non-ethnic' image as essential. This comes back to an acceptance of the Bradley Report finding that a broadening of the support base beyond ethnic communities is required for soccer to become a leading professional sport. While this is regarded as commercial common sense within soccer circles, Mosely (1995) has recently argued that, even from a commercial position, soccer should maintain an appeal to ethnic communities as a means of capturing niche markets. Beyond this, however, and in keeping with the brief of this paper, the concern remains that a focus on the commercial expansion of soccer does coincide with an abandonment of the particular 'community' tradition which nurtured the sport in Australia in the post-war period.

Symbolic Resistance and Social Identity

The BBB contend that, as the change from ethnic names marks the first step toward a total discarding of ethnic identity within soccer, the Sydney United name should have been rejected. Prior to the taking of the vote the BBB mounted a limited campaign for the name Sydney Diaspora. This was regarded as a name which would comply with soccer officialdom's dictates for entry to the NSL and maintain an undeclared linkage to Croatian identity. According to a prominent BBB member, 'It's not really an ethnic name, but it captures the idea of what it is about to be a Croatian in Australia ... in that way its very ethnic.' To the disappointment of BBB members they were not afforded an opportunity to speak for this proposal at the general meeting and the Sydney United name was carried as a *fait accompli*. Despite retaining a dissatisfaction with the name, most BBB members are resigned to accepting it. Consolation was found in a subtextual reading of the name. These members choose to concentrate on the letter U in United. By doing so the name can signify a desired association with the Ustashi movement. Accordingly, a banner has been designed featuring a large letter U painted in black. Similarly, a number of banners have been designed which, although not breaking the letter of soccer officialdom's ruling (prohibiting 'national flags' and banners carrying 'political' connotation), still defy it in spirit. A prominent BBB member refers to this as 'keeping ethnicity in on the sly'. He sees this as the BBB's mission, elaborating: 'They can make as many rules as they like but they can't stop us from doing shit like that. They can stop the club from calling itself Croatia but they can't stop Sydney United from being a Croatian club. It's always up to the supporters just what a club stands for.'

This creative type of resistance involving the display of banners, the performing of nationalistic chants and songs, and the parading of national colours can be described as a form of 'grounded aesthetics' which characterize a sub-cultural identity (see Willis 1990). The BBB is perhaps better able to negotiate the 'modernising' forces within soccer than their community elders. Their adopted 'hooligan' identity facilitates an accommodation of the changes which come to bear with an ongoing celebration of ethnicity framed within the guise of contemporary youth culture. This is not to suggest that their expression of Croatian ethnicity is tokenistic. It would even be incorrect to contend that the culturally hybrid display of the BBB is indicative of what Gans (1979) has referred to as 'symbolic ethnicity'. Gans uses the term to describe the social situation whereby some third-generation Americans use symbols and recognizable aspects of the ancestral culture to give themselves a distinct identity in American society. 'Symbolic ethnicity' is distinguished from 'ethnic identity' (ibid.: 1) because, while the latter involves a reliance on 'ethnic cultures and organisations' within the host society, the former does not require such supports. 'Symbolic ethnicity' involves dipping into the parent culture at will. The young men of the BBB cannot be depicted in this way. While Gans' study focused on upwardly mobile adults who had established organizational support networks removed from their parent culture, BBB members give no indication of experiencing this kind of shift in affiliation from ethnic community. For these young Australian Croatians the organizations of the local Croatian community (namely, the Croatian Roman Catholic Church, Croatian youth clubs and Croatian soccer clubs) remain integral to their social world. As such, they have neither the luxury nor the inclination to drift in and out of their ethnic identity. Theirs is certainly a 'practiced culture' which is incorporated into all aspects of everyday life.[12]

The term 'symbolic ethnicity' remains relevant in the more general sense that the BBB draw selectively on Croatian cultural symbols as a means of identity construction. However, this borrowing should not be construed as resulting in a representation which is culturally unauthentic. Rather, the mixing of symbols from the parent culture with icons of contemporary youth culture creates a 'new stylistic ensemble' (Hebdige 1979: 87) which is uniquely Croatian. It is so because for the young men of the BBB it denotes what 'being Croatian' is about in the social life of western Sydney. Like members of other youth sub-cultures the BBB member is a 'bricoleur' who 'disrupts and re-organises meaning' (ibid.: 106). Images which might appear incompatible to the outside observer communicate a 'secret identity' to those within the sub-culture. The wearing of a Glasgow Celtic replica shirt might appear incongruous with a Sydney United scarf draped over the shoulder, particularly so given the unsightly clash of Celtic's green and white with United's red, white and blue. However, this sartorial combination needs to be understood in view of the BBB's intended identification with the supporters of a team which is famous for its linkage to Roman Catholicism.

The projection of a distinct style promotes a recognizable 'collective solidarity' amongst sub-cultural members (Clarke 1976a: 99). The soccer stadium provides an arena in which this can be displayed by the young men of the BBB. In terms of familiar soccer hooligan types the BBB assume a 'traditional' rather than 'casual' guise.[13] As unfashionable as this might sound to hooligans, and their observers, elsewhere, it is understandable given the link to ethnic background which the BBB seek to maintain. The militaristic look of the traditional hooligan is attractive to young Australian Croatian men who wish to pursue the 'heroic ideal' within the soccer stadium. This strong attachment to ethnicity precludes the adoption of the casual hooligan mode which would see the abandonment of Croatian national colours. As one member declared, 'Without our colours we don't stand for anything.' Indeed, the resentment expressed toward the committee of Sydney United is an expression of concern felt by these young men that they might be denied the one social forum where they are able to stand and declare their Croatianness. It is unlikely that the space for making such an expression can be found in other social arenas more attuned to the Anglo-cultural mainstream.

While the BBB's celebration of 'being Croatian' is decidedly peculiar to their sub-cultural formation, and understandably offensive to some who would also claim a Croatian identity, their ambition to represent a community tradition is undeniably genuine. Their cries of C-R-O-A-T-I-A from the hill of their home ground need to be considered in light of the challenge to the ongoing ethnic affiliations of Australian soccer clubs. Indeed, this cry should register a note of solidarity with others in the Croatian community who would want to keep the soccer stadium as a place where the experience of 'being Croatian' can be enjoyed. The BBB may be engaged in a 'magical recovery of community' but they at once engage a most evocative 'resistance through ritual'.

Notes

1. BBB members support their claim to hooligan identity with reference to activities in which they engage during soccer support. Some of these are exclusive to the away match experience, others are relevant to both home and away experiences. *Inter alia*, the 'taking over' of part of a rival stadium, the display of banners which challenge the directives of the Australian Soccer Federation (ASF), the verbal abuse of rival (non-hooligan) supporters, the vandalizing of property such as seats, and the threatening of and physical confrontation with members of rival supporter groups, have been mentioned as activities indicative of a collective hooligan persona.

2. BBB members make repeated reference to males of their parents' generation as 'old Cro. builders'. Some of the elaborative terms used to indicate the admiration held for men so perceived are: 'hard-working', 'tough', 'pioneer', and 'rough cunt'. Pioneer is, perhaps, the most elucidatory of these terms. The 'old Cro Builder', in this light, is seen as the forbear of an imagined Croatian cultural tradition in Australia.

3. The most comprehensive historical account of the development of soccer in post-war Australia is given by Philip Mosely (1995).

4. The report's author was an academic commissioned by the Australian Soccer Federation (ASF) to provide recommendation for future directions of the sport.

5. An affiliation with competition soccer is enjoyed by various other ethnic groups through an association with teams playing at different levels of state leagues throughout Australia. Most state soccer federations have followed the lead of the national body the Australian Soccer Federation (known since mid-1995 as Soccer Australia) in prohibiting the use of 'ethnic' team names.

6. This finding is drawn from the fieldwork for my doctoral research (Hughson 1996) which has involved speaking to academics, journalists, soccer club officials, soccer supporters and members of the Croatian community in general.

7. This point is pursued in my doctoral thesis (Hughson 1996) via a discussion of John Bale's (1994) application of the concept of topophilia. A related consideration of the notion of 'heimat' as developed in the work of Mosely and Robins (1990) is also made.

8. Definitions of violence are debated in my doctoral thesis (Hughson 1996). In agreement with other writers on 'soccer hooliganism' such as Archetti and Romero (1994) and Finn (1994), and in disagreement with Mosely (1994), I would favour a definition which sees violence as involving physical contact.

9. Clarke (1976a: 101) makes a similar suggestion in relation to skinheads with his reference to the inheritance of an oral tradition from the parent culture.

10. Youth supporters of the White Eagles have been covertly observed at the Serbian Sports Centre prior to the commencement of my study of the BBB.

11. Some figures from matches at the time of writing illustrate the point on low attendances at ASL matches. The aggregate rate for all matches (six) was 24,810, at an average of 4,135. For the match between Sydney United and West Adelaide at Edensor Park the rate was 2,798. This compares with 7,140 for the match between The Melbourne Knights and South Melbourne at the Croatian Sports Centre in Melbourne, which was a derby match. The only lower attendance rate for the weekend round was 1,591 at the game between the Morwell Falcons and Wollongong City. However, this was played in rural Victoria between two teams at the wrong end of the table.

12. Prominent Australian anthropologist Gillian Bottomley (1979) has referred to such a reliance on the ethnic community as

being indicative of the membership of a 'community-type network'. This is to be contrasted with membership of a 'loose-knit network' which will be experienced by those individuals who establish contacts outside the ethnic community through work and non-ethnic social organizations.

13. See Redhead (1986: 102) for a distinction between the mid-1980s 'casual' hooligan style, in contrast to the 'traditional hooligan stereotype of the tabloid newspapers'. The casual style involves a 'whole new look to soccer fashions', most particularly the abandonment of team colours and motifs in favour of expensive sportswear and menswear.

Chapter 13

Soccer's Racial Frontier: Sport and the Suburbanization of Contemporary America

David L. Andrews, Robert Pitter, Detlev Zwick and *Darren Ambrose*

For a month in the summer of 1994, world football's gaze was trained upon a nation which embodies commercial capitalism in its most advanced, manipulative, and often outlandish forms. True to form, the 1994 World Cup in the United States was, in a more concerted fashion than any of its predecessors, devoured by the marketing impulses and schemes of corporate capitalism (Redhead 1994; Wagg 1995a). In their visually pleasing photographic compilation, *This is soccer: Images of World Cup USA '94*, Cheeseman et al. (1994) brought together a series of images which expressed their interpretation of the tournament's essence as it unfolded on American soil. As could perhaps be expected from a *When Saturday Comes* publication, the images and accompanying textual vignettes painted an irreverent, ironic, and amusing narrative. Nevertheless the book's undoubted humour belied a pointed condemnation of the crass Americanization of the World Cup, and thereby the wider commercial exploitation of football itself. Images of a smirking Bill Clinton juggling a football, patrons at Michael Jordan's restaurant in Chicago watching the USA v Switzerland game on a video wall, an Adidas poster for 'The Alexei Lalas Experience', and, most poetically, the figure of a Bulgarian player lying prone beneath a horizontally laid billboard poster of an ice-cold bottle of Coca-Cola, all conjoined to illustrate that the 'World Cup (in its hyper-commercial American reincarnation) fitted the United States like fingers in a snug glove' (Barclay 1994: 6). However, if the crass commercialism of the event is what made the World Cup USA '94 a distinctly American spectacle then, as I believe Redhead (1994) was intimating, we are resigned to the fact that every subsequent tournament is to be held in America.

From the edifice of World Cup '94, it is possible to discern the essence of a thriving transnational post-industrial culture, which commandeers and reworks major sporting events as global spectacles designed to seduce and thereby exploit the global market-place (Wagg 1995a). Nevertheless, the tournament demonstrated little of the peculiar place occupied by football – henceforth referred to in the American vernacular as soccer – within contemporary American culture. In a very real sense, soccer is at one and the same time a distinctly un-American and explicitly American cultural practice. The game has long been associated with the waves of immigrants – initially drawn in greatest numbers from Europe and latterly central and south America – who came to America over the last 120 years (see Mormino 1982; Sugden 1994). For many of these 'hyphenated Americans' (Anon 1993: 100), especially those arriving in the decades spanning the turn of the twentieth century, soccer had not long (if at all) been an identifiable aspect of everyday existence in their respective nations of origin. Nevertheless, once confronted with the homogenizing impulses of new-world culture, many (but certainly not all) American immigrants enthusiastically appropriated soccer as an expression of national cultural Otherness. Through this association soccer became identified as the 'sport of urban immigrants' (Post 1994: 61), be they English, Scottish, German, Polish, Italian, Spanish, Columbian, or Mexican.

In recent decades, soccer's culturally differentiating un-American identity has comfortably coexisted with the game's emergence as perhaps the sporting practice and symbol of fin-de-millennium suburban America. Indeed, such is soccer's material and symbolic incursion into the middle-American lifestyle, that Post's identification of the game as a 'mini-passion of suburban America' (1994: 61) represents a considerable understatement. Whilst not envisioned as part of the suburban American dream (see Jackson 1985), soccer, like the detached family home, the reliance on the automobile, the shopping mall, and a preoccupation with material consumption, has become a core constituent of suburban American reality.

Without wishing to deny the cultural significance of American soccer in its residual multi-ethnic manifestation(s) (see Hayes-Bautista and Rodriguez 1994; Malone 1994), this project concentrates on youth soccer's emergence and influence as a sporting symbol of America's suburban crabgrass frontier (Jackson 1985). According to Hersh, 'soccer in the US is essentially a white, middle-class, suburban sport, just the opposite of the game's demographics in most of the world' (1990: 1). Strangely, although widely acknowledged and discussed by the popular media (see Gardner 1993) soccer's prominent location within the cultural landscape of contemporary suburban America has yet to be the focus of a thorough, intellectual examination.[1]

In Bourdieu's words, this chapter offers a substantive explication of how 'people acquire the "taste" for sport, and for one (soccer) rather than another' (1978: 820). In order to facilitate such a project, and as Grossberg pointed out, 'Understanding a practice involves theoretically and historically (re)constructing its context' (1992: 55). Yet, this core element of critical cultural analysis does not merely involve locating a cultural practice within its context. Rather, it implores us to map out the conjunctural relationships through which *'identities, practices, and effects generally, constitute the very context within which they are practices, identities or effects'* (Slack 1996: 125, italics added). Uppermost in terms of contextualizing any aspect of contemporary American culture is the need to discern the intersecting manifestations of class and race, which profoundly influence the experiencing of everyday existence. As Thomas Dumm correctly noted, 'Class cannot be a substitute for race' (1993: 191). Hence, given the racial complexion of the American class formation (see Wilson 1993a; Omi and Winant 1994), any analysis of soccer's widespread appropriation by a predominantly white suburban middle class, has to acknowledge and interrogate soccer as a point of intersection between class and race. Hence, this chapter locates soccer within the ongoing classed and raced process of American suburbanization.[2] Such a project is designed to interrogate the extent to which soccer contributes to what Frankenberg described as the symbolic construction of whiteness (1993). The first step in this examination would appear to be an empirically based exposition of soccer's position within the American suburban environment.

Soccurbia, USA: Memphis, Tennessee

From the 1930s onwards there have been numerous attempts to establish a professional soccer league in the United States, all of which subsequently failed. Although these aspiring professional leagues sought to capitalize upon soccer's popularity within certain ethnic minority groups, more pertinent to their success was the attraction of the expanding disposable leisure incomes of America's swelling suburban market. The most prominent of these leagues, and therefore the one which had the most visible and public demise, was the North American Soccer League. Founded in 1968, the NASL's popularity peaked in the mid to late 1970s, with the signings of Pelé, Franz Beckanbauer, and a host of foreign soccer mercenaries. Whilst 77,691 witnessed the New York Cosmos winning the NASL play-off game in 1976, average attendance for the 1977 NASL season approached a respectable 15,000 per game. Such was the optimism which enveloped soccer's future as a popular American spectator sport, that Phil Woosnam, then Commissioner of the NASL, stated 'Every sport seems to have a five-year explosive period . . . And all signals indicate now we have just had our first year of that period' (quoted in Anon 1977: 100). By the mid-1980s, such optimism had proved to be misguided, and in 1985 the NASL folded, the victim of overspending, over-expansion, and an accelerated player turnover (Toch 1994).

Despite its ignominious demise, the NASL left a 'significant American legacy' (Hersh 1990: 1) through its comprehensive network of grass-roots youth soccer programmes. Designed to stimulate mass youth interest in the NASL, these promotional programmes profoundly contributed to the growing interest in soccer as a participant sport within the crucial suburban market. By the mid-1980s, 'All that NASL missionary work, all those clinics, were beginning to bear fruit' (Gardner 1993: 225). Between 1981 and 1991 participation in high-school soccer rose from 190,495 to 350,102, an increase of 83.78 per cent. This staggering growth was even more remarkable given the fact that high-school basketball (-2.07 per cent), baseball (-2.07 per cent), and basketball (-7.56 per cent) experienced declines in participation during the same period (Pesky 1993b). At the collegiate level, there are now more National Collegiate Athletic Association (NCAA) representing men's soccer than American football programmes (Pesky 1993a). As well as the promotional machinations of the NASL, soccer's popularity – especially amongst the female population – was stimulated by the passing of Title IX of the Education Amendments Act of 1972. This legislation sought to equalize the funding for male and female programmes in federally financed institutions. Although the practical implementation of Title IX was delayed for six years by political wrangling, the Act had a dramatic effect on female athletic participation in general. In high schools alone, this rose from 294,000 (4 per cent of the female school-age population) in 1972, to 1.8 million (26 per cent of the female school-age population) in 1987 (Messner and Sabo 1990). As a direct result, soccer gained increased popularity as a female sport in part because it represented a socially acceptable outdoor team game to counter the expansive and expensive presence of all-male football programmes. As well as surging in popularity within the nation's high schools, female soccer also expanded in universities where the number of women's programmes exploded from eighty in 1982 to 446 in 1995 (Schrof 1995).

By 1995, soccer had been firmly established as the second most popular team sport for Americans under twelve years of age, with 7.7 million annual participants: a figure which dissected basketball (9.7 million) and softball (5.3 million), activities more commonly associated with American youth culture (Anon 1995). As one commentator wryly noted, 'Generation X may not be soccer-crazy, but Generations Y and Z have got the bug' (Anon 1994: 100). The game's soaring suburban popularity even spurred Hank Steinbrecher, executive director and general secretary of the United States Soccer Federation, to proclaim that one fifth of the US population were somehow embroiled in American soccer culture. Of these reported 45 million 'Soccer Americans', 18 million were comprised of individuals who played the game (70 per cent of which were under the age of eighteen), and 27 million represented the all important 'involved family members' (Steinbrecher 1996).

Given the gender breakdown of soccer participants, which approximately equates to 60 per cent male and 40 per cent female, the game is widely touted as a 'non-gender discriminatory sport unlike any other' (Steinbrecher 1996; see also Schrof 1995). Such claims of inclusion cannot be made with regard to soccer's racial complexion. A 1994 National Family Opinion Survey for the Soccer Industry Council of America described 75.6 per cent (83 per cent) of Americans who played soccer at least once a year as being 'white', and 5.2 per cent (12.5 per cent) 'African American' (Harpe

1995: C3).[3] Evidently, explanations for the racial breakdown of American soccer participants can be gleaned from the fact that the game's remarkable emergence over the last twenty years, has been concentrated within very definite socio-spatial locations, and amongst clearly defined socio-economic sectors of the American populace. According to Hank Steinbrecher:

> What has happened is that soccer was viewed by the general populous (*sic*) as ethnic, urban and very blue collar. What we find, however, is that while there is still a base of ethnic and urban supporters, the reality is that soccer today is mom and dad, two kids, two lawn chairs, Saturday afternoon with the family dog, watching the kids play, $40,000 income, mini van (quoted in Pesky 1993b: 31).

As Steinbrecher intimated, soccer has become America's suburban, middle-class family game, involving parents and children alike. Up to this point, this exposition of American soccer's demographic profile and location has concentrated on a very general level of analysis. Thus, it is necessary to further this examination by focusing on the socio-spatial distribution of soccer within a specific metropolitan area. For this reason, we turn to a brief case study of Memphis, Tennessee.

Constituted by the City of Memphis and parts of Shelby County, metropolitan Memphis comprises some 779,169 people. Bounded to the west by the Mississippi River, in earlier times the city expanded both northward and southward. Post-war expansion has been dominated by the phenomenon of 'white flight' (Marshall 1979) to easterly suburban peripheries, as white (sub)urban Memphians sought refuge from the perils of the inner city, and the economic/racial insecurities represented by ageing inner suburbs. Bordered by a curtain of vibrant suburban employment and housing communities located on the eastern edge of the metropolitan area, contemporary Memphis represents an archetypal decentred and fragmented metropolitan space, whose constituent sectors have evolved along very definite class and racial lines. Within the boundaries of metropolitan Memphis, unofficial capital of the mid-south region, soccer is most definitely alive and kicking, thus refuting Sugden's (1994) assertions as to the underdeveloped nature of the game within the southern United States. Yet, as within the majority of America's metropolitan spaces, soccer is firmly anchored in some Memphis communities, and most noticeably absent from others.

Of the total estimated population for metropolitan Memphis, 54.04 per cent (421,031) are white and 44.66 per cent (348,014) are black. Predictably this population is not equally distributed, but spatially segregated along very definite race and socio-economic class lines. This can be illustrated by contrasting two residential zones, South Memphis and East Suburban Memphis. The former comprises some 186,806 people, and the later 305,411. Whereas South Memphis is predominantly black (some 170,667 people or 91.36 per cent of the zone's population), East Suburban Memphis is predominantly white (some 259,319 people or 84.90 per cent of the zone's population). This racial bifurcation is also expressed in socio-economic terms. Whereas the per capita income of the majority black population in South Memphis is $7,583 p.a. ($14,751 p.a. for the zone's minority white population), that for the majority white population in East Suburban Memphis is $21,456 p.a. ($13,344 p.a. for the zone's minority black population). With regard to soccer, 3,067 (89.89 per cent) of the metropolitan youth soccer players reside in East Suburban Memphis, where 79,171 (37.01 per cent) of the under eighteen population of the entire metropolitan area reside. Conversely, although incorporating 58,002 (27.11 per cent) of the under eighteen population of metropolitan Memphis, the predominantly black and largely impoverished area of South Memphis contains only eighteen (0.53 per cent) of the metropolitan youth soccer players.

Despite not having figures available for the racial composition of registered youth soccer players, the vast over-representation of players from East Suburban Memphis compounded by the statistical dominance of the white population within this residential zone, would inalienably suggest that, as in the rest of America, soccer in metropolitan Memphis has become the domain of the white suburban middle class. However, as Stuart Hall (1986) would advance, there was no guarantee of either occurrence. The emergence of affluent and largely racially exclusive suburbs as the symbolic and material core of post-industrial America, and the development of soccer's seemingly natural association with this white suburban space, were both the result of corresponding intersections of social, economic and political forces. Reconstructing the (sub)urban American context, and hence the logics, out of which soccer's suburban identity – and thereby raced demeanour – emerged, provides the focus for the following section.

Territorializing the Raced Metropolis: Producing (Sub)Urban Space

Perhaps the most suggestive framework pertaining to the study of modern metropolitan spaces has been offered by Mark Gottdiener (1985). This text promotes a synthetic understanding of the production of urban space based on:

> an integrated understanding of the three-dimensional nature of socio-spatial organization as deploying hierarchical linkages to places as well as contextual or interactive relations, such as those which foster agglomeration. Furthermore, this three-dimensional array, the spatio-temporal matrix of social activities which surrounds places, involves an interrelated meshing of cultural, political, and economic forces.

> (1985: 198)

Following Gottdiener, in order to understand fully the convergence of class and race around soccer within suburban America, it would appear necessary to – however briefly – highlight the social, economic and political contingencies that fashioned the idealized post-war suburban space (Wright 1983). This can only be achieved by recognizing the conjoined, contiguous and hierarchical relations that emerged in the post-war era between increasingly decaying and demonized urban cores, and evermore affluent and exalted suburban peripheries. This project provides a platform for understanding soccer's emergence as a marker of the culturally domineering, economically empowering, and racially differentiating, middle American suburban agglomeration.

Between 1950 and 1970, America's suburban population grew from 41 million to 76 million, which equated to 27 per cent of the nation's population in 1950, and 37 per cent in 1970. By 1970, and for the first time in the evolution of the planet, the suburban population of a nation-state accounted for more than either its urban (31 per cent) or rural populations (Holleb 1975). By the advent of the 1990s, the number of American suburban dwellers was nearing an absolute majority of the national population (Kleinberg 1995).

While earlier phases in the history of American suburbanization were engineered to accentuate very definite class and race divisions, the sheer scale of post-war suburbanization wrought the most profound influence on differentiating the collective experiences of class and race in (sub)urban America. Whereas the bulk of the American population living in the low-density, relatively affluent, suburban peripheries of the nation's 320 metropolitan areas are white, the nation's urban environments have become the site of highly concentrated black and hispanic poverty (Jacobs 1992). In 1991, 42.4 per cent of the black population (roughly half of which were located in inner-city areas) lived in poverty, compared with 21.9 per cent of the white population (Fainstein 1995: 127). As Rusk (1995: xv) noted:

> In urban America, there are 10.8 million poor Whites compared with 6.9 million poor Blacks and 4.8 million poor Hispanics. In a typical metropolitan area, however, three out of four poor Whites live in middle-class neighbourhoods scattered widely across the whole area; by contrast, three out of four poor Blacks and two out of three poor Hispanics live in poverty-impacted, inner-city neighborhoods.

According to McCarthy et al. (1996), this racial divide has created a widening gulf between the experiences of predominantly white suburban dwellers and predominantly black or hispanic inner-city residents. There are numerous interrelated reasons for the post-war deconcentration of American metropolitan space (McKay 1977; Jacobs 1992; Wit 1993; Neisser and Schram 1994). The cumulative result of concerted post-war neglect has been most visibly and catastrophically manifested in polarized patterns and experiences of post-industrial suburban socio-economic growth and urban socio-economic decline (Wacquant and Wilson 1989; Wacquant 1993, 1994; Kleinberg 1995). Predominantly white and smugly affluent distending 'technoburbs' (Lemann 1989), have evolved in stark contrast to largely black (in some cities, hispanic) 'hyperghettos' crippled by the ravages of federal and corporate disinvestment (Wacquant 1994).

Normalizing Suburban Space: All-Consuming Lifestyles and Soccer

Perhaps the most profound separation between urban and suburban spaces has formed around the uneven redistribution of capital between the two populations (Squires 1994). In stark contrast to the fiscal disinvestment experienced by America's rapidly declining inner-urban cores, the genesis and flowering of suburban culture was realized through a post-war ethos of unbridled economic expansion. In this era, not far removed from the deprivations of the Great Depression, commodity consumption was advanced as the American way of life, and suburban existence became distinguished by the material commodities which conspicuously defined such lifestyles (see Ewen 1976; Lasch 1979). Previously class-exclusive goods such as refrigerators, televisions and latterly, video-recorders, became available to a broader spectrum of the population; middle-class consumption practices became ever more sophisticated in their search for class distinction, especially with regards to the advancement of differentiating lifestyle patterns (Bourdieu 1984; Lee 1993).

As the twentieth century entered its final quarter, American middle-class consumption became increasingly motivated by an ethos of cultural cosmopolitanism, through which the project of the self was fabricated via lifestyle markers of worldly sophistication and refinement. Clarke (1991) argues that this commodified cosmopolitanism distinguishes and incorporates a new – reconfigured along emerging race and gender lines – American middle class. However, in terms of race, there appears little to suggest that the presence of a growing black suburban middle class (Chideya 1995) has had any effect upon dismantling the racially charged, demonizing, celebration of the 'image of suburbia as a place of refuge for the problems of race, crime, and poverty' (Jackson 1985: 219). Indeed, it could be argued that the co-option of the black middle class, as atypical embodiments and exponents of the America's neo-cosmopolitan suburban *Zeitgeist*, has evermore seductively reinforced the racial 'borderline between the suburbs and the traumatized inner city' (McCarthy et al. 1996: 138).

In Foucaultian fashion, Dumm (1993) identified how the process of racially territorializing suburban space was realized through the circulation and consumption of an economy of commonly accepted lifestyle practices, values and identities. These observable markers of suburban existence coalesced the fragmented subjectivities of America's suburban population into a necessarily imagined normalized community, which underpinned the normality of whiteness. Bounded by a normalized middle-class lifestyle that mobilized operations of racial inclusion and exclusion, this practice of territorialization effectively separated 'those who live in the suburbs from urban others' (Dumm 1993: 189).

Undoubtedly the formation of normalized post-war suburban spaces of consumption have served as compelling markers of the distance from the perceived 'perdition' of inner-urban material deprivation, structural decay, and moral decline, travelled by the suburban dweller (McCarthy et al. 1996: 122). As Cole identified, the meaning of racially coded spaces, the raced bodies who inhabit them, and the raced practices with which they are associated are necessarily relational, for 'the meaning of identity is not self-evident or self-contained, but is dependent on difference' (1996: 25). Thus, post-war (white) suburban bodies, practices and spaces have, in large part, been fabricated in response to their (black) inner-urban equivalents. On the one hand, America's new cultural racism (see Denzin 1991; Reeves and Campbell 1994; Smith 1994) fused the moral panics that enveloped issues of urban crime, violence, drug abuse, and welfare dependency, around the 'soft bodied' irresponsibility, indolence, deviance and promiscuity (Jeffords 1993) of the stereotypical non-white urbanite. In response, middle-class norms have mobilized around the hard bodied white suburbanite, who is necessarily 'middle-class, straight, and law-abiding' (Dumm 1993: 189).

Within this reconfiguring consumer culture, the healthy body has been rendered a conspicuous symbolic expression of lifestyle choice, morality, and thereby status (see Ingham 1985; Howell 1990). For, as Bourdieu noted, the space of sport and physical activity is 'not a universe closed in on itself. It is inserted into a universe of practices and consumptions themselves structured and constituted as a system' (1990: 159). Hence, the practice of particular sports and particular physical activities became synonymous with the emergence of this 'consumerist body culture' (Ingham 1985: 50), whose various physical manifestations represent compelling markers of normalized suburban existence. The most celebrated derivatives of the rigidly class-based fitness movement which enveloped suburban American life from the mid-1970s onwards include jogging, aerobics (Whitson 1994; Markula 1995), and the expanding corporate health and fitness industry (Howell 1990, 1991). Nevertheless, the rise of soccer within suburban America cannot be divorced from the metamorphosis of the body into a corporeal commodity through which self-worth is expressed.

The particular class articulation of soccer in the United States is reflective of a particular relation to the body, which is itself related to the suburban middle-class habitus – the system of dispositions, tastes and preferences – which forms the basis of the suburban middle-class lifestyle (see Bourdieu 1978, 1980a, 1984, 1988). Bourdieu pointed out that the different classes possess differing expectations with regard to the 'perception and appreciation of the immediate or deferred profits accruing from the different sporting practices' (1978: 835). Put crudely, Bourdieu posited the working class as possessing an instrumental relation to the body, and hence to sport. This manifests itself in an orientation towards practical sporting goals, i.e. the viewing of sport as an accepted path toward financial security. Conversely, the economic stability proffered by membership of the relatively privileged middle class, allows for the development of relationships with the body, based upon sports' ability to further the interrelated health and aesthetic dimensions of physical existence. Both of which act as further sources of social distinction and differentiation.

Within the American suburban context, the bodies of the middle classes and indeed those of their children, are markers of upward social mobility, status and achievement, that are self-actualized through involvement in the right healthy lifestyle practices (Howell 1991). As Bourdieu noted, 'Class habitus defines . . . the social value accruing from the pursuit of certain sports by virtue of the distinctive rarity they derive from their class distribution' (Bourdieu 1978: 835). Soccer's particular class distribution within an American context has ensured that it contributes toward demarcating suburban bodies and spaces. Therefore, youth soccer participation has become an integral part of a normalized culture that marks suburban status and sameness, as the antithesis of urban depravity and difference.

The (Normal) People's: Voices from Middle America

Soccer does not possess any innate, essential qualities that can explain its seeming affinity with the status driven suburban middle-class habitus. Indeed, this articulation was only realized through the game's 'objective polysemia, its partial indeterminacy' (Bourdieu 1990: 163), within a post-Civil Rights American context. Although possessing a superficial ethnic gloss, soccer's indeterminate signification made it available for 'different uses' (Bourdieu 1990: 163), and allowed it to be appropriated by the suburban middle class. In order to interrogate this strategic mobilization of soccer by the middle class, this section borrows more explicitly from roughly twenty hours of non-structured ethnographic interviews (see Denzin 1989; Thomas 1993; Fontana and Frey 1994) with parents of children who play in the various leagues within the Germantown Area Soccer Association. Germantown was chosen as the site for the interviews as it represents the single most affluent community within East Suburban Memphis, and in Philip Langdon's (1995) words, minus the sardonic tone, it is viewed by many Memphians as 'a better place to live'. During the course of this discussion we intend to borrow judiciously from the ethnographic interviews, and strategically position quotes from interviewees in such a way as to underscore, and thereby advance, wider social trends and logics as being responsible for fashioning soccer's suburban deportment.

Germantown's popular status as a suburban utopia is underscored by its self-conscious affluence, and homogenous racial composition. With regard to the former, whereas the average per capita income in 1989 for East Suburban Memphis as a whole was $19,687 p.a., that for Germantown spiralled to $28,474 p.a. In terms of the latter, Germantown's 1989 population of 33,824 was 95.13 per cent (32,177) white, 1.96 per cent (662) black, and 2.91 per cent (985) other. Germantown's status as an élite suburb demonstrates the diversity between suburban spaces, both in terms of racial and socio-economic factors. As well as being particularly affluent, Germantown also represents the most racially homogenous (in terms of the statistical dominance of the white population) sector within East Suburban Memphis.[4] Equally predictably, given these demographics, Germantown is a bastion of organized soccer, possessing some of the most established, organized, and successful youth soccer programmes in the metropolitan area. Out of the six sectors within East Suburban Memphis, Germantown was one of only two areas whose percentage of the zone's youth soccer players exceeded the percentage of the zone's under eighteen population. Of the 3,067 registered youth soccer players from East Suburban Memphis, 21.1 per cent (646) were located in Germantown, despite the fact that the area contained only 13.3 per cent (10,520) of the residential zone's under eighteen population. Whilst there are no figures available which document the racial composition of the youth soccer-playing population in Germantown, it should be pointed out that of the hundreds of players observed during the course of the interviewing process, only two were black. None of the parents interviewed were black.

Part of soccer's ability to appeal to contemporary suburban values lies in its obtuse relationship with more established elements of American sporting culture. Given its residual indeterminacy, soccer was able to occupy a symbolic space created by vectors of popular opposition targeted at more traditionally American sporting pursuits. Specifically, both American football and basketball did not rest easily with the superficially progressive (often cloaked in a neo-reactionary traditionalism) mores of America's maturing (white) suburban hegemony. The exaggerated hyper-masculinity and female marginalization celebrated by American football became increasingly incongruous with post-1960s parents, many of whom strove for a semblance of gender equality in their children's lives, if not their own. Within this climate of increased gender awareness and activity in the realm of sport, and emerging as it was in the shadow of American football's physical and symbolic chauvinism, soccer assumed the mantle of the gender inclusive American sport *par excellence*:

> It's a sport that is not unfeminine, it's a good challenging sport that can be accepted. It's not a contact sport, or something like that, but it's a high quality game. I think people like it once it gets competitive, because it's something everyone can do.

The tendency toward celebrating soccer as an agent of gender equality is countered by attitudes which divulge ingrained assumptions towards female physicality, and correspondingly advance revealing attitudes toward soccer as a physical activity:

> She does not have the interest or the skills. She likes it because it is fun. She is on a team and she gets to play with the other kids. It is nothing that she takes seriously.

> I don't know the reason why my daughter plays. It's just because the kids she goes to school with play, and it's something to do.

> This is a kids sport. It's not violent. They get exercise and she's on a team, so I think it's perfect for kids.

The same rationale that made soccer a suitable physical activity for girls – its perceived encouragement of non-aggressive behaviour, sociability, and the all important fun – similarly made it attractive to parents seeking an alternative to American football for their sons. According to Wagg, '"soccer" appeals to liberal and/ or Democratic families concerned to promote equal opportunities but deterred by the aggressive masculinity' embodied within American football (1995a: 182). As Hornung (1994: 39) noted, soccer is 'a sport preferred by middle and upper middle-class parents who want to protect their kids from the savagery of American football.' Certainly, the thoughts of Germantown parents echoed similar sentiments:

> I've seen too many children playing football they hurt their knees . . . It's physically a pretty punishing game, and I think a lot of them have this dream, 'Oh I am going to be a Heisman Trophy[5] winner and I'm going on to the NFL', but statistically very few of them can do it, and a lot them end up with broken bodies along the way.

> Not like football where you are using your upper body to knock people down. I mean, sometimes you knock people down but, not like that. But, he likes it . . . He did not play football and I am happy about that. As a mother I am pretty protective physically. The objective of soccer is not to knock someone down. That is really the major difference.

Soccer was thus popularized because it appeared to offer the right type of aerobic health benefits for boys and girls (Bondy 1992; Pesky 1993b), as dictated by the aesthetic and health directives of the suburban middle-class habitus:

> I think it provides overall higher aerobic exercise, conditioning, and co-ordination development than any of the other sports. I think it does more for them than any other sport.

> I think it's a conditioning sport and I think if you go out and do weights all day it's not going to help you as much as going out and running all the time, and being able to run and keep moving.

> I don't think it's a physical sport, but I think it's good for their bodies other than physical contact sports.

Good team work, and the co-ordination, and the aerobic workout, it's a wonderful sport.

It is a lot of running and endurance. I like to be outside . . . you do not see any fat kids here playing soccer.

According to a 1977 article in *U.S. News and World Report*, 'Another possible reason for the growth of soccer in some suburbs – one that the game's proponents do not discuss publicly, but a few say privately – is that some white youths and their parents want a sport not as dominated by blacks as football and basketball' (Anon 1977: 100). Over the last three decades a racially charged 'national fantasy' (Berlant 1991) has enveloped basketball. This centred upon the popular fears and fascinations associated with the perceived natural physicality of the urban African American athlete, who, were it not for sport, would unerringly be involving his body in more deviant, promiscuous and irresponsible pursuits (see Reeves and Campbell 1994; Cole 1996; Cole and Andrews 1996; McCarthy et al. 1996). Unquestionably, the racial signifiers contained within popular basketball (and to a lesser extent American football) discourse have, in opposition, influenced soccer's symbolic location within the contemporary popular imaginary. In spatial (suburban/urban), racial (white/black), and corporal (cerebral/ physical) senses, soccer became the antithesis of basketball:

> Yes, this is more of your suburban type of sport, it's not an urban sport. It's mainly a white thing, there's not many blacks at all in Germantown, and there's no blacks in soccer here.

> There's a lot of families, you know, you know it's mostly for white players. You don't have a lot of black players in soccer right now, so the city, you know isn't as strong.

As well as valorizing the suburban American family (which will be discussed later), soccer was also cast as the appropriate activity for the normal suburban athlete, whose innate intelligence was counterpoised, even in absentia, by the natural athletic ability of the black urbanite:

> I think it takes a quicker mind, I mean to pick up where the play is going and to set your things up. In basketball and football there is a plan. With soccer, the sport is so fast, much like ice hockey, that it just

happens and you have to be prepared for what's going to happen, and know how to interact with your teammates.

In soccer you have got to control two body parts, your head and your feet.

Kids that do well are the ones that use their head. You can run all day but if you don't use your head you're not going to necessarily do well. So as far as the physical requirements, you need the mental requirements as well, if not more.

I don't believe that any of these kids have a burning desire to play soccer specifically, they just like playing a sport and this is one that you don't have to have a whole lot of expertise in. Anybody can play it, not necessarily well, but anybody can play.

There also appears to be a widespread assumption that the standard of US soccer is hampered by the type of athlete (i.e. white/suburban/cerebral) who is presently dominating the game, and that soccer in the US would undoubtedly improve if the right populations (i.e. black/urban/physical) were encouraged to take up the sport. Accordingly, a *Chicago Sun-Times* columnist noted, 'soccer will never take off in America until the talent that still resides within our cities is fully tapped and discovered . . . Somewhere in the Robert Taylor Homes are a handful of Pelés' (Hornung 1994: 39).

Soccer also provided the suburban middle class with an opportunity for distancing itself from the instrumental relation to the body exemplified by the pragmatic habitus of the black urban working class:

You don't get the big money . . . You don't get 30 million dollars or 40 million dollars, for playing soccer as you do being a quarter back on the NFL or any professional sports, something in basketball . . . Usually black kids have something to look up to in football and basketball, because mainly, I would say probably 70 per cent of all basketball teams are black.

In Memphis, a lot of the economic and racial considerations are that people look at traditional sports – football, baseball and mostly basketball – as the way to go on to big money. Soccer is played in the local setting for sport.

Yeah, Germantown in all has better sports programs both in the schools and in the community, but I think you're dealing with a higher educated group of people that want their children to be involved in some type of sport. That's what it all boils down to. Basically, out of all of the parts of Memphis, the community supports all types of activities. Germantown has a swim team, they have a lot of diversified athletics and other community things like theater and choirs and things like that. We pay higher taxes for this type of thing.

Evidently soccer is celebrated as a symbolic site for reaffirming the ascendant position of the suburban middle-class lifestyle. On a more pernicious level, the use of soccer in sustaining the imagined and normalized suburban community, necessarily – if discreetly – advances notions of the moral and cultural superiority of (white) suburban practices, institutions and individuals in relation to their (black) urban counterparts. Soccer is part of a middle-class lifestyle 'that separates those who live in the suburbs from urban others. Those who are different . . . perceived as dangerous' (Dumm 1993: 189). This is most vividly expressed in attitudes toward the family, and child-rearing responsibilities. The hegemonic 'pro-family' agenda, popularized by the intersecting forces of the Christian Right and the Reagan administration in the 1980s (Diamond 1995), has seemingly infused every aspect of suburban existence. Soccer is no exception:

It's good like I said, it's a family affair here in Germantown.

It keeps the community close, keeps everybody . . . a big family.

The family support is big. If the kid is out here and he doesn't have parents watching he may not really care as much.

I think the people here are more family orientated.

Such pro-family suburban sentiments are clearly fashioned in opposition to the zone of racial difference represented by the ghettos of inner-urban America (Giroux 1994). The New Right castigated the black urban populace for lacking the family orientated values, practices and responsibilities, which were incredulously posited as the reasons for America's neglected, deteriorating and hence threatening, inner cities. In response to this popular racial demonizing of anti-family urban spaces, many suburban dwellers display a hostility, resentment and contempt for the urban populace (McCarthy et al. 1996). This frequently manifests itself in a conceited and self-righteous reinforcement of suburbanites own status as responsible and caring members of the American family:

There's nothing more important than raising your kids.

Memphis is so diverse as far as the population, but also you don't have a lot of communities where you have a clump of middle-aged folks where they can all come together... You have to have commitment from the parents and you may not get that in the inner city.

In this area there's a lot more of a commitment to children in general ... there's a lot more, there's a little more money.

The parents see that the kids have the opportunity if they want to take part, so people like me who are really too busy to do all of this, and to coach baseball and that sort of thing, we just say it's the most important thing that we're going to do besides making a living. This is a well to do community, and the parents are very motivated to see the kids happy.

As many of the quotes in this section suggest, soccer's articulation to suburban whiteness is rarely, if ever, expressed in overtly racial terms. Rather, racial/class references and hierarchies are more frequently inferred or implied through euphemistic (dis)association. In a Derridean sense, white suburban discourse is manufactured out of *différance* to the black urbanite, who is always already there (Smith 1994).

In conclusion, this chapter has attempted to offer a preliminary examination of the ways soccer became complicit in the process of American suburban normalization, precisely because the game was able to resonate with the practices, values and institutions, that marked the boundaries of normalized suburban existence. In other words, the game became a sporting touchstone of racially subdivided America (Jackson 1985), and assumed the mantle of yet another taken-for-granted prerequisite of that mythologized existence:

Germantown is primarily a middle-age, family-type community and everybody has two or three kids. You play soccer in the fall and spring, and basketball leagues in the winter, and everybody plays baseball. You see the same people and the same parents throughout the different sporting seasons. I think it's good.

As an increasingly conspicuous presence in contemporary middle-class suburban American existence, soccer is heavily involved in the hierarchical territorialization of white suburban culture within the national popular imaginary. In rather trite, but nevertheless revealing, terms, Lawson commented, 'soccer became a minor snob prop, like pet alligators and Tuscan extra virgin olive oil' (Mark Lawson 1993, quoted in Sugden 1994: 247). Soccer's explicit articulation within the consumerist lifestyle (Clarke 1991) – which demarcates the normalized racially coded inventory of suburban experience – resulted in the game being both articulated and experienced as the antithesis of America's unravelling urban dystopia. Participation in soccer expresses the type of normalized cultural values and ideals prized by suburban middle-class mores. Thus, as with the other manifestations of the middle-class suburban habitus, soccer is nonchalantly, if unwittingly, experienced and advanced as a compelling popular euphemism for both class and race superiority.

Notes

1. This chapter represents a general introduction to a larger project that focuses on a critical ethnographic analysis of soccer within metropolitan Memphis. This broader study is itself part of a larger project that develops a social cartography of sport within Memphis.
2. As well as loosely drawing from ethnographic data derived from ongoing fieldwork carried out in the Memphis metropolitan area, this project is also informed by varied participatory experiences with youth soccer, in Connecticut, Illinois, and South Carolina.
3. Figures in parenthesis refer to the racial breakdown of US population as a whole (US Census Bureau Data, 1996).

4. Interestingly, and as with some of America's élite suburban communities, the average per capita income of Germantown's miniscule black population actually exceeds that of the white population.
5. The Heisman Trophy is awarded on an annual basis to the best collegiate American football player.

Bibliography

Abu-Lughod, L., and C.A. Lutz. 'Introduction: Emotion, Discourse, and the Politics of Everyday Life' in C.A. Lutz and L. Abu-Lughod (eds), *Language and the Politics of Emotion*, Cambridge, Cambridge University Press; Paris Editions de la Maison des sciences de l'homme, 1990

Adorno, T. *Prisms*, London, Spearman, 1967

Agar, M. *Professional Stranger*, New York, Academic Press, 1980

Akindutire, I.O. 'The Historical Development of Soccer in Nigeria: an appraisal of its emerging prospects', *Canadian Journal of the History of Sport*, 22(1), 1991

Al Nahar, H., and D. Witt. 'History of Sport in Jordan' in H. Uberhorst (ed.), 1989

Allison, L. (ed.), *The Changing Politics of Sport*, Manchester, Manchester University Press, 1993

Alvim, R. *Constituição da Família e Trabalho Industrial*, unpublished PhD thesis, Rio de Janeiro, Museu Nacional, 1985

Alvim, R., and J.S. Leite Lopes. 'Familles Ouvrières, Familles d'Ouvrières', *Actes de la Recherche en Sciences Sociales*, 84 (September 1990)

Amnesty International *Sierra Leone. Prisoners of War? Children detained in barracks and prison*, London, International Secretariat of Amnesty International, 1993

Anderson, B. *Imagined Communities*, London, Verso, 1983

Anderson, B. *Imagined Communities*, revised edition. New York, Verso, 1991

Anon. 'From kids to pros . . . : Soccer is making it big in U.S.', *U.S. News & World Report*, 17 October 1977

Anon. 'Soccer's last frontier', *The Economist*, 4 December 1993

Anon. 'Stateside Soccer: Will the World Cup diminish soccer in America?', *The Economist*, 18 June 1994

Anon. 'Database', *U.S. News & World Report*, 28 August 1995

Arbena, J.L. 'Sport and the Study of Latin American Society: an overview' in J.L. Arbena (ed.), *Sport and Society in Latin America: diffusion, dependency, and the rise of mass culture*, Westport, Greenwood Press, 1988

Archetti, E., and A. Romero. 'Death and Violence in Argentinian Football' in R. Giulianotti, N. Bonney and M. Hepworth (eds), 1994

Archetti, E. *Violencia y fútbol*, Buenos Aires, SEDES, 1985

Archetti, E. 'Argentinian Football: a ritual of violence?', *International Journal of the History of Sport*, 9(2), 1992

Archetti, E.P. (1994a) 'Masculinity and Football: the formation of national identity in Argentina', in R. Giulianotti and J. Williams (eds), 1994(b)

Archetti, E.P. 'Idioms and Rituals of Manhood: the worlds of tango and football in Argentina' University of Oslo, Department of Anthropology, unpublished paper, 1994(b)

Archetti, E.P. (1994c) 'Argentina and the World Cup: in search of national identity', in J. Sugden and A. Tomlinson (eds), 1994(a)

Archetti, E.P. 'Estilos y virtudes masculinas en *El Gráfico*: la creación del imaginario del fútbol argentino', *Desarrollo Económico*, 35(139), 1995

Archetti, E.P. 'Playing Styles and Masculine Virtues in Argentine Football' in M. Melhuus and K.A. Stølen (eds), *Machos, Mistresses, Madonnas, Contesting the Power of Latin American Gendered Imagery*, London, Verso, 1996(a)

Archetti, E.P. 'The Moralities of Argentinian Football' in S. Howell (ed.), *The Ethnography of Moralities*, London, Routledge, 1996(b)

Arens, W. 'Professional Football: an American symbol and ritual' in W. Arens and S.P. Montague (eds), *The American Dimension: cultural myths and social realities*, Port Washington, Alfred Publishing Co, 1976

Armstrong, G. 'False Leeds: The Construction of Hooligan Confrontation' in R. Giulianotti and J. Williams (eds), *Game Without Frontiers*, Aldershot, Arena, 1994

Armstrong, G. *Football Hooligans: An Anthropological Case Study – The Blades of Sheffield United*, University College, London, Department of Anthropology, unpublished PhD thesis, 1996

Armstrong, G., and R. Giulianotti. 'Avenues of Contestation: football hooligans running and ruling urban spaces', paper to the British Sociological Association Annual Conference, *Contested Cities: social process and spatial forms*, University of Leicester, 10–13 April 1995

Armstrong, G., and R. Harris. 'Football Hooligans: theory and evidence', *Sociological Review*, 39(3), 1991

Armstrong, G., and D. Hobbs. 'Tackled from Behind' in R. Giulianotti, N. Bonney and M. Hepworth (eds), 1994

Artusi, L., and S. Gabrielli. *Calcio storico fiorentino ieri e oggi*, Florence, Comune di Firenze, 1986

Ashry, A. 'Where are the homegrown soccer stars?' *The Middle East*, 110 (December 1983)

Atkinson, P. *The Ethnographic Imagination: textual constructions of reality*, London, Routledge, 1990

Augé, M. *Non-Places*, London, Verso, 1995

Bachelard, G. *The Poetics of Place*, Boston, Beacon, 1969

Baker, W.J. *Sports in the Western World*, Urbana, University of Illinois Press, 1988

Bakhtin, M. *Rabelais and His World*, Massachusetts, Massachusetts Institute of Technology Press, 1968

Bale, J. *Sport and Place: a geography of sport in England, Scotland and Wales*, London, Hurst, 1982

Bale, J. (1991) 'Playing at Home: British football and a sense of place' in J. Williams and S. Wagg (eds), 1994

Bale, J. *Landscapes of Modern Sport*, Leicester, Leicester University Press, 1994

Bale, J., and J. Maguire (eds), *The Global Sports Arena*, London, Cass, 1994

Banck, G.A. 'Mass Consumption and Urban Contest in Brazil: some reflections on lifestyle and class', *Bulletin of Latin American Research*, 13(1), 1994

Barclay, P. 'Foreword' in D. Cheeseman et al., 1994

Barley, N. *The Innocent Anthropologist*, Harmondsworth, Penguin, 1986

Barthes, R. *The Pleasure of the Text*, New York, Hill and Wang, 1975

Bateson, G. *Steps to an Ecology of Mind*, London, Intertest, 1972

Baudrillard, J. *The Transparency of Evil: essays on extreme phenomena*, London, Verso, 1993

Bauman, Z. *Legislators and Interpreters*, Oxford, Blackwell, 1987

Bayart, J.F. 'One-Party Government and Political Development in Cameroun', *African Affairs* 72(287), 1973

BBC *Kicking and Screaming*, football documentary series, 1995

Beck, U., A. Giddens and S. Lash. *Reflexive Modernization*, Cambridge, Polity, 1994

Beckles, H., and B. Stoddart (eds), *Liberation Cricket: West Indies cricket culture*, Kingston, Ian Randle Publishers, 1995

Bedecki, T. 'Sport and Nationalism' in J.C. Pooley and C.A. Pooley (eds), *Proceedings of the Second International Seminar on Comparative Physical Education and Sport (September 23–27, 1980)*, Halifax, Dalhousie University Printing Centre, 1982

Bengtsson, E. *Heja röda vita laget*, Uddevalla, Författarförlaget, 1975

Benzaquem de Araújo, R. 'Os Gênios da Pelota: Um Estudo do Futebol como Profissão', Rio de Janeiro, Museu Nacional-UFRJ (unpublished M.A. Dissertation in Social Anthropology), 1980

Berlant, L. *The Anatomy of National Fantasy: Hawthorne, utopia, and everyday life*, Chicago, University of Chicago Press, 1991

Bernstein, B. *Class, Codes and Control*, (3 vols) London, Routledge & Kegan Paul, 1975

Blanchard, K. 'Sport and Ritual: a conceptual dilemma', *Journal of Physical Education, Recreation and Dance* 59(9), 1988

Blanchard, K. *The Anthropology of Sport: an introduction*, Westport,

Connecticut, Bergin & Garvey, 1995

Block, R. 'EC's timber imports fuel Liberia civil war', *the Independent on Sunday*, 22 November 1992

Bogard, W. *The Simulation of Surveillance: hypercontrol in telematic societies*, Cambridge, Cambridge University Press, 1996

Bondy, F. 'Soccer: now kids, that's the way to use your heads!', *New York Times*, 24 December 1992

Bottomley, G. *After the Odyssey: a study of Greek Australians*, St Lucia, University of Queensland, 1979

Bottomley, G. *From Another Place*, Cambridge, Cambridge University Press, 1992

Bourdieu, P. 'Sport and Social Class', *Social Science Information*, 17(6), 1978

Bourdieu, P. (1980a) 'A Diagram of Social Position and Lifestyle', *Media, Culture and Society*, 2, 1980

Bourdieu, P. (1980b) 'Comment Peut-On Être Sportif?' in *Questions de Sociologie*, Paris, Minuit, 1980

Bourdieu, P. *Distinction: a social critique of the judgement of taste*, Cambridge, Harvard University Press, 1984

Bourdieu, P. 'Program for a Sociology of Sport', *Sociology of Sport Journal*, 5(2), 1988

Bourdieu, P. 'Program for a Sociology of Sport' in *In Other Words: essays toward a reflexive sociology*, Stanford, Stanford University Press, 1990

Bourdieu, P. *Language and Symbolic Power*, Cambridge, Polity Press, 1991

Boyle, R. 'We are Celtic supporters . . . : questions of football and identity in modern Scotland' in R. Giulianotti and J. Williams (eds), 1994

Bradley, G. *Final report to the Australian Soccer Federation*, Sydney, ASF, 1990

Bradshaw, S. 'The Coming Chaos?', *Moving Pictures Bulletin*, 25, February 1996

Brand, L.A. *Palestinians in the Arab World. Institution Building and the Search for State*, New York, Colorado University Press, 1988

Brand, L.A. 'Palestinians and Jordanians: A Crisis of Identity', *Journal of Palestine Studies*, XXIV(4), 1995

Bredekamp, H. *Calcio Fiorentino. Il Rinascimento dei giochi*, Genoa, Il Melangolo, 1995

Brockmann, D. 'Sport as an Integrating Factor in the Countryside', *International Review of Sport Sociology*, 4 (1969)

Bromberger, C. (1987a) 'Allez l'OM' 'Forza Juve!' La passion du football à Marseille et à Turin', *Terrain*, 8 (April 1987)

Bromberger, C. (1987b) 'L'Olympique de Marseille, la Juve et le Torino: variations ethnologiques sur l'engouement populaire pour les clubs et les matches de football', *Esprit*, April 1987

Bromberger, C. 'Pour une ethnologie du spectacle sportif: les matches de football à Marseille, Turin et Naples' in B. Michon and C. Faber (eds), *Sciences Sociales et Sport*, Strasbourg, University of Strasbourg Press, 1988

Bromberger, C. 'Ciuccio e fuochi d'artificio. Indagine sul rapporto fra la squadra di calcio napoletana e la sua città', *MicroMega*, 4 (1990)

Bromberger, C. 'Le football comme vision du monde', *Le Monde diplomatique*, 10–11 June 1992. [Reprinted 1994 as 'Football Passion and the World Cup: why so much sound and fury?' (translated by Christopher Young) in J. Sugden and A. Tomlinson (eds), 1994(a)]

Bromberger, C. (1993a) '"Allez l'O.M., Forza Juve": the passion for football in Marseille and Turin' in S. Redhead (ed.), 1993

Bromberger, C. (1993b) 'Fireworks and the Ass' in S. Redhead (ed.), 1993

Bromberger, C. 'Foreign Footballers, Cultural Dreams and Community Identity in some North-western Mediterranean Cities' in J. Bale and J. Maguire (eds), 1994

Bromberger, C. *Le Match de Football: ethnologie d'une passion partisane à Marseille, Naples et Turin*, Paris, Editions de la Maison des sciences de l'homme, 1995(a)

Bromberger, C. 'Lo spettacolo delle partite di calcio' in A. Roversi and G. Triani (eds), *Sociologia dello sport*, Napoli, ESI, 1995(b)

Budak, L. 'Post-war Croatian Settlement' in J. Jupp (ed.), *The Australian People: an encyclopedia of the nation, its people and their origins*, North Ryde, Angus & Robertson, 1988

Caldas, W. *O Pontapé Inicial; Memória do Futebol Brasileiro (1894–1933)*, São Paulo, Ibrasa, 1990

Cameron, A. *Circus Factions: Blues and Greens at Rome and Byzantium*, Oxford, Clarendon Press, 1976

Canter, D., M. Comber and D. Uzzell. *Football in its Place*, London, Routledge, 1989

Carter, J.M., and A. Krüger (eds), *Ritual and Record: sports records and quantification in pre-modern societies*, Westport, Greenwood Press, 1990

Caselli, G.P. 'Il calcio da sport a impresa capitalistica' in R. Grozio and F. Portinari (eds), *Catenaccio e contropiede. Materiali e immaginari del football italiano*, Rome, Antonio Pellicani, 1990

Cashman, R. *Paradise of Sport: the rise of organised sport in Australia*, Melbourne, Oxford University Press, 1995

Cashmore, E.E. *Making Sense of Sport*, 2nd edn, London, Routledge, 1996

Chakra, A.A. 'Sport' in T. Mostyn (exec. ed.), *The Cambridge Encyclopedia of the Middle East and North Africa*, Cambridge, Cambridge University Press, 1988

Chalaby, J.K. '"Knowledge is Power": the working class "unstampeds" as an example of public discourse', *Working Papers*, London School of Economics, Department of Sociology, 1995

Chambers, I. *Migrancy, Culture, Identity*, London, Routledge, 1994

Cheeseman, D., M. Alway, A. Lyons and P. Cornwall (eds), *This is Soccer:*

images of World Cup USA '94, London, Gollancz/Witherby, 1994

Cheska, A.T. 'Sports Spectacular: the social ritual of power', *Quest*, 30, 1978

Chideya, F. *Don't Believe the Hype: fighting cultural misinformation about African-Americans*, New York, Penguin, 1995

Clarke. J. 'Football Hooliganism and the Skinheads', Stencilled occasional paper No.42, Birmingham: Centre for Contemporary Cultural Studies, University of Birmingham, 1973

Clarke, J. 'The Skinheads and the Magical Recovery of Community' in S. Hall and T. Jefferson (eds), 1976(a)

Clarke, J. 'Style' in S. Hall and T. Jefferson (eds), 1976(b)

Clarke, J. 'Football and Working Class Fans: tradition and change' in R. Ingham (ed.), 1978

Clarke, J. *New Times and Old Enemies: essays on cultural studies and America*, London, Harper Collins, 1991

Clayton, A. 'Sport and African Soldiers: the military diffusion of Western sport throughout Sub-Saharan Africa' in W.J. Baker and J.A. Mangan (eds), *Sport in Africa: Essays in Social History*, New York, Africana Publishing Company, 1987

Clifford, J., and G.E. Marcus. *Writing Culture: the poetics and politics of ethnography*, Berkeley, University of California Press, 1986

Clignet, R., and M. Stark. 'Modernisation and Football in Cameroun', *Journal of Modern African Studies*, 12(3), 1974

Cohen, A. *Two Dimensional Man*, London, Routledge & Kegan Paul, 1974

Cole, C.L. 'P.L.A.Y., Nike, and Michael Jordan: national fantasy and the racialization of crime and punishment', *Working Papers in Sport and Leisure Commerce*, The University of Memphis, Bureau of Sport and Leisure Commerce, 1(1), 1996

Cole, C.L., and D.L. Andrews. '"Look-Its NBA ShowTime!": Visions of race in the popular imaginary', *Cultural Studies*, 1(1), 1996

Coles, R.W. 'Football as a Surrogate Religion' in M. Hill (ed.), *Sociological Yearbook of Religion in Britain*, vol. 8, London, SCM Press, 1975

Collin, R.O. 'The Blunt Instruments: Italy and the police' in J. Roach and J. Thomaneck (eds), *Police and Public order in Europe*, London, Croom Helm, 1985

Collins, J. *Migrant Hands in a Distant Land: Australia's post-war immigration*, Sydney, Pluto, 1991

Colome, G. 'Il Barcelona e la società catalana' in P. Lanfranchi (ed.), 1992

Cook, B. 'Football Crazy', *New Society*, 44(819), 15 June 1978

Corrêa, F.P. *Grandezas e Misérias do nosso Futebol*, Rio de Janeiro, Fores & Mano, 1933

Coutinho, E. *Maracanã, Adeus (Onze Histórias de Futebol)*, published as *Bye, Bye Soccer*, Austin, Texas, Host Publications, 1980

Curren, M., and L. Redmond. 'We'll Support You Evermore? Football club allegiance: a survey of *When Saturday Comes* readers', University of Leicester, Sir Norman Chester Centre for Football Research, 1991

Da Matta, R. *Relativizando: uma Introdução à Antropologia Social*, Petrópolis, Vozes, 1981

Da Matta, R. 'Notes sur le Futebol brésilien', *Le Débat*, 19 (1982)

Dal Lago, A. *Descrizione di una battaglia*, Bologna, Il Mulino, 1990

Dal Lago, A. 'Il voto e il circo', *Micromega*, 1, 1994

Dal Lago, A., and R. De Biasi. 'Italian Football Fans: culture and organization' in R. Giulianotti, N. Bonney and M. Hepworth (eds), *Football, Violence and Social Identity*, London, Routledge, 1994

Davidson, B. *The Black Man's Burden: Africa & the curse of the nation state*, London, James Currey, 1992

Davies, C. 'The Protestant Ethic and the Comic Spirit of Capitalism', *British Journal of Sociology*, 43, 1992

De Biasi, R. *Le Culture del Calcio: un'analisi comparatiba dei rituali e delle forme del tifo calcistico in Italia e in Inghilterra*, unpublished PhD thesis in Sociology, University of Trento, 1993

De Biasi, R. 'The Policing of Hooliganism in Italy', paper to the international symposium, *The Policing of Mass Demonstrations in Contemporary Democracies*, Florence, European University Institute, 13–14 October 1995

De Certeau, M. *The Practise of Everyday Life*, Berkeley, California, University of California Press, 1984

De Wit, W. 'The Rise of Public Housing in Chicago, 1930–1960' in J. Zukowsky (ed.), *Chicago Architecture and Design 1923–1993: reconfiguration of an American metropolis*, Munich, Prestel, 1993

Della Porta, D. 'Police Knowledge and Public Order', paper to the international symposium, *The Policing of Mass Demonstrations in Contemporary Democracies*, Florence, European University Institute, 13–14 October 1995

Denzin, N.K. 'The Research Act: a theoretical introduction to sociological methods', Englewood Cliffs, Prentice Hall, 1989

Denzin, N.K. *Images of Postmodern Society: social theory and contemporary cinema*, London, Sage, 1991

Descola, P. *The Spears of Twilight: life and death in the Amazon jungle*, London, Harper Collins, 1996

Diamond, S. *Roads to Dominion: right-wing movements and political power in the United States*, New York, Guilford Press 1995

Dini, V. 'Maradona, héros Napolitain', *Actes de la Recherche en Sciences Sociales*, 103 (1994)

Dini, V., and O. Nicolaus (eds), *Te Diegum: genio, sregolatezza e bacchetoni*, Milan, Leonardo, 1991

Dodd, P.C. 'Family Honour and the Forces of Change in Arab Society', *International Journal of Middle East Studies*, 4 (1973)

Donnelly, P. 'Resistance through Sports: sport and cultural hegemony' in Sports et Sociétés Contemporaines (8th International Symposium of the International Committee for Sociology of Sports). Paris, Société Française de Sociologie du Sport, 1983

Douglas, M. *Purity and Danger: an analysis of concepts of pollution and taboo*, Harmondsworth, Penguin, 1970

Douglas, M. *How Institutions Think*, London, Routledge, 1987

Dujovne Ortiz, A. *Maradona C'est Moi*, Paris, Editions La Découverte, 1992

Duke, V., and L. Crolley. *Football, Nationality and the State*, London, Longman, 1996

Dumm, T.L. 'The New Enclosures: racism in the normalized community' in R. Gooding-Williams (ed.), *Reading Rodney King: reading urban uprising*, New York, Routledge, 1993

Dunning, E. 'La Dynamique du Sport Moderne' in N. Elias and E. Dunning, 1994

Dunning, E., P. Murphy and J. Williams (eds), *The Roots of Football Hooliganism: an historical and sociological study*, London, Routledge, 1988

Eco, U. *Travels in Hyperreality*, London, Picador, 1986

Elias, N., and E. Dunning. 'The Quest for Excitement in Unexciting Societies' in G. Lüschen (ed.), *The Cross-Cultural Analysis of Sport and Games*, Champaign, Illinois, Stipes, 1970

Elias, N., and E. Dunning. *Sport et Civilization: la violence maîtrisée*, Paris, Fayard, 1994

Ellis, S. 'Liberia 1989–1994: a study of ethnic and spiritual violence', *African Affairs*, 94(375), 1995

Evans-Pritchard, E.E. *Witchcraft, Oracles and Magic among the Azande*, Oxford, Oxford University Press, 1937

Evans-Pritchard, E.E. *Kinship and Marriage among the Nuer*, Oxford, Clarendon, 1951

Evans-Pritchard, E.E. *Essays in Social Anthropology*, London, Faber, 1962

Evens, T.M.S. *Two Kinds of Rationality. Kibbutz Democracy and Generational Conflict*, Minneapolis, University of Minnesota Press, 1995

Ewen, S. *Captains of Consciousness: advertising and the social roots of the consumer culture*, New York, McGraw-Hill, 1976

Fainstein, N. 'Black Ghettoization and Social Mobility', in M.P. Smith and J.R. Feagin (eds), *The Bubbling Cauldron: race, ethnicity, and the urban crisis*, Minneapolis, University of Minnesota Press, 1995

Fairgrieve, J. *The Boys in Maroon. Heart of Midlothian: The Authorized Inside Story of an Unforgettable Season*, Edinburgh, Mainstream/HMFC, 1986

Fairgrieve, J. (1976) 'Out of the East' in S.F. Kelly (ed.), *The Kingswood Book of Football*, London, The Kingswood Press, 1992

Faris, J.C. 'Occasion and Non-Occasion' in M. Douglas (ed.), *Rules and Meanings*, Harmondsworth, Penguin, 1968

Fentress, J., and C. Wickham. *Social Memory*, Oxford, Blackwell, 1992

Fernandez, J.W. 'Symbolic Consensus in a Fang Reformative Cult', *American Anthropologist*, 67 (1965)

Ferrarotti, F., and O. Beha. *All'Ultimo Stadio: una repubblica fondata sul calcio*, Milan, Rusconi, 1983

Filho, M. *Viagem em tôrno de Pelé*, Rio de Janeiro, Editora do Autor, 1963

Filho, M. *O Negro no Futebol Brasileiro*, Rio de Janeiro, Civilização Brasileira, 1964

Finn, G.P.T., and R. Giulianotti. 'Scottish Fans, Not English Hooligans! Scots, Scottishness and Scottish Football' in R. De Biasi (ed.), *Il Mito Del Tifo Inglese*, Milan, Sheke, 1996

Finn, G.P.T. 'Racism, Religion and Social Prejudice: Irish Catholic clubs, soccer and Scottish society. (I) – The Historical Routes of Prejudice, (II) – Social identities and conspiracy theories', *International Journal of the History of Sport*, 8(3), 1991

Finn, G.P.T. (1994a) 'Football Violence: a societal psychological perspective' in R. Giulianotti, N. Bonney and M. Hepworth (eds), 1994

Finn, G.P.T. (1994b) 'Sporting Symbols, Sporting Identities: soccer and intergroup conflict in Scotland and Northern Ireland' in I.S. Wood (ed.), *Scotland and Ulster*, Edinburgh, Mercat Press, 1994

Fishwick, N. *English Football and Society 1910–50*, Manchester, Manchester University Press, 1989

Fiske, J. *Power Plays, Power Works*, London, Verso, 1993

Fontana, A., and J.H. Frey. 'Interviewing: the art of science' in N.K. Denzin and Y.S. Lincoln (eds), *Handbook of Qualitative Research*, Thousand Oaks, California, Sage, 1994

Forsyth, R. *The Only Game: the Scots and world football*, Edinburgh, Mainstream, 1991

Foucault, M. *The Order of Things: an archaeology of the human sciences*, New York, Pantheon Books, 1970

Foucault, M. *Discipline and Punish: the birth of the prison*, London, Lane, 1977

Foucault, M. *Power/Knowledge: selected interviews and other writings* (edited by G. Gordon). Brighton, Harvester Press, 1980

Fox, N. 'Sport International: progress in the Third World', *International Journal of Physical Education*, 15(3), 1978

Fox, R. 'Pueblo Baseball: a new use for old witchcraft', *Journal of American Folklore*, 74 (1961)

Frankenberg, R. *Village on the Border: a study of religion, politics and football in a North Wales community*, London, Cohen & West, 1957

Frankenberg, R. 'The Social Construction of Whiteness: white women, race matters', Minneapolis, University of Minnesota Press, 1993

Frazer, J. (1922) *The Golden Bough*, London, Macmillan, 1974

Furley, O. 'Child Soldiers in Africa' in O. Furley (ed.), *Conflict in Africa*,

London, Tauris, 1995

Fyfe, C. *A Short History of Sierra Leone*, London, Longman, 1979

Gans, H. 'Symbolic Ethnicity: the future of ethnic groups and cultures in America', *Ethnic and Racial Studies*, 2(2), 1979

Garcia, A., Jr. *Libres et Assujettis*, Paris, Editione de la Maison des Sciences de l'Homme, 1989

Gardner, P. *The Simplest Game*, New York, Collier Books, 1993

Geertz, C. 'The Integrative Revolution: primordial sentiments and civil politics in new states' in C. Geertz (ed.), *Old Societies and New States: the quest for modernity in Asia and Africa*, Glencoe, Free Press, 1963

Geertz, C. 'Deep Play: notes on the Balinese cockfight', *Daedalus*, 101 (1972)

Geertz, C. *The Interpretation of Cultures*, New York, Basic Books, 1973

Geertz, C. *The Interpretation of Cultures*, London, Hutchinson, 1975

Gehrmann, S. 'Football and Identity in the Ruhr: the case of Schalke 04' in R. Giulianotti and J. Williams (eds), 1994

Ghirelli, A. *Intervista sul Calcio Napoli*, Bari, Laterza, 1978

Ghirelli, A. *Storia del calcio in Italia*, Turin, Einaudi, 1990

Giddens, A. *Modernity and Self-Identity: self and society in the late modern age*, Oxford, Polity, 1991

Giddens, A. 'Living in a Post-Traditional Society' in U. Beck, A. Giddens and S. Lash (eds), 1994

Gilen A.N. *Finding Ways: Palestinian coping strategies in changing environments*, Oslo, Fafo report 177 (1994)

Giles, H.A. 'Football and Polo in China', *The Nineteenth Century and After*, vol. 59 (1906)

Ginsborg, P. *Storia d'Italia dal dopoguerra ad oggi*, Turin, Einaudi, 1989

Giroux, H.A. *Disturbing Pleasures: learning popular culture*, New York, Routledge, 1994

Giulianotti, R. 'Scotland's Tartan Army in Italy: the case for the carnivalesque', *Sociological Review*, 39(3), 1991

Giulianotti, R. (1993a) 'Soccer Casuals as Cultural Intermediaries' in S. Redhead (ed.), 1993

Giulianotti, R. (1993b) 'A Model of the Carnivalesque?: Scottish football fans at the 1992 European Championship Finals in Sweden', *Working Papers in Popular Culture*, no. 5, Manchester Metropolitan University

Giulianotti, R. 'Social Identity and Public Order: political and academic discourses on football violence' in R. Giulianotti, N. Bonney and M. Hepworth (eds), *Football, Violence and Social Identity*, London, Routledge, 1994

Giulianotti, R. 'Football and the Politics of Carnival: an ethnographic study of Scottish fans in Sweden', *International Review for the Sociology of Sport*, 30(2), 1995

Giulianotti, R. *A Sociology of Scottish Football Fan Culture*, University of

Aberdeen, Department of Sociology, unpublished PhD thesis, 1996 (a)

Giulianotti, R. 'Back to the Future: an ethnography of Ireland's Football Fans at the 1994 World Cup Finals in the USA', *International Review for the Sociology of Sport*, 31(3), 1996(b)

Giulianotti, R. (1997) '"All the Olympians, a thing never known again?": Reflections on Irish football culture and the 1994 World Cup Finals', *Irish Journal of Sociology*, 1997

Giulianotti, R., N. Bonney and M. Hepworth (eds), *Football, Violence & Social Identity*, London, Routledge, 1994

Giulianotti, R., and J. Williams (eds), *Game Without Frontiers: football, identity and modernity*, Aldershot, Arena, 1994

Gluckman, M. *Custom and Conflict in Africa*, Oxford, Blackwell, 1955

Gluckman, M., and M. Gluckman. (1977) 'On Drama, and Games and Athletic Contests' in S.F. Moore and B.G. Meyerhoff (eds), 1977(b)

Goffman, E. *Encounters: two essays on the sociology of interaction*, Indianapolis, Bobbs-Merrill, 1961

Goffman, E. *Frame Analysis: an essay on the organization of experience*, New York, Harper & Row, 1974

Goodwin-Gill, G., and I. Cohn. *Child Soldiers: the role of children in armed conflicts*, Oxford, Clarendon Press, 1994

Gorn, E.J., and W. Goldstein. *A Brief History of American Sports*, New York, Hill & Wang, 1993

Gottdiener, M. *The Social Production of Urban Space*, Austin, Texas, University of Texas Press, 1985

Grossberg, L. *We Gotta Get Out of This Place: popular conservatism and postmodern culture*, London, Routledge, 1992

Grueninger, R.W. 'Sport and Physical Education in Bahrain' in W. Johnson (ed.), *Sport and Physical Education around the World*, Champaign, Illlinois, Stipes Publishing Co., 1980

Guedes, S. 'O "povo brasileiro" no campo de futebol', *À Margem: Revista de Ciências Humanas*, s/n, Rio de Janeiro, 1993

Guttmann, A. *From Ritual to Record: the nature of modern sports*, New York, Columbia University Press, 1978

Guttman, A. *Sports Spectators*, New York, Columbia University Press, 1986

Guttman, A. *A Whole New Ball Game: an interpretation of American sports*, Chapel Hill, University of North Carolina Press, 1988

Guttmann, A. *Games and Empires: modern sports and cultural imperialism*, New York, Columbia University Press, 1994

Hall, S. 'The treatment of "Football Hooliganism" in the Press' in R. Ingham (ed.), 1978

Hall, S. 'The Problem of Ideology: Marxism without guarantees', *Journal of Communication Inquiry*, 10(2), 1986

Hall, S., and T. Jefferson (eds), *Resistance through Rituals: youth subculture in post-war Britain*, London, Hutchinson, 1976

Harpe, M. 'Soccer dollar limits blacks', *News & Record*, Greensboro, North Carolina, 28 May 1995

Harris, J.C. 'Sport and Ritual: a macroscopic comparison of form' in J.W. Loy (ed.), *The Paradoxes of Play: proceedings of the sixth annual meeting of the Association for the Anthropological Study of Play*, West Point, Leisure Press, 1982

Hayes-Bautista, D.E., and G. Rodriguez. 'L.A. story: Los Angeles, CA, soccer and society', *the New Republic*, 19 (4 July 1994)

Haynes, R. 'Vanguard or Vagabond? A History of *When Saturday Comes*' in S. Redhead (ed.), *The Passion and the Fashion*, Aldershot, Avebury, 1993

Haynes, R. *The Football Imagination: the rise of football fanzine culture*, Aldershot, Arena, 1995

Hebdige, D. 'The Meaning of Mod' in S. Hall and T. Jefferson (eds), 1976

Hebdige, D. *Subculture: the meaning of style*, London, Methuen, 1979

Hebdige, D. *Hiding in the Light: on images and things*, London, Routledge, 1988

Hersh, P. 'Soccer in U.S. at Crossroads: World Cup seen as last resort to stir fan sport', *Chicago Tribune*, 3 June 1990

Herzfeld, M. *The Social Production of Indifference*, Oxford, Berg, 1992

Hoggart, R. *The Uses of Literacy*, Harmondsworth, Penguin, 1969

Hognestad, H. *The Jambo Experience. Identity, meaning and social practice among supporters of Heart of Midlothian Football Club*, University of Oslo, Dept. and Museum of Anthropology, unpubl. thesis, 1995

Holleb, D.B. 'The Direction of Urban Change' in H.S. Perloff (ed.), *Agenda for the New Urban Era*, Chicago, American Society of Planning Officials, 1975

Holt, R. 'Working Class Football and the City: the problem of continuity', *British Journal of Sport History*, 3(1), 1986

Holt, R. *Sport and the British*, Oxford, Oxford University Press, 1989

Holt, R. 'La tradition ouvriériste du football anglais', *Actes de la recherche en sciences sociales*, 103 (1994)

Home Affairs Committee *Policing Football Hooliganism. Memoranda of Evidence*, London, HMSO, 1990

Hopcraft, A. *The Football Man*, London, Simon & Schuster, 1968

Horne, J., and D. Jary. (1994) 'Japan and the World Cup: Asia's first World Cup final hosts?' in J. Sugden and A. Tomlinson (eds), 1994(a)

Hornung, M.N. '3 billion people can't be wrong', *Chicago Sun-Times*, 17 June 1994

Howell, J. '"A Revolution in Motion": advertising and the politics of nostalgia', *Sociology of Sport Journal*, 8 (1991)

Howell, J.W. 'Meanings Go Mobile: fitness, health and the quality of life debate in contemporary America', Urbana, Illinois, University of Illinois at Urbana-Champaign, unpublished PhD thesis, 1990

Hughson, J. 'Australian Soccer: ethnic or Aussie? The search for an image', *Current Affairs Bulletin*, 68(10), 1992

Hughson, J. 'Mad Boys, Bad Boys and Stallions: male youth supporter groups and ethnic identity in the Australian National Soccer League', paper to the *International Conference: Youth 2000*, Teeside University, July 1995

Hughson, J. *A Feel for the Game: an ethnographic study of soccer support and social identity*, University of New South Wales, School of Sociology, unpublished PhD thesis, 1996

Huizinga, J. (1949) *Homo Ludens. A Study of the Play Element in Culture*, London, Routledge & Kegan Paul, 1980

Humphrey, J. 'Brazil: football, nationalism and politics' in A. Tomlinson and G. Whannel (eds), *Off the Ball*, London, Pluto Press, 1986

Humphrey, J. (1994) 'Brazil and the World Cup: triumph and despair' in J. Sugden and A. Tomlinson (eds), 1994(a)

Humphreys, L. *Tearoom Trade: impersonal sex in public places*, Chicago, Aldine, 1970

Hutchinson, J. 'Some Aspects of Football Crowds before 1914', paper to the conference, *The Working Class and Leisure*, University of Sussex, 1975

Ibrahim, H. 'Leisure and Islam', *Leisure Studies*, 1 (1982)

Igbinovia, P. 'Soccer Hooliganism in Black Africa', *International Journal of Offender Therapy and Comparative Criminology*, 29 (1985)

Ilmarinen, M. (ed.), *Sport and International Understanding*, Berlin, Springer-Verlag, 1984

Ingham, A.G. 'From Public Issue to Personal Trouble: well-being and the fiscal crisis of the state', *Sociology of Sport Journal*, 2(1), 1985

Ingham, A.G., and J. Loy. 'Sport Studies through the Lens of Raymond Williams' in A. Ingham and J. Loy (eds), *Sport in Social Development: traditions, transitions and transformations*, Champaign, Illinois, Human Kinetics, 1993

Ingham, R. (ed.), *Football Hooliganism: the wider context*, London, Interaction, 1978

Inglis, S. *The Football Grounds of Europe*, London, Collins Willow, 1990

Jackson, K.T. *Crabgrass Frontier: the suburbanization of the United States*, New York, Oxford University Press, 1985

Jackson, M. *Paths Toward a Clearing: radical empiricism and ethnographic enquiry*, Bloomington, Indiana University Press, 1989

Jacobs, B.D. *Fractured Cities: capitalism, community and empowerment in Britain and America*, London, Routledge, 1992

Jarvie, G., and J. Maguire. *Sport and Leisure in Social Thought*, London, Routledge, 1994

Jarvie, G. 'Sport, Nationalism and Cultural Identity' in L. Allison (ed.), 1993

Jary, D., J. Horne and T. Bucke. 'Football "Fanzines" and Football Culture: a case of successful "cultural contestation"', *Sociological Review*, 39(3), 1991

Jary, D., and J. Jary. *Collins Dictionary of Sociology*, Glasgow, HarperCollins, 1991

Jeffords, S. *Hard Bodies: Hollywood masculinity in the Reagan era*, New Brunswick, Rutgers University Press, 1993

Jeffrey, I. 'Street Rivalry and Patron-Managers: football in Sharpeville, 1943–1985', *African Studies*, 51(1), 1992

Johnson, F. (1939) *A Standard Swahili–English Dictionary*, Dar-es-Salaam and Nairobi, Oxford University Press, 1990

Jones, R., and P. Moore. '"He only has eyes for Poms"': soccer, ethnicity and locality in Perth', *Australian Society for Sports History: Studies in Sports History*, 10 (1994)

Jones, S.G. *Sport, Politics and the Working Class*, Manchester, Manchester University Press, 1989

Kaplan, R. D. 'The coming anarchy: how scarcity, crime, overpopulation, and disease are rapidly destroying the social fabric of our planet', *Atlantic Monthly*, February 1994

Kerr, J. *Understanding Soccer Hooliganism*, Milton Keynes, Open University Press, 1994

Kertzer, D.I. *Ritual, Politics and Power*, New Haven, Yale University Press, 1988

Klapp, O.E. *The Collective Search for Identity*, New York, Holt, Rinehart & Winston, 1969

Klein, A.M. *Sugarball: the American game, the Dominican dream*, New Haven, Yale University Press, 1991

Kleinberg, B. *Urban America in Transformation: perspectives on urban policy and development*, Thousand Oaks, California, Sage, 1995

Knappert, J. *The Aquarian Guide to African Mythology*, London, Aquarian Press, 1990

Kohn, M. (1994) 'Trouble with Funny Hats', review of C. Townshend, *Making the Peace: public order and public securities in modern Britain*, in *Independent on Sunday*.

Korr, C. *West Ham United: the making of a football club*, London, Duckworth, 1986

Kovacevic, M., and M. Gladovic (eds), *Croatians in Australia: as printed in the Sydney Morning Herald*, Sydney, Croatian Resource Centre, 1990

Kozanoglu, C. 'Beyond Erdine: football and the national identity crisis in Turkey', unpublished paper, 1996.

Krieger, M. 'Cameroon's Democratic Crossroads 1990–4,' *Journal of Modern African Studies*, 32(4), 1994

Kuper, A. *An African Bourgeoisie: race, class and politics in South Africa*, New Haven, Yale, 1965

Kuper, A. *Anthropology and Anthropologists: the modern British school*, London, Routledge & Kegan Paul, 1983

Kuper, S. *Football Against the Enemy*, London, Orion, 1994

Kyröläinen, H., and T. Varis. 'Approaches to the Study of Sports in International Relations', *Current Research on Peace and Violence*, 4(1), 1981

La Nouvelle Expression, no.174, 26 July–1 August 1994

Lackoff, G., and M. Johnson. *Metaphors We Live By*, Chicago, Illinois, University of Chicago Press, 1980

Lambert, J. 'Musiques Régionales et Identité Nationale' in M. Tuchscherer (ed.), 1994

Lane, J.-E. (ed.), *Understanding the Swedish Model*, London, Cass, 1991

Lanfranchi, P. *Il calcio e il suo pubblico*, Napoli, ESI, 1992

Lanfranchi, P. 'The Migration of Footballers: the case of France 1932–1982' in J. Bale and J. Maguire (eds), 1994

Lanfranchi, P. 'I giochi con la palla all'epoca del calcio fiorentino e lo sport moderno' in *Tempo libero e società di massa nell'Italia del Novento*, Milan, Franco Angeli, 1995

Langdon, P. *A Better Place to Live: reshaping the American suburb*, New York, HarperPerennial, 1995

Larsen, K. *Where Humans and Spirits Meet: incorporating difference and experiencing otherness in Zanzibar Town*, Doctoral thesis, University of Oslo, 1995

Lasch, C. *The Culture of Narcissism: American life in an age of diminishing expectations*, New York, W. W. Norton, 1978

Lash, S., and J. Urry. *Economies of Signs and Space*, London, Sage, 1993

Last, M., and P. Richards. *Sierra Leone 1787–1987: two centuries of intellectual life*, Manchester, Manchester University Press, 1987

Leach, E. *Pul Eliya, a Village in Ceylon: a study in land tenure and kinship*, Cambridge, Cambridge University Press, 1961

Leach, J.W., and G. Kildea (eds), *Trobriand Cricket: An indigenous response to colonialism, structure and message in Trobriand cricket*, Berkeley, University of California Media Center, 1974

Leatherdale, C. *The Aberdeen Football Companion*, Edinburgh, John Donald, 1986

Lee, M.J. *Consumer Culture Reborn: the politics of consumption*, London, Routledge, 1993

Leite Lopes, J.S. *O 'vapor do diabo': o trabalho dos operários do açúcar*, [The 'Devil's Steam': the labour of sugar workers], Rio de Janeiro, Paz e Terra, 1976

Leite Lopes, J.S. *A tecelagem dos conflitos de classe na cidade das chaminés*, [The Weaving of Class Conflict in 'Chimneys' City], São Paulo, Marco Zero/Editora da UnB, 1988

Leite Lopes, J.S. 'Lectures savantes d'un syndicalisme paradoxal: la

formation de la classe ouvrière brésilienne et le syndicat "officiel"',
Genèses, 3 (1991)

Leite Lopes, J.S. 'A vitória do futebol que incorporou a *pelada*; a invenção
do jornalismo esportivo e a entrada dos negros no futebol brasileiro',
São Paulo, *Revista USP*, 22(3), 1994

Leite Lopes, J.S. 'Esporte, en ɔção e conflito social', Rio de Janeiro, *Mana:
Estudos em Antropologia Social*, 1 (1995)

Leite Lopes, J.S., and J.P. Faguer. 'L'invention du style brésilien: sport,
journalisme et politique au Brésil', *Actes de la Recherche en Sciences
Sociales*, 103 (1994)

Leite Lopes, J.S., and S. Maresca. 'La disparition de la joie du peuple:
notes sur la mort d'un joueur de football', *Actes de la Recherche en
Sciences Sociales*, 79 (1987)

Lemann, N. 'Stressed Out in Suburbia: a generation after the postwar
boom, life in the suburbs has changed, even if our picture of it hasn't',
The Atlantic, 34 (November 1989)

Leseth, A. *Bevegelseskultur. Et antropologisk perspektiv på kroppslig bevegelse
i Dar-es-Salaam, Tanzania*. University of Oslo, Dept and Museum of
Anthropology, unpubl. thesis, 1995

Lever, J. 'Soccer: opium of the Brazilian people?', *Transaction*, 7 (1969)

Lever, J. *Soccer Madness*, Chicago, University of Chicago Press, 1983

Lévi-Strauss, C. *The Raw and the Cooked*, London, Jonathan Cape, 1970

Linde-Laursen, A., and J.-O. Nilsson (ed.), *Nationella identiteter i Norden
– ett fullbordat projekt?* Nordiska Rådet, 1991

Luttwak, E. N. 'Great-powerless days', *Times Literary Supplement*, 16 June
1995

Lutz, C. *Unnatural Emotion*, Chicago, University of Chicago Press, 1988

Lyotard, J.-F. *The Postmodern Condition*, Manchester, Manchester University
Press, 1983

Lyotard, J.-F. *Peregrinations: law, form, event*, New York, Columbia
University Press, 1988

Lyra Filho, J. *Taça do Mundo, 1954*. Rio de Janeiro, Irmãos Pongetti, 1954

MacAloon, J.J. 'The Ethnographic Imperative in Comparative Olympic
Research', *Sociology of Sport Journal*, 9(2), 1992

McCarthy, C., A. Rodriguez, S. Meacham, S. David, C. Wilson-Brown,
H. Godina, K.E. Supryia and E. Buendia. 'Race, Suburban Resentment
and the Representation of the Inner City in Contemporary Film and
Television' in N.K. Denzin (ed.), *Cultural Studies*, vol. 1, Greenwich,
Connecticut, JAI Press, 1996

MacClancy, J. (ed.), *Sport, Identity and Ethnicity*, Oxford, Berg, 1996

McDonald, M. 'The Construction of Difference: an anthropological
approach to stereotypes' in S. Macdonald (ed.), 1994

Macdonald, S. (ed.), *Inside European Identities*, Oxford, Berg, 1994

McKay, D.H. *Housing and Race in Industrial Society: civil rights and urban policy in Britain and the United States*, London, Croom Helm, 1977

Mackie, A. *The Hearts: the story of the Heart of Midlothian F.C.*, London, Stanley Paul, 1959

Maffesoli, M. *The Time of the Tribes*, London, Sage, 1996

Maguire, J. 'Towards a Sociological Theory of Sport and the Emotions: a process-sociological perspective' in E. Dunning and C. Rojek (eds), 1992

Malcolmsen, R. 'Popular Culture and Social Change', *Journal of Popular Culture*, 14(4), 1971

Malinowski, B. *Argonauts of the Western Pacific*, London, Routledge & Kegan Paul, 1922

Malinowski, B. *Magic, Science and Religion*, New York, Doubleday, 1926

Malone, M. 'Soccer's Greatest Goal: cultural harmony through sports', *Americas*, 64, May–June 1994

Marchi, V., A. Roversi and F. Bruno. *Ultrà: le sottoculture giovanili negli stadi d'Europa*, Instituto di studi politici economici e sociali, Roma, Koinè, 1994

Marcuse, H. *Eros and Civilisation*, London, Allen Lane, 1970

Markula, P. 'Firm but Shapely, Fit but Sexy, Strong but Thin: the postmodern aerobicizing female bodies, *Sociology of Sport Journal*, 12(4), 1995

Marri, F. 'Metodo, sistema e derivati nel linguaggio calcistico', *Lingua Nostra*, XLIV (1983)

Marsh, P. *Aggro: the illusion of violence*, London, Dent, 1978

Marsh, P., E. Rosser and R. Harré. *The Rules of Disorder*, London, Routledge & Kegan Paul, 1978

Marshall, H. 'White Movement to the Suburbs: a comparison of explanations', *American Sociological Review*, 44 (1979)

Martin, P.M. 'Colonialism, Youth and Football in French Equatorial Africa', *The International Journal of the History of Sport* 8(1), 1991

Marzola, P.G. *L 'Industria del Calcio*, Rome, La Nuova italia Scientifica, 1990

Mason, T. *Association Football and English Society*, Brighton, Harvester, 1980

Mason, T. 'Football' in T. Mason (ed.), *Sport in Britain: a social history*, Cambridge, Cambridge University Press, 1989

Mason, T. 'Football on the Maidan: cultural imperialism in Calcutta' in J.A. Mangan (ed.), *The Cultural Bond: sport, empire, society*, London, Frank Cass, 1992

Mason, T. *Passion of the People? Football in South America*, London, Verso, 1994

Matteucci, H. *Memórias de Mário Américo: o massagista dos reis*, São Paulo, Cia. Editôra nacional, 1986

Mauss, M. 'Les techniques du corps' in *Sociologie et Anthropologie*, Paris, Presses Universitaires de France, 1968

Mbiti, J.S. *African Religions and Philosophy*, Nairobi, East African Educational publishers, 1969

Melucci, A. 'The New Social Movements: a theoretical approach', *Social Science Information*, 19(2), 1980

Melucci, A. 'The Symbolic Challenge of Contemporary Social Movements', *Social Research*, 52(4), 1985

Merton, R.K. *On Theoretical Sociology*, Glencoe, Free Press, 1967

Mesaki, S. *Witch-killings in Sukumaland, Tanzania*. Department of Sociology, University of Dar-es-Salaam, Tanzania, 1992

Messner, M.A., and D.F. Sabo. 'Introduction: toward a critical feminist reappraisal of sport, men, and the gender order' in M.A. Messner and D.F. Sabo (eds), *Sport, Men and the Gender Order: critical feminist perspectives*, Champaign, Human Kinetics, 1990

Miller, T. 'The Unmarking of Soccer: making a brand new subject' in T. Bennett, P. Buckridge, D. Carter and C. Mercer (eds), *Debating the Nation: a critical study of Australia's Bicentenary*, Sydney, Allen & Unwin, 1992

Monnington, T. 'Politicians and Sport: uses and abuses' in L. Allison (ed.), 1993

Moolenijzer, Nicolaas J., and Swanpo Sie. 'Sport and physical education in Indonesia' in W. Johnson (ed.), *Sport and Physical Education Around the World*, Champaign, Stipes Publishing Co, 1980

Moore, S.F., and B.G. Meyerhoff (eds), *Secular Ritual*, Assen/Amsterdam, Van Grocum, 1977(b)

Moore, S.F., and B.G. Myerhoff. (1977a) 'Introduction: secular ritual: forms and meanings' in S.F. Moore and B.G. Myerhoff (eds), 1977(b)

Morley, D., and K. Robins. 'No Place like *Heimat*: images of home(land) in European culture', *New Formations*, 12 (Winter 1990)

Mormino, G.R. 'The Playing Fields of St. Louis: Italian immigrants and sport, 1925–1941', *Journal of Sport History*, 9 (1982)

Morris, D. *The Soccer Tribe*, London, Jonathan Cape, 1981

Mosely, P. *A Social History of Soccer in New South Wales: 1880–1957*, University of Sydney, unpublished PhD Thesis, 1987

Mosely, P. 'Balkan Politics in Australian Soccer', *ASSH Studies in Sports History*, 10 (1994)

Mosely, P. *Ethnic Involvement in Australian Soccer: a history 1950–1990*, Canberra, Australian Sports Commission, 1995

Murdock, G.P. 'Anthropology's Mythology', *Proceedings of the Royal Anthropological Institute*, London, 1971

Murphy, P., J. Williams and E. Dunning (eds), *Football on Trial: spectator violence and development in the football world*, London, Routledge, 1990

Murray, B. *The Old Firm: Sectarianism, Sport and Society in Scotland*, Edinburgh, John Donald Publishers, 1984

Murray, B. *Football: a history of the world game*, Hampshire, England, Scolar Press, 1994

Neisser, P.T., and S.F. Schram. 'Redoubling Denial: industrial welfare policy meets postindustrial poverty', *Social Text* (41), 1994

Niola, M. 'San Gennarmando: le disavventure del simbolo' in V. Dini and A. Nicolaus (eds), *Te Diegum*, Milan, Leonardo, 1991

Norton, A. (1988), *Reflections on Political Identity*, Baltimore, The John Hopkins University Press, 1993

Ntonfo, A. *Football et Politique du Football au Cameroun*, Yaoundé, Editions du CRAC, 1994

Oakley, J. *Morality and the Emotions*, London, Routledge, 1993

Oliveira, M. de 'Bangú: de fábrica-fazenda e cidade-fábrica a mais uma fábrica na cidade', Federal University of Rio de Janeiro, M.A. Geography dissertation, 1991

Omi, M., and H. Winant. *Racial Formation in the United States: from the 1960s to the 1990s*, New York, Routledge, 1994

Pálsson, G. *Beyond Boundaries: understanding, translation and anthropological discourse*, Oxford, Berg, 1993

Paoletti, P. *Il mio Re*, Naples, Edizione Europee, 1993

Paric, L., D. Boon, A. Henjak and I. Buljan. *Croats in the Australian Community*, draft report by the Australian Croatian Community Services to the Australian Federal Bureau of Immigration, Population and Multicultural Research, 1996

Parren, M. P. E., and N.R. de Graaf. *The quest for natural forest management in Ghana, Côte d'Ivoire and Liberia*, Wageningen, Netherlands, Tropenbos Foundation, Series 13, 1995

Patterson, O. 'The Cricket Ritual in the West Indies', *New Society*, 352 (1969)

PEA. *Bras, Greens and Ballheads: interviews with Freetown 'street boys'*, Freetown, People's Educational Association of Sierra Leone, 1989

Pearson, G. *Hooligan: a history of respectable fears*, London, Macmillan, 1983

Pearson, H. *The Far Corner: a mazy dribble through north-east football*, London, Little, Brown & Co, 1994

Perkin, H. 'Teaching the Nations How to Play: sport and society in the British Empire and Commonwealth, *International Journal of the History of Sport*, 6(2), 1989

Pesky, G. (1993a) 'The changing face of the game', *Sporting Goods Business*, 32 (March 1993)

Pesky, G. (1993b) 'On the attack: The growth of soccer in the United States', *Sporting Goods Business*, 31 (April 1993)

Pitt-Rivers, J. 'Honour and Social Status' in Peristiany (ed.), *Honour and Shame*, Chicago, University of Chicago Press, 1966

Pivato, S. *Sia lodatto Bartali*, Rome, Edizioni del Lavoro, 1985

Pivato, S. *I terzini della borghesia*, Milan, Leonardo, 1991

Pivato, S. *La bicicletta e il sol dell'avvenire. Sport e tempo libero nel socialismo della Belle-Epoque*, Florence, Ponte alle Grazie, 1992

Pivato, S. 'Italian Cycling and the Creation of Catholic Hero: The Bartali Myth' in R. Holt, J.A. Mangan and P. Lanfranchi (eds), *European Heroes*, London, Cass, 1996

Podravac, V. 'Occupational Structure (Croatians)' in J. Jupp (ed.), *The Australian People: an encyclopedia of the nation, its people and their origins*, North Ryde, Angus & Robertson, 1988

Pooley, J.C. 'Ethnic Soccer Clubs in Milwaukee: a study in assimilation' in M. Hart (ed.), *Sport in the Sociocultural Process*, Dubuque, Iowa, Wm. Brown, 1976

Popplewell, O. *Committee of Inquiry into Crowd Safety and Control of Football Grounds* (Final Report), London, HMSO, 1986

Popplewell, O. Lord Justice (Chairman) *Inquiry into the Crowd Safety and Control at Sports Grounds*, London, HMSO, 1986

Porro, N. 'From Local to Global: spectacular football in Italy as "political discourse" and the organizational paradigm', paper to the International Committee for the Sociology of Sport conference, Bielefeld, 18-23 July 1994

Porro, N. *Identità, Nazione, Citadinanza. Sport, società e sistema politico nell'Italia contemporanea*, Rome, Seam, 1995

Portelli, A 'The Rich and the Poor in the Culture of Football' in S. Redhead (ed.), 1993

Pospisil, M. *Croatia Sydney 1958–1988,* Sydney, independently published, 1988

Post, T. 'Feet of the future', *Newsweek Special Issue*, Spring, 1994

Poster, M. *The Second Media Age*, Cambridge, Polity, 1995

Powell, D. *Out West: perceptions of Sydney's western suburbs*, Sydney, Allen & Unwin, 1993

Putnam, R.D. *Making Democracy Work: civic traditions in modern Italy*, Princeton, New Jersey, Princeton University Press, 1993

Redhead, S. *Sing When You're Winning*, London, Pluto, 1986

Redhead, S. *Football with Attitude*, Manchester, Wordsmith, 1991(a)

Redhead, S. (1991b) 'An Era of the End or the End of an Era: football and youth culture in Britain' in J. Williams and S. Wagg (eds), 1991

Redhead, S. (1991c) 'Some Reflections on Discourses on Football Hooliganism', *Sociological Review*, 39(3), 1991

Redhead, S. (ed.), *The Passion and the Fashion: football fandom in the new Europe*, Aldershot, Arena, 1993

Redhead, S. (1994) 'Media Culture and the World Cup: the last World Cup?' in J. Sugden and A. Tomlinson (eds), 1994(a)

Reed, J.D. 'The Name of the Game is Petrosports', *Sports Illustrated* 53(21), 17 November 1980

Reeves, J.L., and R. Campbell. *Cracked Coverage: television news, the anti-cocaine crusade, and the Reagan legacy*, Durham, Duke University Press, 1994

Reno. W. 'Foreign firms and the financing of Charles Taylor's NPFL', *Liberian Studies Journal*, 18(2), 1993

Ribeiro, A.D. *Atletas de Cristo*. São Paulo, Editora Mundo Cristão, 1994

Ribeiro, P. *Didi, o gênio da folha sêca*. Rio de Janeiro, Imago, 1994

Richards, P. 'Videos and Violence on the Periphery: Rambo and war in the forests of the Sierra Leone–Liberia border', *IDS Bulletin, Knowledge is Power? the use and abuse of information in development*, ed. Susanna Davies, 25(2), 1994

Richards, P. *Fighting for the Rain Forest: war, youth and resources in Sierra Leone*, London, James Currey for the International African Institute, 1996(a)

Richards, P. (1996b) 'Chimpanzees, Diamonds and War: the discourses of global environmental change and local violence on the Liberia–Sierra Leone border' in H. Moore (ed.), *The Future of Anthropological Knowledge*, London, Routledge, 1996

Richards, P. (1996c) 'Small Wars and Smart Relief: radio and local conciliation in Sierra Leone', *Creative Radio for Development*, International Workshop and Conference, Birmingham, 12–15 May 1996

Riches, D. 'The Phenomenon of Violence' in D. Riches (ed.), *The Anthropology of Violence*, Oxford, Blackwell, 1986

Riess, S.A. *City Games: the evolution of the American urban society and the rise of sports*, Urbana, University of Illinois Press, 1991

Riordan, J. 'State and Sport in Developing Societies', *International Review for the Sociology of Sport*, 21(4), 1986

Rodrigues, N., and M. Filho. *Fla-Flu: e as multidões despertaram*, Rio de Janeiro, Editora Europa, organizado por Oscar Maron Filho e Renato Ferreira, 1987

Rogers, A., and S. Vertovec (eds), *The Urban Context: ethnicity, social networks and situational analysis*, Oxford, Berg, 1995

Romero, A. *Las barras bravas y la 'contrasociedad deportiva'*, Buenos Aires, Centro Editor De America Latina, 1994

Rosandich, T.J. 'Sports in Society: the Persian Gulf countries', *Journal of the International Council for Health, Physical Education and Recreation*, 27(3), 1991

Rosenfeld, A. *Negro, Macumba e Futebol*, São Paulo, Perspectiva, 1993

Roversi, A. 'Calcio e Violenza in Italia' in A. Roversi (ed.), *Calcio e Violenza in Europa*, Bologna, il Mulino, 1990

Roversi, A. *Calcio, Tifo e Violenza*, Bologna, il Mulino, 1992

RUF/SL *Footpaths to Democracy: toward a new Sierra Leone*, place of publication unknown ['The Zogoda'?], The Revolutionary United Front of Sierra Leone, 1995

Rusk, D. *Cities without Suburbs*, Baltimore, Maryland, Woodrow Wilson Center Press, 1995

Sage, G.H. *Power and Ideology in American Sport: a critical perspective*,

Champaign, Illinois, Human Kinetics, 1990

Sangren, P.S. 'Power against Ideology: a critique of Foucaultian usage', *Cultural Anthropology*, 10(1), 1995

Santos, W.G. *Cidadania e Justiça*, Rio de Janeiro, Campus, 1979

Saudi Arabian Ministry of Information. 'Part 14: Achievements: Youth Programs', in *Twenty Yea : of Achievements in Developmental Planning (1390–1410 H)(1970–1989)*, Riyadh, Arabian Encyclopedia House for Publishing and Distribution, 1991

Sayigh, R. *From Peasants to Revolutionaries*, London, Zed Press, 1979

Schmitt, C. *Der Begriff des Politischen*, Archiz fur Social Wissenschaft und Sozial Politik, 1 (1927)

Schrof, J.M. 'American women: Getting their kicks', *Science & Society*, 118 (19 June 1995)

Scotch, N.A. 'Magic, Sorcery and Football among the Urban Zulu: a case of reinterpretation under acculturation' in M. Truzzi (ed.), *Sociology and Everyday Life*, Englewood Cliffs, New Jersey, Prentice Hall, 1968

Scott, J.C. *Weapons of the Weak: everyday forms of peasant resistance*, New Haven and London, Yale University Press, 1985

Scott, J.C. *Domination and the Arts of Resistance: hidden transcripts*, New Haven and London, Yale University Press, 1990

Seban, M.M. 'Political Ideology and Sport in the People's Republic of China and the Soviet Union' in M. Hart (ed.), *Sport in the Sociocultural Process*, Dubuque, Wm. C. Brown, 1976

Seyferth, G. 'As Ciências Sociais no Brasil e a questão racial' in *Cativeiro e Liberdade*, Rio de Janeiro, UERJ, 1989

Seyferth, G. 'Os paradoxos da miscigenação: observações sobre o tema imigração e raça no Brasil', *Estudos Afro-Asiáticos*, 20 June 1991

Seyferth, G. 'A invenção da raça e o poder discricionário dos estereótipos', *Anuário Antropológico 93*, Rio de Janeiro, Ed. Tempo Brasileiro, 1995

Shields, R. *Places on the Margin: alternative geographies of modernity*, London, Routledge, 1991

Shimoni, Y. *Political Dictionary of the Arab World*, New York, Macmillan, 1987

Sie, S. 'The Problem of Sport and Nation Building in Southeast Asia' in B. Love, D.B. Kanin, and A. Strenk (eds), *Sport and International Relations*, Champaign, Illinois, Stipes Publishing Co, 1978

Skrbis, Z. 'National Self-Determination Today: problems and prospects', conference paper delivered at Macquarie University, Sydney, 6–7 November 1993

Slack, J.D. 'The Theory and Method of Articulation in Cultural Studies' in D. Morley and K.H. Chen (eds), *Stuart Hall: critical dialogues in cultural studies*, London, Routledge, 1996

Smith, A.M. *New Right Discourse on Race and Sexuality: Britain, 1968–1990*, Cambridge, Cambridge University Press, 1994

Smith, S. 'Where to Draw the Line: a geography of popular festivity' in A. Rogers and S. Vertovec (eds), 1995

Sociological Review *Cultural Aspects of Football*, 39(3), 1991

Soldati, M. *Le due città*, Milan, Garzanti, 1964

Sports in the GDR. 'Great prospects for sport in PDR Yemen', *Sports in the German Democratic Republic*, 1 (1982)

Squires, G.D. *Capital and Communities in Black and White: the intersection of race, class, and uneven development*, Albany, New York, State University of New York Press, 1994

Stedman Jones, G. 'Working-class culture and working-class politics in London, 1870–1900: notes on the remaking of a working class', *Journal of Social History*, 7 (1974)

Steinbrecher, H. 'Getting in on Soccer: the hottest sport to reach international markets', unpublished paper presented at the Marketing with Sports Entities, Swissotel, Atlanta, Georgia, February 1996

Stokvis, R. 'Conservative and Progressive Alternatives in the Organization of Sport', *International Social Science Journal*, 34(2), 1982

Storch, R.D. 'The Plague of Blue Locusts: police reform and popular resistance in northern England 1840–57', *International Review of Social History*, 20 (1976)

Strathern, M. *Kinship at the Core: an anthropology of 'Elmdon', a village in north-west Essex in the 1960s*, Cambridge, Cambridge University Press, 1982

Stratton, J. *The Young Ones: working class culture, consumption and the category of youth*, Perth, Black Swan Press, 1992

Strauss, A., L. Schateman, R. Bucher, D. Ehrlich and M. Sabshin. *Psychiatric Ideologies and Institutions*, New York, Free Press, 1964

Strinati, D. *An Introduction to Theories of Popular Culture*, London, Routledge, 1995

Sugden, J., and A. Tomlinson (eds), 1994(a) *Hosts and Champions*, Aldershot, Arena

Sugden, J. (1994) 'USA and the World Cup: American nativism and the rejection of the people's game' in J. Sugden and A. Tomlinson (eds), 1994(a)

Sugden, J., and A. Tomlinson (1994b) 'Soccer Culture, National Identity and the World Cup' in J. Sugden and A. Tomlinson (eds), 1994(a)

Suttles, G. *The Social Order of Communities*, Chicago, Chicago University Press, 1972

Symonds, M. 'Imagined Colonies: on the social construction of Sydney's western suburbs', *Communal/plural*, 1 (1993)

Tarr, S.B. 'The ECOMOG Initiative in Liberia: a Liberian perspective', *Issue: A Journal of Opinion*, 21(1–2), 1993

Taylor Report *The Hillsborough Stadium Disaster*, London, HMSO, 1989

Taylor, I. 'Soccer Consciousness and Soccer Hooliganism' in S. Cohen (ed.), *Images of Deviance*, Harmondsworth, Penguin, 1971

Taylor, I. 'English Football in the 1990s: taking Hillsborough seriously?' in J. Williams and S. Wagg (eds), 1991

Taylor, R. *Football and its Fans: supporters and their relations with the game, 1885–1985*, Leicester, Leicester University Press, 1992

Teno, J.-M. (ed.), *Mr. Foot*, London, South Productions, 1991

Theroux, P. *The Kingdom by the Sea: a journey around the coast of Great Britain*, London, Hamish Hamilton, 1983

Thomas, J. *Doing Critical Ethnography*, Newbury Park, Sage, 1993

Tillich, P. *Dynamics of Faith*, New York, Harper & Row, 1957

Tiltnes, A. *Regimelegitimitet og demokratisering i Jordan.* (Regime legitimacy and democratization in Jordan.) Cand. Polit. thesis in Political Science. University of Oslo, 1994

Tkalcevic, M. *Croats in Australian Society*, Canberra, Australian Government Publishing Services, 1989

Toch, T. 'Football? In short pants? No helmets?', *Science & Society*, 116 (13 June 1994)

Tomlinson, A. (1994) 'FIFA and the World Cup: the expanding football family' in J. Sugden and A. Tomlinson (eds), 1994(a)

Trivizas, E. 'Offences and Offenders in Football Crowd Disorders', *British Journal of Criminology*, 20 (1980)

Tsanga, S. *Le Football Camerounais*, Des Origines à L'Independance, Yaoundé, 1969

Tuan, Y.F. *Space and Place: the perspective of experience*, London, Edward Arnold, 1977

Turner, R. *In Your Blood: football culture in the late 1980s and early 1990s*, London, Working Press, 1990

Turner, V. *The Ritual Process: structure and anti-structure*, Chicago, Illinois, University of Chicago Press, 1964

Turner, V. *The Ritual Process*, New York, Cornell University Press, 1969

Turner, V. *Dramas, Fields and Metaphors: symbolic action in human society*, New York, Cornell University Press, 1974

Turner, V. 'Comments and Conclusions' in B. Babcock (ed.), *The Reversible World: symbolic inversion in art and society*, Ithaca, New York, Cornell University Press, 1978

Turner, V. *Process, Performance and Pilgrimage*, New Delhi, Concept, 1979

Turner, V. *From Ritual to Theatre: the human seriousness of play*, New York, Performing Arts Journal Publications, 1982

Tylor, E.B. (1871) 'The Science of Culture' in M. Fried (ed.), *Readings in Anthropology*, vol. 2: *Cultural Anthropology*, New York, Crowell, 1968

Uberhorst, H. (ed.), *Geschichte der Leibesübungen, 6*, Berlin, Verlag Bartels and Wernitz GmbH, 1989

Unikoski, R. *Communal Endeavours: migrant organisation in Melbourne*, Canberra, Australian National University Press, 1978

UNRWA (1994) Map of UNRWA's area of operations 30.6.1994, Public Information Office UNRWA H.Q. (Vienna)

Urry, J. *The Tourist Gaze: leisure and travel in contemporary societies*, London, Sage, 1990

Vagnuzzi, U. *Quelli del calcio*, Padua, Italy, Centro Editoriale Cattolico Carroccio, 1992

Vamplew, W. 'Sports Crowd Disorder in Britain 1870–1914: causes and controls', *Journal of Sport History*, 7(1), 1980

Vamplew, W. *Play Up and Play the Game: professional sport in Britain 1875–1914*, Cambridge, Cambridge University Press, 1988

Vamplew, W. 'Wogball: ethnicity and violence in Australian football' in R. Giulianotti and J. Williams (eds), 1994

Van der Merwe, F. 'Afrikaner Nationalism in Sport', *Canadian Journal of History of Sport*, 22(2), 1991

Van Gennep, A. *The Rites of Passage*, London, Routledge and Kegan Paul, 1960

Vargas Llosa, M. *Making Waves*, London, Faber & Faber, 1996

Various Authors, (apresentação de João Saldanha) *Na Bôca do Túnel*, Rio de Janeiro, Livraria Editôra Gol, 1968

Väyrynen, R. 'Nationalism and Internationalism in Sport' in M. Ilmarinen (ed.), 1984

Vinnai, G. *Football Mania*, London, Ocean, 1971

Vinokur, M.B. *More than a Game: sports and politics*, Westport, Greenwood Press, 1988

Vrcan, S. 'Dal Tifo Aggressivo alla Crisi del Pubblico Calcistico: il caso jugoslavo', *Rassegna Italiana di Sociologia*, 33(1), 1992

Wacquant, L. 'Pugs at Work: bodily capital and bodily labour among professional boxers', *Body and Society*, 1(1), 1995

Wacquant, L.J.D., and W.J. Wilson. 'Poverty, Joblessness, and the Social Transformation of the Inner City' in P.H. Cottingham and D.T. Ellwood (eds), *Welfare Policy for the 1990s*, Cambridge, Massachusetts, Harvard University Press, 1989

Wacquant, L.J.D. 'The Cost of Racial and Class Exclusion in the Inner City' in W.J. Wilson (ed.), 1993(b)

Wacquant, L.J.D. 'The New Urban Color Line: the state and fate of the ghetto in postfordist America' in C. Calhoun (ed.), *Social Theory and the Politics of Identity*, Oxford, Blackwell, 1994

Waddington, P.A.J. *Liberty and Order: public order policing in a capital city*, London, University College, London, 1994

Wagg, S. *The Football World: a contemporary social history*, Brighton, Harvester Press, 1984

Wagg, S. (1995a) 'The Business of America: reflections on World Cup '94' in S. Wagg (ed.), 1995(b)

Wagg, S. (ed.), *Giving the Game Away: football, politics and culture on five continents*, Leicester, Leicester University Press, 1995(b)

Wagner, E.A. (ed.), *Sport in Asia and Africa: a comparative handbook*, Westport, Greenwood Press, 1989

Wahl, A. *La balle au pied: histoire du football*, Paris, Découvertes Gallimard, 1990

Walker, G. 'There's not a team like Glasgow Rangers: football and religious identity in Scotland' in T. Gallagher and G. Walker (eds), *Sermons and Battle Hymns*, Edinburgh, Edinburgh University Press, 1990

Walter, T.O., B. Brown and E. Grabb. 'Ethnic Identity and Sports Participation: a comparative analysis of West Indian and Italian soccer clubs in Metropolitan Toronto', *Canadian Ethnic Studies*, 23(1), 1991

Walvin, J. *The People's Game: a social history of British football*, London, Allen Lane, 1975

Walvin, J. *The People's Game: the history of football revisited*, Edinburgh, Mainstream, 1994

Weber, M. *The Protestant Ethic and the Spirit of Capitalism*, London, Allen & Unwin, 1930

Weber, M. *From Max Weber*, edited by H.H. Gerth and C.W. Mills, London, Routledge & Kegan Paul, 1948

Webster, J. *Another Grain of Truth*, London, Collins, 1988

Webster, J. *The Dons: the history of Aberdeen Football Club*, Revised Edition, London, Stanley Paul, 1990

White, J. *A Socio-Legal Approach to Football Hooligans*, University of Edinburgh, Department of Law, unpublished PhD Thesis, 1984

Whitson, D. 'The Embodiment of Gender: discipline, domination, and empowerment' in S. Birrell and C.L. Cole (eds), *Women, Sport, and Culture*, Champaign, Illinois, Human Kinetics, 1994

Wild, R.A. *Australian Community Studies and Beyond*, Sydney, Allen & Unwin, 1981

Williams, J. 'Having an Away Day: English football spectators and the hooligan debate' in J. Williams and S. Wagg (eds), 1991

Williams, J. 'The Local and the Global in English Soccer and the Rise of Satellite Television', *Sociology of Sport Journal*, 11 (1994)

Williams, J., E. Dunning and P. Murphy (eds), *Hooligans Abroad: the behaviour and control of English fans in continental Europe*, London, Routledge, 1984

Williams, J. and R. Giulianotti. 'Stillborn in the USA?' in R. Giulianotti and J. Williams (eds), 1994

Williams, J. and S. Wagg (eds), *British Football and Social Change: getting into Europe*, Leicester, Leicester University Press, 1991

Williams, R. *A Protestant Legacy: attitudes to death and illness among older Aberdonians*, Oxford, Clarendon, 1990

Willis, P. *Learning to Labour: how working class kids get working class jobs*,

Westmead, Farnborough, Saxon House, 1977

Willis, P. *Common Culture*, Milton Keynes, Open University Press, 1990

Willis, P. 'Ethno-Cultural Studies', plenary paper to the conference *Crossroads in Cultural Studies*, Finland, University of Tampere, July 1996

Wilson, K.B. 'Cults of Violence and Counter-Violence in Mozambique', *Journal of Southern African Studies*, 18(3), 1992

Wilson, W.J. (1993a) 'The Underclass: issues, perspectives, and public policy' in W.J. Wilson (ed.), 1993(b)

Wilson, W.J. (ed.), *The Ghetto Underclass: social science perspectives*, Newbury Park, California, Sage, 1993(b)

Winch, P. 'Understanding a Primitive Society' in B.R. Wilson (ed.), *Rationality*, Oxford, Blackwell, 1979

Wohl, A. 'Integrational Functions of Competitive Sport and its Role in Shaping International Competition, Co-operation and Mutual Understanding' in M. Ilmarinen (ed.), 1984

Wren-Lewis, J. and A. Clarke. 'The World Cup: a political football?', *Theory, Culture & Society*, 1(3), 1983

Wright, G. *Building the Dream: a social history of housing in America*, Cambridge, Massachusetts, MIT Press, 1983

Yeebo, Z. *Ghana: the struggle for popular power*, London and Port of Spain, New Beacon Books, 1991

Young, M. *An Inside Job: policing and police culture in Britain*, Oxford, Clarendon, 1991

Young, M. *In the Sticks: cultural identity in a rural police force*, Oxford, Clarendon, 1993

Young, M. 'The Police, Gender and the Culture of Drug Use and Addiction' in M. McDonald (ed.), *Gender, Drink and Drugs*, Oxford, Berg, 1994

Zack-Williams, A.B. *Tributors, Supporters and Merchant Capital: mining and under-development in Sierra Leone*, Aldershot, Avebury Press, 1995

Zizinho. *Zizinho, o mestre Ziza*, Rio de Janeiro, Editora do Maracanã, Secretaria de Estado de Esporte e Lazer, 1985

Index